RIVERS OF DISCORD

GREG SHAPLAND

Rivers of Discord

International Water Disputes in the Middle East

HURST & COMPANY, LONDON

First published in the United Kingdom by
C. Hurst & Co. (Publishers) Ltd.,
38 King Street, London WC2E 8JZ
© 1997 by Greg Shapland
All rights reserved.
Printed in India
ISBN 1-85065-214-7

PREFACE AND ACKNOWLEDGEMENTS

My interest in the geography and politics of the Middle East began over two decades ago, when I studied for an M.A. at the School of Oriental and African Studies (SOAS) in the University of London. Only later did this interest come to focus particularly on the question of water resources, as my work in the Foreign and Commonwealth Office (FCO) on Egypt and Sudan led me to look at how the River Nile affected the relationships between the states which shared it.

It was also clear that water was an important factor in inter-state relations elsewhere in the Middle East. As well as having a major impact on relations between Turkey, Syria and Iraq, water appeared to be a serious obstacle in the path of any settlement of the Arab-Israel dispute. At the same time, there seemed to be no general work dealing with all three of these major areas of dispute over water. The present book represents an attempt to fill that gap for readers with no previous acquaintance with the subject.

Many people have helped me to produce this book, although I bear sole responsibility for its shortcomings. A number of technical experts and practitioners, both within the Middle East and beyond, have shared their knowledge and experience with me. I am grateful to them all, but (in this sensitive subject) have only quoted them where they have given me explicit permission to do so. I should also like to thank those who have been kind enough to read the manuscript in whole or in part and to offer comments on it, especially Professors Allan and McLachlan of SOAS, and Martin Fuller, formerly of the FCO's Research and Analysis Department. I should like to express my appreciation of the efforts of Catherine Lawrence of SOAS who drew the maps and Jon Wild (formerly of SOAS) who gave me invaluable help in sorting out word-processing problems.

Thanks are due also to the FCO, which generously paid my salary while I spent a year at SOAS researching and writing this book, and funded a research visit to the Middle East. However, the opinions expressed are my own, and should not be taken as an expression of official government policy.

CONTENTS

Preface and Acknowledgements	*page* v
Abbreviations and Conversion Factors	xi

Chapters

1.	Introduction: Water and Politics in the Middle East	1
	The time-scale	3
	Difficulties of data	4
2.	Water in the Arab-Israel Dispute	5
	The Historical Background	5
	The Resources in Question	8
	— *Surface waters*	8
	— *The Litani*	10
	— *Ground-water*	11
	— *Water resources and boundaries*	12
	Disputing the Waters – up to June 1967	13
	Disputing the Waters – June 1967 to the Madrid Peace Process	17
	— *Surface waters*	17
	— *The West Bank aquifers*	20
	— *The Gaza Strip*	25
	— *Water on the Golan*	27
	Water in the Madrid Peace Process	28
	— *The Jordan-Israel peace treaty, 26 October 1994*	29
	— *Israeli-Palestinian negotiations on water*	31
	— *The Syrian and Lebanese tracks*	38
	— *Bilateral versus comprehensive*	40
	The Challenge of the Future	41
	— *Population growth*	41
	— *Balancing supply and demand*	43
	— *Increasing supply through conventional methods*	43

	— Importing water	45
	— Non-conventional methods	47
	— Conserving water	50
	— Managing demand	50
	— Cooperative management	54
	Water, War and Peace	55
3.	The Nile	57
	The Geopolitics of the Nile Basin	57
	The Contribution of the States of the Basin	59
	Regulating the Nile	60
	— Egypt	61
	— Sudan	66
	— Further upstream	68
	— The quality of the Nile waters	68
	Treaties and Disputes	69
	— Agreements from the colonial period	69
	— The 1959 agreement between Egypt and Sudan	72
	— The attitude of other riparians	74
	— The states of the upper White Nile basin	75
	— Ethiopia	77
	— Questions of quality	82
	Meeting New Demands	82
	— The upper White Nile basin	85
	— Ethiopia	87
	— Sudan	89
	— Climatic change	90
	— Making more water available	91
	— Re-allocation	96
	— Enough water for all?	97
	—The outlook	98
4.	The Tigris-Euphrates Basin	103
	The Geopolitics of the Tigris-Euphrates Basin	103
	— The Euphrates	103
	— The Tigris	105
	— The Karun	106
	Using the Rivers	107

	— Syria	109
	— Turkey	111
	— Iran	114
	— The impact of use on water quality	115
	Agreeing and Disagreeing	115
	— Developments since 1980	118
	Downstream Fears	123
	— Future Turkish consumption	124
	— Syria's needs	125
	— Iraq's needs	129
	— The effect of pollution	132
	— Strategic questions	134
	— Conclusions	137
	The Outlook: Policy Responses Downstream	138
5.	The Orontes (Asi)	144
6.	Ground-water Disputes	148
	The Qa Disi aquifer: Jordan and Saudi Arabia	148
	Other shared aquifers	150
7.	Some Common Themes	152
	Geographical-cum-hydrological factors	153
	Economic and financial factors	156
	Political and legal factors	159
	Military strength	164
	The changing picture	165
8.	Outlook	166
Bibliography		169
Index		177

MAPS

1. The basin of the River Jordan 6
2. The aquifers shared by Israel and the Palestinians 21
3. The Nile basin 58
4. The Nile basin: Sudan and Ethiopia 84
5. The Tigris-Euphrates basin 104
6. The Tigris-Euphrates basin: southern Turkey and northern Syria 112

TABLES

1. Flows in the basin of the River Jordan 10
2. Population growth in Israel and neighbouring countries 42
3. Agricultural sector as % of total economies in Israel and neighbouring countries 54
4. Chronology of major works on the Nile 62
5. Population growth in the Nile basin 83

ABBREVIATIONS AND CONVERSION FACTORS

Abbreviations
km.: kilometre
km.^{2}: square kilometre
ha.: hectare
mg./l.: milligrams per litre
ppm.: parts per million
mcm.: million cubic metres
DMZ: Demilitarised zone
PNA: Palestinian National Authority

Conversion factors
1 hectare = 2.4 acres
1 acre = 0.42 ha.
1 hectare = 10 dunums (Palestinian)
1 dunum (Palestinian) = 0.1 ha.
1 hectare = 2.31 feddans
1 feddan = 0.43 ha.
1 mile = 1.625 km.
1 kilometre = 0.615 miles

1

INTRODUCTION: WATER AND POLITICS IN THE MIDDLE EAST

The Middle East is the most arid of the world's major regions. Except in Turkey and a few mountainous areas, rainfall is generally inadequate to support agriculture without irrigation. The flow of major Middle Eastern rivers such as the Nile and the Euphrates comes to a large extent from rain and snow that fall outside the region.

The position of boundaries between the states of the region means that they have to share the waters of these rivers not only with states outside or on the fringes of the region – such as Ethiopia and Turkey – but also with each other. Moreover, political boundaries divide many of the basins of the smaller rivers which rise wholly within the region, such as the Jordan and the Orontes, as well as many of the aquifers.

As a result, most states of the region are dependent on water supplies from beyond their boundaries. But the degree of dependence varies greatly: at one extreme, all Lebanon's water rises on its national territory; at the other is Egypt, where 95% of the water the country consumes comes from outside its boundaries. In between are states that have supplies of water within their boundaries but are also dependent to a significant extent on flows of rivers (or ground-water) from other states: Iraq may depend on such 'outside' sources for around two-thirds of its water consumption, while in Syria the equivalent figure may be less than a quarter.[1]

This complex picture would produce knotty problems for regions with a tradition of international co-operation. In the Middle East, the dismal reality is that relations between states are more often soured by long-standing antagonisms that are exacerbated by disputes over specific issues. Indeed, the region has been the scene of half-a-dozen substantial outbreaks of armed conflict since the Second World War, two of which involved intervention by forces from outside.

These conflicts did not break out over water. But the disputes which

---

[1] See Kolars (1992), Table 1. Different sources may give different figures: for example, the Iraqi Minister of Irrigation has said that 75% of Iraq's water resources come from outside the country (Iraqi News Agency, 28 February 1994, translated by BBC, Monitoring *SWB* ME/1935, 2 March 1994).

lay behind them – especially the dispute between Israel and its Arab neighbours – have engendered attitudes that often make it difficult for policy-makers to co-operate over water. The region's leaders are frequently suspicious of one another, if not downright hostile. Megaphone diplomacy has been more common than the sort of easy and regular communication which makes for calm discussion and negotiation. Moreover, there are no effective regional structures that include all the region's major competitors for water: the largest organisation of states in the region, the Arab League, of course does not include Ethiopia, Turkey or Israel. Its effectiveness even as a means of resolving inter-Arab disputes is debatable, especially given the divisions among the Arab states caused by Iraq's invasion of Kuwait.

While these disputes rumble on, water resources are coming under increasing pressure from population growth, economic development and expectations of higher standards of living. In some Middle Eastern countries, the rate of natural population growth is so high that there will be twice as many peoples to cater for in twenty years' time. In Israel and Jordan, particular circumstances have led to sudden increases in population through immigration. Independent status for the Occupied Territories as a result of a peace settlement would probably lead to a similar phenomenon there. Urbanisation, industrialisation and greater use of fertilisers, pesticides and herbicides mean that issues of water quality will take their place in Middle Eastern water disputes along with questions of quantity.

At the same time, there are no major opportunities for increasing the supply of water in the Middle East. As well as finding ways of agreeing on the fair division of the water resources they share, the states of the region face the challenge of having to manage their economies with fewer cubic metres of water per citizen.

The aim of this study, then, is to examine the present state of disputes between Middle Eastern states over water and to consider how they may develop. The list of water sources selected for examination is not comprehensive, but certainly includes all the currently significant disputes involving states in the core area of what is normally defined as the Middle East.[2]

The disputes which form the subject of this study are over fresh water as a resource for consumption, whether agricultural, domestic or industrial. Its main concern is thus the way in which shared sources of water are divided in terms of volume. Trans-boundary pollution is also increasingly part of the picture, however: pollutants originating in

---

[2] This core area is interpreted here as comprising Egypt, Israel, the Occupied Territories, Jordan, Lebanon, Syria, Iraq and the Arabian peninsula.

one country may affect the quality of water available for use in another, and water may be rendered unfit for some or even all uses.

These are not the only kinds of international dispute which relate to water. Navigation, fisheries or boundaries in bodies of water are common sources of discord between states. In the Middle East, however, navigation and fisheries are comparatively minor uses of international rivers; boundaries are another question altogether.

Considerations of internal politics may well impose constraints on foreign policies relating to water. For instance, a powerful agricultural lobby, anxious to protect its supply of irrigation water, might inhibit a government from making concessions to another riparian state over the sharing of a source of water that it would otherwise be prepared to offer in the interests of good bilateral relations. Although this book is about international water disputes, these aspects of domestic politics cannot be wholly excluded.

Shared fresh-water sources take two forms: surface flow (rivers and lakes) and ground-water (aquifers). Both are included here.

The approach taken in this study is a pragmatic one. Rather than follow any formal analytical framework, it seeks in the case of each dispute to identify the issues which confront decision-makers in the region, and the factors which constrain their freedom of action. Nonetheless, some common themes emerge. As these may be interest to those working on water disputes in other parts of the world, they are considered later in the book (in Chapter 7).

The time-scale

The different factors which play a part in the politics of international water-sharing change over very different time-scales. The evolution of two crucial elements can be predicted with some confidence as much as two decades ahead. The first is population growth: the population which most of the states concerned will have to provide for in the year 2010 or 2020 can be determined with a reasonable degree of accuracy. The second is the number and location of the large dams and other installations which control the flow of shared rivers. A major dam project can easily take ten or fifteen years from the initial consideration to the point where it is generating hydro-power or storing water for irrigation. This gestation period may even be longer if the opposition of other riparian states leads to lengthy wranglings about the provision of international funding.

Great leaps forward in technology are less predictable, but there is generally quite a long time-lag between a new discovery and its commercial application. For example, it is highly unlikely that new sources of energy will lower the cost of desalinating sea-water over the next decade or two to the point where it can be economically used for irrigating crops.

Other elements may be subject to more rapid change. The most important of these are political: the policies of regimes in the region, their relationships with one another and their relationships with outside powers. There have been dramatic changes in the international politics of the Middle East and East Africa in the last few decades. The recent breakthroughs in the Middle East peace process suggest that another such change is currently under way. Predicting such changes is virtually impossible. Nevertheless, it is necessary to be aware that they do occur and that political relationships can change almost overnight, with important consequences for policies on water.

All these considerations suggest that a time-horizon of around two decades is reasonable, although with increasing caution about predictions as that horizon is approached. Beyond that point, there are too many unknowns, and forecasting becomes little more than guess work.

Difficulties of data

The vital statistics of Middle Eastern rivers and aquifers are often uncertain. In some cases (aquifers especially) this may be because the water source has not been fully studied over a period sufficiently long for reliable statements to be made. In other cases, figures for the same water-course may vary because different 'runs' of years have been used to establish an average.

Data may be presented in different ways for political reasons. For example, an upstream state may wish to show that there is ample water in a shared river for both its proposed projects and those of downstream states. It would thus have an interest in promoting the acceptance of a high figure for the river's average annual flow. A downstream state that wanted to obstruct its upstream neighbour's plans would have an interest in demonstrating that the average flow was much lower. Data may also be withheld, wholly or partly, to weaken another riparian's ability to prepare a case in negotiations.

The difficulty of obtaining precise, agreed data hinders scientific work on rivers and aquifers in the region. The lack of agreement between figures published by official bodies in different states frequently causes arguments between governments and other political actors in the region. For the purposes of the present study, however, orders of magnitude rather than exact statistics are sufficient to illustrate the issues. Where data from different sources vary so much as to make it impossible to settle on a single approximate figure, or where the variations form part of the dispute, this will be made clear.

2

WATER IN THE ARAB-ISRAEL DISPUTE

The Historical Background

Jews had continued to live in the area between the Mediterranean and the River Jordan after the Diaspora which followed the collapse of the Bar Kochba revolt in AD 135. But by the 19th century, these Jews were an urban not an agricultural people; they were concentrated particularly in the cities of Jerusalem, Hebron, Safad and Tiberias.

The Zionist project to revive the Jewish presence in what had become the Districts of Jerusalem, Acre and Balqa of the Ottoman Empire was not simply a desire to bring in large numbers of Jews.[1] The project included a strong element of social engineering: the Jews were to be revived as a people by the establishment of a healthier social structure, and would become farmers as well as city-dwellers (as they were – generally – in Europe and Middle East, as well as the Holy Land). Agriculture was also seen as a means of cementing the attachment to the land of the 'new Jews' and securing the Zionist claim to and control of it.

There was a substantial Arab population in the Holy Land (probably around 600,000 people) when Jewish immigration began in the second half of the nineteenth century.[2] Arab agriculture was, however, mainly of a subsistence character, and the Arabs' standard of living was low. For a sizeable Jewish population to be settled on the land at a standard of living acceptable to immigrants from Europe, much higher productivity would be necessary. Only large-scale irrigation could make this possible in the semi-arid conditions of the Holy Land. Hydro-electricity was seen as a major source of power for Jewish homes and industries. Water was thus an integral part of Zionist plans – and therefore of the Arab-Israel dispute – from the beginning.

---

[1] The Districts (*sanjaks*) of Acre and Balqa (Nablus) were part of the Province (*vilayet*) of Beirut. The Sanjak of Jerusalem was an independent district in the sense that it was not tributary to a provincial capital but directly to Istanbul.

[2] No reliable figures are available for the Arab population at this time. An official Ottoman estimate in 1914 put the total population of Palestine at 689,000, of whom 604,000 were Arabs. The Arab population is unlikely to have changed much over the preceding half century. See Government of Palestine (1946/7).

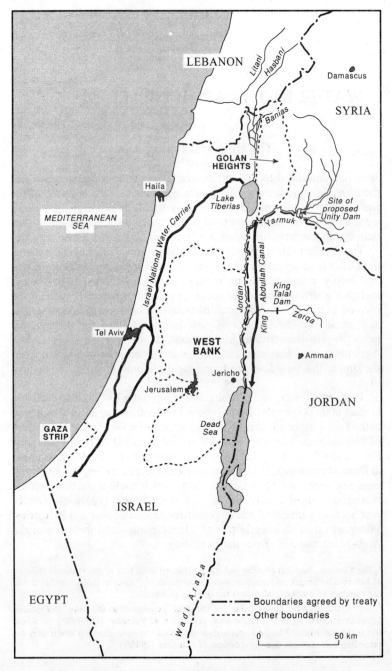

Map 1. BASIN OF THE RIVER JORDAN

The Historical Background

In 1917, British troops under General Allenby drove the Ottoman army out of the Holy Land. For reasons mainly connected with imperial communications, Britain resolved to keep control of the area (as well as the lands to the east of the River Jordan, and Mesopotamia), using a mandate issued by the League of Nations to legitimise its actions. France was similarly determined to establish control over the northern Levant, in the area which has since become Syria and Lebanon.

As part of its mandatory obligations in the Holy Land, Britain was required to support 'the establishment in Palestine of a National Home for the Jewish people'. In order to secure the most favourable resource base for the proposed National Home, the Zionists pressed the British government to obtain, in negotiations with France, boundaries for Palestine that would include the headwaters of the Rivers Jordan and Yarmuk, as well as the lower course of the Litani. At the Paris Peace Conference of 1919, the World Zionist Organisation's Memorandum declared that it was 'of vital importance not only to secure all water sources already feeding the country, but also to be able to conserve and control them at their sources.'[3]

In this endeavour, the Zionists were only partly successful, as the British had to balance Zionist aspirations with the demands of the French (for the most part unrelated to water). After many attempts to draw mutually acceptable boundaries between their respective mandates, Britain and France finally settled on lines that:

– left the Litani wholly within Lebanon;

– left the upper reaches of the Rivers Hasbani and Banias in French-controlled Lebanon and Syria respectively; and

– excluded from Palestine all but the last 10 km. or so of the main stream of the Yarmuk (dividing the rest between Syria and Transjordan); but

– incorporated within Palestine the Dan spring, the largest and most regular of the headwaters of the Upper Jordan River (that part of the river above Lake Tiberias), and the whole of Lake Tiberias; and

– divided the Lower Jordan River (the part of the river below Lake Tiberias) between Palestine and Transjordan, the boundary following the river as far as the Dead Sea.

During the period of British rule, from 1917 until 1948, both the indigenous Arabs and the Jewish immigrants made use of water abstracted from wells. While Arab use remained essentially at its traditional levels,

---

[3] The World Zionist Organisation's Memorandum to the Supreme Council at the Peace Conference, quoted by Hurewitz (1956).

Jewish agricultural development took rapidly growing volumes of ground-water. In the 1930s, Jewish settlers began using ground-water to irrigate orange groves in the Tel Aviv area. By 1948, settlers were already consuming a significant portion of the aquifers' safe yield, from springs, rivers and deep wells.

Until they gained the control which came with statehood, the Zionists' ability to undertake major hydraulic projects to make use of the rivers of Palestine was severely limited. The largest works were constructed by the Palestine Electric Corporation. Their main purpose was the generation of electricity, although one of the schemes also supplied water for irrigation.[4]

During the Mandate, despite official restrictions, the Jewish population increased rapidly, mainly through immigration. The Arab population also grew, through natural increase. In 1944, there were 554,000 Jews in Palestine, and 1,179,000 Arabs.[5] The flight of the Arabs during the fighting of 1948/9 changed their distribution, but left most of them dependent on the same water resources, whether in the West Bank, the Gaza Strip or Transjordan.[6] The establishment of the state of Israel in May 1948 was followed by the mass immigration of Jews from elsewhere in the world, 687,000 arriving by the end of 1951.[7]

This growing pressure on water resources was accompanied by a political situation that made cooperation apparently impossible. Not only had the Zionist armed forces fought against the Arabs of Palestine and the neighbouring Arab states: those states continued to resist the very idea of a Jewish state, while the displacement of the Palestinian Arab population made any solution of the dispute doubly difficult.

The Resources in Question

Surface waters

The water supplies at stake are small. The largest river basin in the area, that of the Jordan, is tiny by world standards, covering only some 18,000 km.^{2}, as compared with 3,100,000 km.^{2} for that of the Nile. The Jordan basin is small in terms of total flows, as well as in areal extent: the Nile has about forty-five times the flow, the Euphrates over

---

[4] The Rutenberg Concession on the River Jordan below Lake Tiberias was the main electricity-generating scheme. The one which provided water for irrigation as well as hydro-power was in the Auja basin. See Government of Palestine, 1946/7.
[5] Government of Palestine, 1946/7.
[6] The Emirate of Transjordan became the Hashemite Kingdom of Jordan in June 1949, and annexed the West Bank in April 1950.
[7] Eban (1972).

twenty. That we are dealing with a much smaller order of magnitude is clear from the fact that flows in the Jordan basin are normally given in *millions* of cubic metres, as opposed to the billions of cubic metres used for the larger rivers of the region.

The main headwaters of the Jordan are the Dan, the Banias and the Hasbani (see Map 1). Below the confluence of these headwaters at a point 6 km. south of Israel's border with Lebanon, the main stream of the Jordan flows southwards through Lake Huleh (formerly a much larger area of swamp, drained in the 1950s) and into Lake Tiberias.

The Yarmuk is the Jordan's main tributary, its flow coming from a watershed divided between Syria and the Kingdom of Jordan, with four-fifths in Syria. After its outflow from Lake Tiberias, in addition to the water which it receives from the Yarmuk, the Jordan also gets water (mainly in the form of winter floods) from wadis on both sides of the valley. The greater part of this flood water comes from the eastern side (as the western side of the valley is in the rain-shadow of the West Bank hills); the most important of these tributaries is the Zerqa.

In terms of flow, the largest of the headwaters of the Upper Jordan (i.e., above Lake Tiberias) is the Dan: on average, it contributes about 40% of the water which flows into the lake. It is also the least variable of the headwaters from years to year. The Hasbani and the Banias account for around 20% each.[8]

There is considerable disagreement about what the annual average volume of water in the Jordan system was in its natural state, that is before the development of large-scale abstractions. This disagreement applies to both the basin as a whole and its constituent parts. For the former, figures vary from as low as 1,113 mcm. to 1,850 mcm.[9] For the latter, the inflow into Lake Tiberias illustrates the point: while one source gives 500 mcm. another gives 790 mcm.[10]

For the purposes of this study, the author has adopted the figures in Table 1 as a working approximation of the average natural flows within the basin.

There are large annual variations in the volume of water in the Jordan and its tributaries: total surface flow in low years is about one-third less that the average annual flow. Runs of dry years may be followed by flows that are much higher than average. Thus the 1980s were characterised by low rainfall and hence low flows. By the winter of

---

[8] The balance is made up by run-off between the confluence of these headwaters and the lake, together with rainfall on the surface of the lake itself.

[9] The lower figure is cited by Wishart (1990), the higher figure by Smith (1966).

[10] The lower figure is from Inbar and Maos (1984), the higher from Naff and Matson (1984).

1990-1 the level of Lake Tiberias had fallen so far that the National Water Carrier, the backbone of Israel's water system, was closed. The following winter brought heavy rain and snow, and river flows that exceeded the capacity of reservoirs to store them. Seasonal variations are large too, with high flows in winter and low flows in summer and autumn.

Table 1. FLOWS IN THE BASIN OF THE RIVER JORDAN

	flow (mcm./year)
Upper Jordan	
River Dan	245
River Hasbani	125
River Banias	120
Springs in Upper Jordan valley, run-off from Golan Heights etc.	110
Total flow into Lake Tiberias	600
Lower Jordan	
River Yarmouk	485
Eastern wadis	200
Western wadis	50
Total flow in Lower Jordan at Allenby Bridge	1,335

The water of the Jordan above Lake Tiberias is of sufficiently high quality for all used; and much less saline than that which flows out from the lake. This is the result of high rates of evaporation from the lake and the inflow from saline springs below its surface. Human action has exaggerated this characteristic, making the Lower Jordan too saline for almost any use.[11] By contrast, the water of the Yarmuk is still of good quality.

The Litani

No mention has so far been made of the Litani, because it is a wholly Lebanese river: throughout its course it is within the boundaries of Lebanon which are, moreover, not contested (see Map 1).[12] Since the early years of the twentieth century, however, it has been seen by Zionist and Israeli leaders as a potential source of additional water for

---

[11] See p. 29.
[12] There may be a connection between the Litani and Jordan basins, in the sense that seepage from the lower Litani may flow underground to feed the Hasbani: see Kolars (1992).

The Resources in Question

Palestine and later Israel: it cannot therefore be excluded from the discussion.[13]

The Litani's average 'natural' flow is around 700 mcm. per year.[14] While not a major river on a regional scale, it is an important element in the Lebanese water 'budget'.

Ground-water

Where ground-water is concerned, there are two main areas of concern: the 'Mountain Aquifer' underlying the West Bank and Israel, and the aquifer which extends beneath Israel's coastal plain and the Gaza Strip. The Mountain Aquifer under the West Bank is in fact three aquifers, divided on the basis of the principal direction of their underground flow (see Map 2). The largest of the three, the Western aquifer, flows towards the west. The North-Eastern aquifer flows northwards under the Vale of Esdraelon.[15] The flow in the Eastern aquifer is towards the Jordan valley. All three aquifers extend into Israel under the line defined by the 1949 Armistice Agreement between Israel and Jordan (under whose control the West Bank came).[16] The Eastern aquifer, however, is almost wholly on the Palestinian side of the 1949 line, extending into Israel only in a small area west of Jerusalem.

Both the Western and North-Eastern aquifers are recharged by precipitation, at most a fifth of which falls on the Israeli side of the 1949 line.[17] The average annual rate of recharge is around 700 mcm.[18] Of course, precipitation over the West Bank varies considerably from year to year, and the rate of recharge varies with it.

While the West Bank is a hilly area, the Gaza Strip is low-lying. As a result, the precipitation which recharges the aquifer under the Strip is a lot lower than that which falls on the West Bank. The average annual recharge is between 55 and 100 mcm., some of which occurs on the Israeli side of the line established by the 1949 Armistice Agreement with Egypt (which controlled, but did not claim sovereignty over, the

---

[13] For an account of Zionist attempts to include the Litani within the area of the British Mandate for Palestine, see Garfinkle (1994).

[14] Comair (1993).

[15] Israelis often refer to the Western and North-Eastern Aquifers as the Yarkon-Taninim and Gilboa-Bet She'an (or Schechem-Gilboa) Aquifers, respectively.

[16] Since Israel occupied the West Bank, this line has often been referred to as 'the Green Line'.

[17] Shuval (1993).

[18] The Interim Agreement gives a figure of 679 mcm. (Annex III, Appendix I, Schedule 10).

Gaza Strip). Most sources give a figure closer to the lower end of this range than to the higher.[19]

The Gazan aquifer is essentially a southward extension of the aquifer which underlies the Israeli coastal plain. Nonetheless, as the flow in the aquifer is mainly east-west, and the degree of transmissibility (the ease with which water flows underground) between different parts of the aquifer is low, Israeli activities to the north have little effect on those parts of the aquifer which lie beneath the Gaza Strip, and vice-versa.

Water resources and boundaries

The relationship of the water-courses and aquifers in the Jordan basin with the political boundaries in the area is a highly complicated one (see Map 1).

The fact that Israel's boundaries are not everywhere agreed only serves to increase this complexity. While Israel's boundaries with Egypt, Jordan and Lebanon are not in dispute, those with Syria and whatever Palestinian entity emerges on the West Bank have yet to be settled.[20]

The basin of the River Jordan is divided between Israel, Lebanon, Syria, Jordan and the West Bank. The main headwaters of the Upper Jordan are the Dan, the Banias and the Hasbani; they rise in Israel, Syria and Lebanon respectively. Since 1967, the Banias has been entirely under Israeli control; the 'security zone' established by Israeli forces in southern Lebanon in 1978 incorporates much of the Hasbani.

Before the war of June 1967, Israeli troops on the Syrian front were confined to the west of a line established by the 1949 Armistice Agreement. For much but not all of its length, this line was the same as that delineated by the 1923 agreement between Great Britain and France (as the mandatory powers for Palestine and Syria respectively). Where the two lines were different, the Armistice Agreement designated the areas between them as a Demilitarised Zone (DMZ). While keeping its forces out of the DMZ, Israel continued to claim sovereignty over it (i.e. up to the 1923 line) and maintained a non-military presence in parts of it. For its part, Syria has rejected the 1923 line and called on

---

[19] Abu-Maila (1991) gives a range between 62 and 77 mcm. Tahal (1990), and Ahiram and Siniora (1992) give 65 mcm. WRAP (1994) suggests that the average annual recharge is between 55 and 70 mcm., which includes return flow from irrigation.

[20] The existence of the Israeli-controlled 'security zone' in southern Lebanon does not mean that the boundary between Israel and Lebanon is in dispute: both states are agreed that the line to which Israel will withdraw is the 1923 boundary established by agreement between Great Britain and France (as the mandatory powers for Palestine and Lebanon respectively). The relationship between the boundaries of Israel and the West Bank and water resources will be dealt with in the sub-section entitled 'Ground-water'.

Israel to withdraw its troops to the positions which they occupied on the eve of the war of June 1967.[21]

The essential difference between the two lines in terms of their relationship with the water resources of the area is that, apart from the Banias spring and the small westward-flowing streams of the Golan, the 1923 line would not give Syria access to the water resources of the Upper Jordan. By contrast, the line claimed by Syria would give Syria a presence on both sides of the Upper Jordan just below Lake Huleh and just above Lake Tiberias. It would also give Syria a shoreline on the lake itself.

From the southern shore of the lake, the Jordan continues southwards for just over 100 km. before ending its course in the Dead Sea, some 400 metres below sea level.[22] From a point about 10 km. below its outflow from Lake Tiberias, near the confluence with the River Yarmuk, the Jordan marks the easternmost extent of Israeli control.[23]

The Yarmuk for the first 40 km. or so of its 50-km. course forms or lies very close to the boundary between Syria and Jordan.[24] Below that point (if the 1923 line is taken as the boundary between Israel and Syria), the Yarmuk forms the boundary between Israel and Jordan, apart from a short section immediately before the river's confluence with the Jordan. Since 1967, Israeli control has extended another 10 km. or so up the northern bank of the Yarmuk. If the line claimed by Syria is taken as the Israeli-Syrian boundary, almost the whole length of the northern bank of the river would lie in Syria.

Disputing the Waters – up to June 1967

After the creation of the state, the Israeli government began the elaboration of a national water plan, along the lines of schemes drawn up during the Mandate. The Israeli plan was based on the idea that water should be conveyed from the north – where it was relatively abundant – to the south, where it could be used to irrigate otherwise uncultivable

---

[21] In 1946, having achieved independence, Syria called on Britain to discuss 'the question of the territories ceded by the French Mandatory Power to Palestine'. See Foreign Office (1946).

[22] The distance between the Lake and the Dead Sea is a straight-line distance: as the river meanders extensively, the distance measured along its course would be much greater.

[23] For the first 25 km., this is the border established by the 1994 treaty between Israel and Jordan, which follows the line of the 1949 Armistice Agreement between the two countries; beyond that point, as far as the Dead Sea, it is the 1967 cease-fire line.

[24] Where the railway line in the Yarmuk valley is closer to the Kingdom of Jordan than is the centre-line of the river, it is the railway line that forms the boundary. At some points, therefore, the Yarmuk is wholly within Syria. The distances given are straight-line measurements.

land. In a favourite phrase of Ben Gurion's, it aimed to 'make the desert bloom'.

Israel's initial proposal for its National Water Carrier involved the diversion of the River Jordan at the Bridge of Jacob's Daughters, a point some 13 km. above Lake Tiberias and within the DMZ.[25] The Israelis began work there in September 1953, but gave in to American pressure, following Syrian protests to the United Nations, to desist.

Like Israel, Jordan also had to cope with a sudden rise in population in its early years. In Jordan's case, this took the form of an influx of refugees from those areas of Palestine which fell under Israeli control. To provide a livelihood for the refugees, and more generally to promote the country's economic advancement, the government was anxious to use the waters of the Jordan basin to develop its own agriculture. To this end, on the advice of an American engineer, Mills Bunger, Jordan proposed to build a dam on the Yarmuk at Maqarin (see Map 1). As one bank of the Yarmuk at this point is Syrian territory, Jordan negotiated an agreement with Syria, signed in 1953, giving Jordan the bulk of the water which would be stored behind the dam; Syria was to have three-quarters of the electricity generated.[26] However, Israeli protests in Washington and to the UN prevented the proposal from going ahead.

It was apparent to the USA that a settlement of the dispute over the River Jordan was a necessary condition of Middle East peace. Indeed, it seemed to offer a means of introducing cooperation into one area of the relationship between Israel and the Arabs. In October 1953, in order to promote such cooperation, President Eisenhower appointed a special envoy, Eric Johnston.

In his discussions with the governments of the region, Johnston took as his starting-point the Main Plan for the Jordan basin, which was published within days of his appointment. The plan itself had been commissioned by the United Nations Relief and Works Administration (UNRWA) from the Tennessee Valley Authority (TVA); the work was done by the American consulting firm of Chas. T. Main Inc. The plan followed the TVA model of seeking the optimum development of a river basin as a single unit.

Johnston's task was to square the Main Plan with the political realities of the region. He came very close to success. After four rounds of shuttle diplomacy in the Middle East, he had narrowed the differences between the respective negotiators to 15 mcm. per year of Yarmuk

---

[25] In Arabic: Jisr Banaat Yaaqub; in Hebrew: Gesher Bnot Yaacov.
[26] Khouri (1981).

water – not much more than one per cent of the total surface flow in the Jordan basin.[27]

During his fourth visit to the region in August and September 1955, Johnston secured the agreement of the Arab League's Technical Committee on the Jordan waters to what became known as the Revised Unified Plan. The Plan shared out the waters of the Jordan basin as follows:

– Lebanon would get 35 mcm. per year, from the Hasbani.
– Syria would get 132 mcm. per year, of which 90 mcm. would come from the Yarmuk, 20 mcm. from the Banias and 22 mcm. from the Upper Jordan. (The water from the Upper Jordan was to be used to irrigate land in the Boteiha area, north east of Lake Tiberias).
– The Kingdom of Jordan's share would be 720 mcm. a year, of which some 470 mcm. would come from the Jordan and Yarmuk rivers (100 from the former and 370 from the letter), the remaining 250 mcm. coming from side-wadis and wells in the Lower Jordan valley. The Kingdom would also have access to 30 mcm. a year from the saline springs beneath the surface of Lake Tiberias.
– Israel would be entitled to take the residue of the flow of the Jordan, and 25 mcm. per year from the Yarmuk.

In addition, the United States offered to finance the construction of a dam on the Yarmuk with a capacity of 300 mcm. Jordan and Syria would have the right to increase the height of the dam later if they wished, at their own expense. A decision on the contentious issue of the use of Lake Tiberias to store Yarmuk floodwater would be deferred for five years.

Despite Johnston's untiring efforts, final agreement at the political level was never reached. Israel seemed poised to accept his proposal, but the Plan proved too bitter a pill for many Arab politicians to swallow.[28] They were influenced by several considerations. They did not wish to see Israel reap the economic benefits of the development of the Jordan waters – benefits which would have have enabled Israel to accommodate more immigrants. Moreover, Arab acceptance of the Revised Unified Plan would have meant implicit acquiescence in the resettlement of the Palestinian refugees in their host countries, and hence the abandonment of the hope of repatriation.

There were domestic and inter-Arab political factors too: Arab leaders

---

[27] For a detailed account of the Johnston mission in its broader political context, see Lowi (1993).

[28] According to Brecher (1974), Israel and the United State had already signed a Draft Memorandum of Understanding containing terms very similar to those which Johnston agreed with the Arab League Technical Committee.

did not wish to bring upon themselves the unpopularity and opprobrium which would have followed a show of willingness to cooperate with Israel.[29] They may even have feared for their physical safety: the assassination of King Abdullah of Jordan after his attempt to negotiate with Israel was probably still fresh in their minds.[30]

In October 1955, the Arab League Council referred the Revised Unified Plan back to the League's Technical Committee for further consideration. In effect, the Plan had been rebuffed.

Nonetheless, in communications with the United States, Israel and Jordan continued to affirm their adherence to the Johnston allocations. For Israel, acceptance of the Revised Unified Plan gave the seal of approval to its 'National Water Carrier', the project to bring water from the Jordan basin to the Negev. Whatever other motivations the two governments may have had, US funding for their water projects depended upon such affirmation. Indeed, it was an explicit condition of the American grant to Jordan for the East Ghor project, which was completed in 1961. This scheme takes water from the Yarmuk some 10 km. as the crow flies above its confluence with the Jordan, and conveys it via the King Abdullah Canal to the eastern floor of the valley.[31]

Satisfied that they were acting in accordance with the Revised Unified Plan, the Israelis began work on that section of the National Water Carrier which was to bring water from Lake Tiberias to central Israel, to link up with the section which had already been built between the coastal plain and the northern Negev. The new section of the Carrier came into operation in 1964.

Despite Jordan's tacit acquiescence in the Israeli project (as a condition of the implementation of Jordan's own plans), other Arab states were not prepared to countenance a development that seemed likely to make a major contribution to Israel's economic growth. Between 1955 and 1964, the Arab League considered both military action and the diversion of the headwaters of the Jordan which lay in Arab lands.

After two summit conferences in 1964, the Arab states accepted that they were not strong enough to thwart the Israeli plan by military force. They therefore chose to implement a scheme that involved the damming of the Hasbani and the Banias, and the diversion of their flow across the plateau of the Golan and into the Yarmuk. A dam was to be build on the Yarmuk to impound the additional water.

---

[29] Lowi (1993), quoting a US diplomatic document from November 1953, says that King Hussein considered that co-operation with Israel would be political suicide.
[30] Saliba (1968).
[31] The canal was originally known as the East Ghor Canal, but was later renamed in honour of Jordan's first monarch.

The Arab states established a unified military command to deter any Israeli attack. It proved ineffective. Israel attacked construction works in Syria on a number of occasions over the next three years.[32] By the time full-scale war broke out between Israel and its Arab neighbours in June 1967, the Arab states had already allowed their diversion plan to wither away.[33]

The Israeli attacks on the diversion works were not isolated incidents along an otherwise peaceful border. Rather, they were part of a pattern of clashes between Israel and Syria. Nor was the dispute over the Arab diversion plan a direct cause of the June 1967 war. Nonetheless, there seems little doubt that the plan – and Israel's reaction to it – played a significant part in the creation of the rising tension which eventually led to that war.

Disputing the Waters – June 1967 to the Madrid Peace Process

Israel's successes in the war of June 1967 gave it greatly increased control over its sources of water. The territory which it occupied included:
– the whole of the Banias;
– an additional 10 or so kilometres along the right (northern) bank of the Yarmuk (these two areas being both part of Syria);
– the whole of the Kingdom of Jordan west of the River Jordan: i.e., the area known as the West Bank; and
– the whole of the Gaza Strip.

Surface waters

The Jordan basin. There was now no possibility of the Banias being diverted to reduce its flow into the Upper Jordan. There was also less opportunity for hostile diversion of the Yarmuk. Nonetheless, in 1975 the Jordanian government returned to the idea of building a dam at Maqarin. The project was included in the Jordan Valley Commission's seven-year plan; a feasibility study was carried out, financed by the United States, which further promised to pay for part of the cost of construction, although this was made conditional on the agreement of the other riparians.

This agreement was not forthcoming. Israel declared that it wished

---
[32] See for example *Daily Telegraph* 15 July 1966: 'Long Israeli-Arab feud over Jordan waters', and Neff (1994).
[33] See *Daily Telegraph* 1 February 1967: 'End of Arabs' scheme to divert Jordan'.

to be cooperative, but expressed concern that the volume of water available to Israeli farmers in the Yarmuk Triangle would fall if the dam were to be built. Israel also claimed that the West Bank (under Israeli occupation) should receive the water which had been allocated by Johnston for the West Ghor Canal project.[34]

There was an inter-Arab dimension to the competition for the waters of the Yarmuk too. Syria began to make use of springs in the Yarmuk basin for irrigation as early as 1946. The development of irrigation schemes using water from the Yarmuk basin has continued up to the present. These schemes are very small in relation to Syria's projects for the Euphrates or even the Orontes. Individually, most of them are small even in comparison with Israeli and Jordanian projects for the use of water from the Jordan basin. Nevertheless, there are now some twenty-five dams on wadis in Syria that feed the Yarmuk, with a total storage capacity of more than 150 mcm. – around three-quarters of the capacity of the reservoir that would be impounded by the proposed dam at Maqarin.

While talks between Israel and Jordan, with US mediation, were taking place in mid-1980, there was a dramatic downturn in Syrian-Jordanian relations. The reasons were completely unconnected with water. Syria accused Jordan of subversion through the Muslim Brotherhood, and the two countries found themselves supporting opposite sides in the war between Iran and Iraq. In the circumstances, bilateral cooperation over the development of water resources was not a possibility.

By the second half of the 1980s, Jordan's relations with Syria were on the mend. In September 1987, the two countries signed an agreement 'for the Utilisation of the Waters of the Yarmuk River'.[35] Under the terms of this agreement, a dam – to be known as the Unity Dam – was to be constructed at the Maqarin site. Jordan was to receive most of the water which would be stored behind the dam, and 25% of the electricity generated there. However, the agreement seemed more favourable to Syria than to Jordan (and for that reason caused controversy in Jordan), since:

---

[34] When Johnston made this apportionment, the West Bank was part of Jordan, and water for the West Ghor would have been included in the Jordanian 'share'. It was not separately mentioned, however, and it is therefore not possible to say precisely how much of the Jordanian share was intended for the West Bank. Elmusa (1993) estimates the West Bank component of the Jordanian share of the waters of the Jordan and Yarmuk at 140 mcm. per year; according to Hillel (1994), the Israeli claim was for 150 mcm.

[35] An English text of the agreement is contained in Garfinkle (1992), Appendix F. The 1987 agreement was very similar to the one which Syria and Jordan had signed in 1953: see page 14.

Disputing the Waters – June 1967 to the Madrid Peace Process 19

- Jordan had to find the money for the project;
- the agreement was structured in such a way that Syria's position would be much more secure that Jordan's in dry years, since the filling of Syrian reservoirs would take precedence over the filling of the reservoir behind the Unity Dam; and
- Jordan had no means of monitoring Syrian compliance with the agreement.

The agreement had a more fundamental drawback: it had been signed by only two of the three riparians. The third, Israel, continued to express reservations about the Unity Dam.[36] The World Bank had offered part of the funding for the project, on condition that all the riparians were in agreement with it. Negotiations between Israel and Jordan were still taking place until in the Summer of 1990, when the crisis caused by Iraq's invasion of Kuwait led to severe difficulties for the Jordanian economy.[37] One of the casualties was the Unity Dam. Once more, the project had been delayed by factors unrelated to water.

The Litani. There have been persistent reports that Israel is tapping the Litani in its 'security zone' by clandestine means of one kind or another.[38] However, no convincing evidence has been produced to support this claim. In any case, there is very little water in the lower Litani. Since the mid-1960s, a substantial part of the flow of the Litani has been impounded by a dam at Qiraoun and diverted through a tunnel into the Awali river to generate hydro-power.[39] Water is also taken from the river's upper basin in the Bekaa, for irrigation projects. As a result, the average annual flow in the lower Litani is much reduced: one Lebanese academic source gives it as under 130 mcm.[40] During the summer and early autumn – the period of peak demand – there is virtually no flow in the lower Litani. For the Israelis to exploit the

---

[36] An Israeli official involved in the talks quoted by Rodan (1995), explained Israel's position as follows: 'Basically, we wanted a share of any additional water that would come as a result of the project. We also wanted to prevent the Jordanians from doing anything that would block off water to Israel.'

[37] In July 1990, the Jordanian Prime Minister blamed Israel for 'obstructing' the Unity Dam project with a view to obtaining a larger share of the water. see BBC Monitoring *SWB* 24 July 1990, quoting a Radio Monte Carlo report for 13 July 1990.

[38] The claim has mostly recently been made in a report by ESCWA (the United Nations Economic and Social Commission for Western Asia) released in May 1994: see *Mideast Mirror*, 1 June 194: 'The great water grab: Lebanon wants the UN to investigate.'

[39] According to Kolars (1992), the volume diverted into the Awali is 236 mcm. a year.

[40] Baasiri (1990). Kolars (1992) puts the flow at 'perhaps 100 mcm. per year'.

Litani, they would need not only a means of conveying the water to Israel, but also a dam to impound winter and spring flows for use later in the year. It is doubtful whether the slim pickings to Israel of tapping the Litani would justify the capital costs involved.[41]

The West Bank aquifers

Israel's control of the West Bank was the most important new element introduced by the war of June 1967 into the Arab-Israel hydro-political equation. In the case of the Banias, Israel had already shown before the war that it was capable of using military force to prevent neighbouring countries from constructing diversionary work to deprive it of water. In the case of the Yarmuk, it was able to obstruct the proposed Unity Dam by blocking Jordan's attempts to secure funding. Preventing a progressive growth in consumption on the West Bank by Palestinians drilling new wells or increasing the capacity of existing ones would have been a different task altogether – and one that would have been virtually impossible without physical control of the area.

Israel's presence on the West Bank after June 1967 enabled it to impose severe restrictions of Palestinian abstractions from the aquifer, and hence to ensure that Israel did not suffer any reduction in the amount of water flowing 'downstream' (albeit underground) to its side of the 1949 Armistice line.

By June 1967, Israel was already drawing some 300 mcm. a year from well and springs within Israel that tapped the Western and North-Eastern Aquifers.[42] This represented around a quarter of Israel's total water supply. At this time, Palestinian consumption from these two shared aquifers, from both springs and wells, was not much more than a tenth of Israeli abstractions. Indeed, it was the fact that Palestinian use of these aquifers was so slight that was responsible for the absence of any dispute over them before the war of June 1967. Abstractions from the Mountain Aquifer as a whole by Palestinians were between 80 and 100 mcm. a year, but most of this came from the Eastern Aquifer, which was hardly shared at all with Israel.[43]

After June 1967, when Israel took control of the West Bank and

---

[41] Hudson (1971). There is also some anecdotal evidence in support of this contention: Yuval Ne'eman, Israel's Minister of Science and Energy in the early 1980s, claimed that Israel's incursion into Lebanon had revealed that there was 'scarcely a trickle' in the lower Litani: see Cooley (1983). Fares Bouez, Lebanon's Foreign Minister, has recently declared 'I can't say that we have evidence that there is a direct theft of water in the south.' (See *Mideast Mirror*, 1 June 1994: 'The great water grab: Lebanon wants the UN to investigate.')

[42] Pearce (1991).

[43] Kahan (1987).

Disputing the Waters – June 1967 to the Madrid Peace Process 21

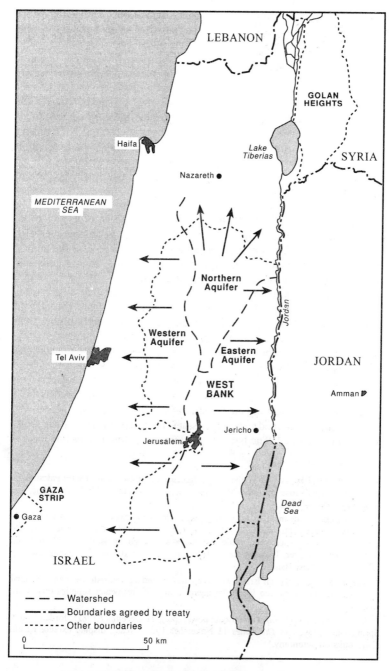

Map 2. THE AQUIFERS SHARED BY ISRAEL
AND THE PALESTINIANS

Gaza Strip, the Israeli authorities imposed regulations that had the effect of severely restraining the growth of Palestinian consumption. These regulations required Palestinians to obtain a licence before drilling new wells or increasing the capacity of existing ones. In practice, licences have only been granted in a few cases, all of them for domestic water; no licence has been granted for the provision of water for agriculture. As a result, there has been a slight fall in the amount of water used in irrigation, while population growth has far outstripped the small increases in domestic supply which have been permitted.[44] Domestic consumption per person has now fallen to between 20 and 30 cubic metres a year – one of the lowest figures in the world. These regulations covered not only the aquifers from which Israel had drawn before the war, but the Eastern Aquifers under the West Bank and the those under the Gaza Strip as well.

Meanwhile, Israeli abstractions from the shared aquifers via wells situated within pre-1967 Israel continued to grow. In an average year, they now total around 440 mcm. accounting for over 65% of the annual recharge.[45] Their relative importance in Israel's total water supply has remained about the same, at around a quarter.[46]

For many years, there has been concern in Israel that abstractions from the Western and North-Eastern Aquifers, and from the coastal aquifer which lies wholly within Israel, were significantly higher than the rate of recharge. A continuation of this state of affairs implies a progressive fall in the water-table, eventually reaching a point at which the aquifers would be unable to meet the demands normally made upon them.

The restrictions which the Israelis imposed became themselves an element in the Arab-Israel dispute, because of the great resentment which they created among the Palestinians of the West Bank. Moreover, the Palestinians blamed excessive Israeli abstractions when their wells and springs ran dry.[47] The Israelis countered that these events had natural

---

[44] According to Elmusa (1993), the total volume of water used annually by Palestinians in the West Bank rose by only 20 mcm. between 1967 and 1993; in that time, the population had doubled.

[45] The figure of 440 mcm. is taken from Schedule 10 of Appendix I of Annex III of the Interim Agreement, which states that 340 mcm. of water from the Western Aquifer are 'used in Israel' each year, while 103 mcm. a year go 'to Israeli users' from the North-Eastern Aquifer. It is not clear whether part of this 103 mcm. is being used by settlers on the West Bank.

[46] That is, a quarter of total Israeli water supplies, including brackish water and recycled waste-water. The proportion would be nearer a third if freshwater supplies only were considered.

[47] See for example Al- Fajr (Palestinian newspaper), 13 December 1987: 'Jordan Valley Spring Goes Dry', and The Times 11 November 1981: 'Water dispute excluded from Cairo talks on autonomy.'

causes. The hydrological evidence available – at least to outsiders – is insufficient to enable a conclusion to be reached on this point.

The Palestinians of the West Bank complained of the hardship which was caused by the regulations. They also pointed to their inequity, since they prevented any significant increase in Palestinian consumption, in contrast to the growth in abstraction on the Israeli side of the 1949 line and the apparently unrestrained consumption of water by the Jewish settlers.

In response, the Israeli authorities pointed to the inefficiency of the traditional forms of irrigation in the West Bank, suggested that the Palestinians could increase their agricultural production without using more water by adopting modern methods and argued that the Palestinians had no ground for complaint, since there was no increase in the volume of water allocated to agriculture on the Israeli side of the 1949 line either.

Nonetheless, there seems little doubt that the Palestinians could have been allowed to increase their consumption of water much more than they were in fact permitted to do, especially from the Eastern Aquifer, where consumption is well below the sustainable annual yield.[48] Moreover, Palestinians could have had considerably more water if the water from deep wells drilled by the Israelis for their settlements had also been supplied to the Palestinians or alternatively (if one accepts the Palestinian hypothesis), if none of these wells had been drilled, as fewer Palestinian wells would have dried up.

Settlers in the West Bank. Before June 1967, as we have seen, Palestinian residents of the West Bank and Israelis living on the other side of the 1949 line made use of water abstracted from the Mountain Aquifer. After 1967, a further category of consumer was added, in the form of Jewish settlers in the West Bank. The earliest settlements in the West Bank were intended to fulfill a defensive function. From the mid-1970s, a different kind of settler movement made its appearance on the West Bank. Motivated mainly by religion, these settlers aimed to establish a permanent Jewish presence throughout the territory (which they regarded as part of the Land of Israel) in order to prevent its return to Arab control. From 1977, when the right-wing Likud party came to power, these settlers received strong official encouragement and their numbers increased rapidly. When the peace process began in late 1991, the total number of settlers in the West Bank (excluding East Jerusalem) had reached 110,000; by 1996 it had risen to 133,000.

---

[48] The data provided in the Interim Agreement of September 1995, in suggesting that there is an average surplus of 78 mcm. a year in the Eastern Aquifer, support this contention: see the section below entitled 'Water in the Madrid Peace Process'.

The only official information available regarding the overall consumption of these settlements comes in the Interim Agreement, which states that 'Israeli users' in the Jordan Valley (presumably all settlers) take 40 mcm. per year from the Eastern Aquifer. Given that there are a large number of settlers outside the Jordan Valley, the total volume of water taken from the Mountain Aquifer by Israeli settlers is likely to be considerably greater than 40 mcm. One well-informed Israeli academic source suggests that the West Bank settlements use around 50 mcm. a year, but this is probably an under-estimate.[49] It is true that some water is piped to West Bank settlers from the Israeli water system, but this is a relatively small quantity: the bulk of the water used by settlements on the West Bank comes from wells drilled into the aquifers below.[50]

As we have seen, the bulk of the water that Israel takes from the shared West Bank aquifers still comes from wells on the Israeli side of the 1949 line. In terms of Israeli abstractions from these aquifers, the settlements are of secondary importance. For Israel, the most important aspect of the occupation of the West Bank in water terms is not that it has enabled additional quantities of water to be abstracted, but rather that it has conferred the control necessary to prevent the Palestinians from increasing their use of the aquifers.

Although the volume of water abstracted from the West Bank aquifers for Jewish settlements is small relative to the volume taken within pre-1967 Israel, it is high compared to the number of settlers and (proportionately) to the quantity of water available to the Palestinians: if around 133,000 settlers on the West Bank (excluding Jerusalem) use 50 mcm. a years, while about 1.6 million Palestinians in the same territory use about 118 mcm., the Palestinian population – twelve times greater than the settler population – is consuming less than two-and-a-half times as much water. Put another way, the settler's consumption per capital is five times that of the Palestinians. For non-Israelis, it is easy to understand the Palestinians' sense of grievance that their own consumption of water is constrained at such a low level, especially as the use of water by the settlers is not subject to any limits. Indeed, the average water consumption per settler is higher than that of Israelis living on the other side of the 1949 line. Palestinian resentment is compounded by the knowledge that the settlers receive water at subsidised rates: for domestic water, they pay one-third of the price per unit paid by the Palestinians.

---

[49] Shuval (1993).
[50] According to the Director of Mekorot (reported in the Jordanian newspaper *Al Rai*, 19 January 1987), Mekorot supplied around 2.5 mcm. of water to settlers on the West Bank in 1986 (and 0.5 mcm. to Palestinians).

On the question of the supply of water to Israeli settlements on the West Bank, the United Nations has asserted that the Israeli occupation should be governed by the Geneva Convention.[51] The Convention does not deal specifically with natural resources under occupation. It is, however, clear on the question of settlements, in that it forbids the occupying power from transferring parts of its own civilian population into the territories which it occupies. Since the settlements are themselves illegal, it follows that supplying water to them from aquifers underlying the occupied territory is illegal too.

The United Nations Security Council has affirmed in two resolutions its view that the 1949 Geneva Convention applies to the territories occupied in 1967. Resolution 446 of 1979 established a commission to examine the question of settlements in those territories. Israel refused to co-operate with the commission. The Security Council passed Resolution 465 the following year, deploring Israel's attitude, and calling for the protection of water resources as well as land and property. Paragraph 8 requested the commission to investigate the depletion of natural resources, especially water, to ensure their protection. Israel maintained its refusal to co-operate with the commission, and made no changes to its practices regarding water (or any other matters) in response to the Council's condemnation.[52]

The Gaza Strip

Israel's occupation of the Gaza Strip conferred no real advantages in hydrological terms. For one thing, any underground flow is westwards, from Israel to the Strip. Control of the Strip did not, therefore, give Israel enhanced ability to protect its sources of water, as control of the West Bank did. Moreover, Israel appears to have made little or no use (to the east of its side of the 1949 line) of the aquifer which it shares with the Strip. According to one official source, it has remained so: it 'is not considered part of the Israel water sector'.[53] While the presence of 3,000-5,000 Israeli settlers is unhelpful (and just as illegal in the eyes of the United Nations as it is in the West Bank), their effect on the water situation is not great. If they consume water at the same rate as the settlers on the West Bank (i.e., around 375 cubic metres per person per year), they would use less than 2 mcm. a year.

---

[51] The Fourth Geneva Convention, 12 August 1949.
[52] Israel's attitude may have been influenced by President Carter's repudiation of Resolution 465, two days after it was passed.
[53] Tahal (1990).

The principal water question in the Strip is not one of water sharing between Palestinians and Israelis. Rather, it centres on pressure on water resources and waste-water treatment facilities caused by rapid population growth in an area that was already overcrowded in June 1967, as a result of the influx of refugees which had taken place at the time of the establishment of Israel. Some 750,000 Palestinians now inhabit 360 square kilometres, making the Strip one of the most densely populated areas of the world. Restrictions on Palestinian use of the aquifer were imposed by the Israeli authorities in the mid-1970s, but never as severely as in the West Bank: as a result, abstraction exceeded replenishment by at least 25%. In May 1994, under the terms of the Gaza/Jericho Agreement, supervision of the abstraction of water was transferred to the Palestinian National Authority (PNA) in that part of the Strip (about two-third of the area of the territory) which came under Palestinian control. This has been followed by a relaxation of controls and a rash of well-digging. While no figures are available, the rate of over-abstraction must have increased markedly since the Palestinian take-over.[54]

In the case of the aquifers under the Israeli coastal plain and the Gaza Strip, there was an additional fear. Ground-water in such a situation has an interface with salt-water in the rocks underlying the coast: the salt-water will intrude into the fresh-water aquifer if the ground-water in the latter is excessively depleted. The first signs of this phenomenon were noted in Palestine in the 1940s.[55] To counter this (as well as to store water against summer demand), the Israeli portion of the coastal aquifer is recharged in winter from the National Water Carrier.

The Gazan portion of the aquifer has not been artificially recharged in this way. For some years, abstraction has exceeded recharge by at least 25%, and possibly more than 50%.[56] The resulting fall in the water-table has allowed sea-water to penetrate into the aquifer up to a distance of 1.5 km. inland, and saline ground-water to intrude from the east.[57] Further reasons for the fall in water quality have been the repeated re-use of water from the aquifer for irrigation, and the lack of waste-water treatment facilities (allowing raw sewage to percolate into the ground).

---

[54] One Israeli source says that some 500 new wells have been dug in the Strip since the PNA take-over (see *Ha'aretz*, 25 August 1995: 'Gaza Strip salinisation said affecting Negev Water Resources', translated by BBC Monitoring *SWB*). There may be political reasons for this development: during the Israeli occupation, Palestinians associated with the PLO were denied permission to drill wells; when the PNA took control, it probably rewarded PLO supporters by allowing them to do so.

[55] Government of Palestine (1946/7).

[56] Ahiram and Siniora (1992) give figures at the lower end of this range, Abu-Maila (1991) at the higher end.

[57] Abu-Maila (1991).

As a result, water used for domestic purposes often has a higher concentration of chlorides and nitrates than is safe for drinking. In 1991, over half the drinking water supplied to Gaza City was unsafe on the basis of international guidelines. There is also a growing risk to health from the consumption of food crops that have been irrigated with ground-water contaminated by the percolation into the sub-soil of untreated sewage. The growing salinity of the aquifer poses an economic threat as well as a health hazard. It will do increasing damage to agriculture in the Strip, especially citrus fruits, the most important crop – and hence to livelihoods.

According to Palestinian sources, the Israelis are not only reducing the inflow of ground-water to the Strip by pumping from twenty-five wells on the Israeli side of the 1949 line, but also abstracting ground-water through deep wells in their settlements in the Strip and selling it to Palestinian refugees through Mekorot.[58] A series of small dams designed to trap storm-water in the Wadi Gaza is also likely to reduce flow (in this case, of surface water) from the Israeli side. But the impact of these activities is almost certainly marginal, compared with the level of Palestinian abstractions within the Gaza Strip. In other words, the territory would continue to have serious water problems even if all Israeli operations affecting the aquifer beneath it were to cease immediately.

Nevertheless, water plays a major part in the environmental degradation in the Strip, which in its turn has an important role in fuelling Palestinian discontent. An improvement in the supply of water and the disposal of waste-water would make an important contribution to the creation of a better life for the Palestinians in the Strip – and hence to the sort of conditions which would increase the chances of the peace being a lasting one.

Water on the Golan

As we have seen earlier in this chapter, the occupation of Syrian territory gave Israel control of the Banias, and an improved position on the Yarmuk. However, the Golan plateau between these two rivers is not rich in water resources. A report in an Arab newspaper, quoting 'Israeli sources', says that, of the 46 mcm. used annually by Israeli settlers on the Golan, 16 mcm. come from Lake Tiberias, 11 mcm. from 'the springs of el-Himmeh [Hamma] and the River Jordan', and 19 mcm. from the rivers and springs of the Golan itself, some of it trapped by small dams constructed by the Israelis.[59] In other words, nearly 60%

---

[58] See for example *Asharq Al-Awsat*, 5 October 1994: 'The Palestinian authority accusses Israel of stealing the water supply in Gaza' (in Arabic).

[59] See *al-Hayat* for 9 March 1995: 'Water and peace in the Golan.'

of the water used by the settlements is pumped uphill to reach them, over 600 metres. The extra expense involved has made farming on the Golan costly: as a result, settler's numbers have stagnated, at between 9,000 and 12,000.[60]

Water in the Madrid Peace Process

The present peace process began with the Madrid conference in 1991. The bilateral talks between the parties immediately involved in the Arab-Israel dispute have been paralleled by multilateral meetings with wider participation, both from within the Middle East and beyond. This multilateral 'track' was designed to find ways in which wider regional co-operation could underpin a settlement between Israel and its Arab neighbours. It has taken the form of five working groups, of which the Water Resources Working Group is one.[61]

As far as water issues are concerned, a division of labour has emerged between the bilateral and multilateral tracks. The Water Resources Working Group has examined ways in which more water could be provided, or more efficient use made of what is already available, leaving the question of 'water rights' (i.e. the way in which existing supplies should be apportioned) to the respective bilateral talks.

The Water Resources Working Group has achieved an unprecedented degree of cooperation among participating countries from the region and beyond (although, at the time of writing, Syria and Lebanon had declined to take part in any of the multilateral groups). Valuable work (albeit so far largely preparatory) has been done on a number of important matters, such as the development and conservation of water supplies, the re-use of water and the sharing of data.

The bilateral talks have reached different stages as far as water is concerned. Jordan and Israel have signed a fully-fledged peace treaty that contains (in an annex) a detailed apportionment of shared sources of water. The Israeli-Palestinian Interim Agreement signed on 28 September 1995 postpones the question of Palestinian 'water rights' to the 'final-status' negotiations which are due to begin by May 1996.[62] On

---

[60] According to an AFP report dated 22 October 1993, three additional water sources capable of yielding around 10.5 mcm. per year had recently been discovered. In the new political context created by the peace process, however, it is highly unlikely that these sources will be drawn on to allow more settlers to establish themselves on the Golan.

[61] The other groups deal with the environment, economic development, refugees and arms control. At the time of writing, Syria and Lebanon had declined to take part in any of the multilateral working groups. On the multilateral track as a whole, see Peters (1994).

[62] The Israeli-Palestinian Declaration of Principles of September 1993 stipulates that talks on final-status issues will begin within two years of the establishment of a Palestinian

the Syrian and Lebanese tracks, water is a secondary (but not insignificant) issue compared to those such as Israeli withdrawal, security and normalisation of relations.

The Jordan-Israel peace treaty, 26 October 1994

In terms of water along, the treaty represents a marked improvement for Jordan compared to the status quo. For Israel, the treaty represents, overall, a change for the worse in respect of water (although this is very small vis-à-vis Israel's total water budget): the compensating gain to Israel lies mainly in the fact that the treaty turns the *de facto* peace with Jordan into a *de jure* one, and provides for normal relations between the two states.

There are a number of gains for Jordan in terms of a more favourable division of existing supplies of water.[63] First, Israel has accepted a ceiling of 25 mcm. on its yearly abstractions from the Yarmuk: 12 mcm. in summer and 13 mcm. in winter.[64] It is particularly important for Jordan that Israel will take only 12 mcm. in summer, the period of maximum demand. The 13 mcm. taken in winter is not so significant, as Jordan has no means of storing winter flows. Moreover, Israel will take an additional 20 mcm. from the Yarmuk each winter and store it in Lake Tiberias until the summer, when it will be released to meet Jordan's needs. A pipeline making the necessary physical connection between the River Jordan immediately below the lake and the King Abdullah Canal was completed in June 1995.[65]

Secondly, the Jordanians can store 20 mcm. of winter floods in the River Jordan, at a point south of the confluence with the Yarmuk. Thirdly, the Jordanians can take, from the Jordan, between its confluence with the Yarmuk and the confluences of Wadi Yabis and Tirat Zvi, a quantity equivalent to that already being taken from that stretch of the river by the Israelis.[66] Fourthly, the Jordanians will receive, each year, 10 mcm. of desalinated water from the saline springs beneath the surface

---

self-governing authority in implementation of the Declaration. This took place in May 1994, with the Israeli withdrawal from part of the Gaza Strip and the environs of Jericho, under the terms of the Gaza/Jericho Agreement. For a fuller description of the framework of the Israeli-Palestinian 'track' of the peace process, see the section below entitled 'Israeli-Palestinian negotiations on water'.

[63] Israel-Jordan peace treaty: Annex II: Water-related matters.

[64] The treaty defines summer as the period from 15 May to 15 October, and winter as being the period from 16 October to 14 May.

[65] See the *Jordan Times*, 21 June 1995: 'Israel starts pumping Tiberias water to Jordan.'

[66] Wadi Yabis joins the Lower Jordan from the East Bank, while Tirat Zvi flows in from Israeli territory. The treaty does not specify the quantity involved but, as the water is of poor quality here and therefore unsuitable for most uses, it is not likely to be large.

of Lake Tiberias that have been diverted by Israel to flow into the Lower Jordan.

As well as these gains, there are other benefits for the Kingdom of Jordan, as follows:

– Israeli assistance in finding an additional 50 mcm. a year of drinkable water (probably mainly from the desalination of brackish ground-water underlying Jordanian soil);

– Israeli agreement to co-operate in the construction of diversion and storage works on the Yarmuk to improve the flow into the King Abdullah Canal, and a system of storage on the Jordan between the confluence of the Yarmuk and the confluences of Wadi Yabis and Tirat Zvi (the latter system being necessary to allow the Jordanians to take from the Jordan the 20 mcm. of Yarmuk winter flows to which the treaty entitles them);

– an improvement in the quality of water in the Lower Jordan, as water from saline springs will no longer flow into the river;

– the possibility (now that the Jordanians have recovered their water rights to their own satisfaction and no longer have inhibitions about working with Israel) of further benefits through co-operating with Israel in water projects, in addition to those specified in the treaty.

For its part, Israel has gained recognition of its right to continue to take a total of 25 mcm. a year from the Yarmuk, and to continue to use water from the Jordan between the confluence of the Yarmuk and Wadi Yabis/Tirat Zvi. The Israelis have also secured Jordan's agreement to their continuing to abstract saline water from wells on Jordanian territory in Wadi Araba (south of the Dead Sea) with the possibility of an increase of 10 mcm. a year above the present quantity abstracted.[67]

The limitation of the Israeli share of the Yarmuk to 25 mcm. a year restores the apportionment on which US envoy Eric Johnston had sought to secure agreement in the mid-1950s.[68] However, the treaty does not (and could not) restore to the Kingdom of Jordan the share of the Yarmuk proposed by Johnston, given that Syria is removing from the headwaters of the river far more than the 90mcm. a year which he envisaged. While it is difficult to establish how much water Syria is taking from the Yarmuk basin at present, one official Syrian source

---

[67] According to Haddadin, the chief Jordanian water negotiator, quoted by Elmusa (1995), the present level of abstraction is around 8 mcm a year.

[68] See the section above entitled 'Disputing the waters – up to June 1967'. See also the *Jordan Times*, 20 October 1994, reporting remarks by Haddadin, on the similarity between the treaty and the Johnston proposals.

gives a figure of 116 mcm. a year; other sources cover a range from 163 to a much as 200 mcm.[69]

The Jordan-Israel treaty is a purely bilateral document, and makes no mention of the status of Lebanon, Syria and the West Bank as riparian territories. Because of their upstream position, Lebanon and Syria are not affected by the water aspects of the treaty.[70]

Israeli-Palestinian negotiations on water

The way in which shared water resources should be apportioned and managed represents one of the most difficult issues in negotiation between the Israelis and Palestinians. At stake are the acceptability to the Israeli public of the peace process with the Palestinians, the future of Israeli-Palestinian cooperation in economic affairs, and the potential of the Palestinian economy to develop.

Negotiations between Israel and the Palestinians over water are taking place within the overall framework of the Palestinian track of the Middle East peace process. Because of the difficulty of the issues involved, that framework phases the negotiations over a number of years. The first agreement between Israel and the PLO, the 'Declaration of Principles' signed on 13 September 1993, provided for a five-year interim or transitional period.[71] In the first phase of this period, the Palestinians would establish their own self-governing authority in the Gaza Strip and an enclave around Jericho in the West Bank. In the second phase, the area controlled by this Palestinian authority would be extended much more widely in the West Bank. Then, two years at the latest after the establishment of the authority in Gaza and Jericho, 'final-status' negotiations would begin. These would deal with those issues deemed to be too contentious to be tackled at the outset, before the parties had built up some measure of confidence in each other's good faith. The Declaration of Principles identified some of these final-status issues (e.g. Jerusalem, Israeli settlements), but did not exclude the addition of others to the list.

The Palestinian track has followed the framework originally envisaged, although the timetable has slipped considerably.

The 'Gaza/Jericho Agreement' of May 1994, which gave the Palestinians a measure of self-government in two-thirds of the Gaza Strip

[69] The official Syrian source is Hadid (1990). Garfinkle (1992) gives 163 mcm; Abu Taleb et al (1991) give 170 mcm. One well-informed Jordanian source, speaking in early 1993, suggested a figure of 180-200 mcm.

[70] For a more detailed analysis of its water-related provisions, see Elmusa (1995).

[71] The Declaration of Principles is also known as the 'Oslo Agreement', as the talks leading up to it took place near Oslo.

and the Jericho enclave, provided for some control over water in these areas.[72] The Agreement provided for a Palestinian Water Authority (PWA) that was to take charge of the supply of water.[73] For the time being, however, the Palestinians in the autonomous areas were not able to escape entirely their hydrological dependence on Israel, which was to continue to provide water on their behalf.[74]

It may be no coincidence that the areas over which the Palestinians gained control had no hydrological implications for Israel, in that both are as far downstream as it is possible to be. Nothing that the Palestinians could do with the water supplies of the Gaza Strip or the Jericho area would have had any effect on Israeli consumers (with the possible exception of a small number of settlements).[75] In any case, the Gaza/Jericho Agreement provides that the PNA shall 'prevent any harm to the water resources'.[76]

On 28 September 1995, Israel and the PLO signed a further agreement, the 'Interim Agreement on the West Bank and the Gaza Strip', formally marking the beginning of the much-delayed interim phase of the process.[77] The main purpose of the Interim Agreement was to extend the PNA's control of civil affairs in the West Bank to most areas inhabited by Palestinians (excluding East Jerusalem). It was inevitable that water would form a significant part of the Agreement. One reason for this was the pressing need for an immediate increase in the quantities of water for the Palestinian population, as a means of producing an improvement in their daily lives (without which the Agreement would probably not have been accepted). Another reason was connected with the extent of the territory above the Mountain Aquifer which was to come under Palestinian administration: to the Israeli negotiators, retention

---

[72] The Agreement is also known as the 'Cairo Agreement' after the city in which it was signed.

[73] Gaza-Jericho accord between Israel and the Palestinians, signed 4 May 1994.

[74] See the *International Herald Tribune*, 5 May 1994; 'Main points of Gaza-Jericho pact', and BBC Monitoring *SWB*, 10 May 1994, quoting the Voice of Israel for 7 May 1994; 'PLO official says service contracts signed with foreign firms'.

[75] Israel's Agriculture Minister, Tzur, was reported by the *Jerusalem Post* to have said that Israeli authorities do not supervise water production in the Gaza Strip because Israel obtains the underground flow first (see *Mideast Mirror*, 21 July 1995: 'No immediate solution on tap'). Not all Israelis have been so sanguine: the Sha'ar Hanegev Regional Council has expressed its concern that continued Palestinian pumping in the Strip will lead to the rapid salinisation of the southern part of the coastal aquifer, to the east of the Strip (see *Ha'aretz*, 25 August 1995: 'Gaza Strip salinisation said affecting Negev water resources', translated by BBC Monitoring *SWB*).

[76] Item 31, Section A.

[77] The Agreement is also known as 'Oslo II' (as being the successor of the first 'Oslo Agreement') or the 'Taba Agreement' (after the Egyptian resort in which the negotiations took place).

of some control was necessary to protect their interest in the ground-water beneath the West Bank.[78]

The water-related provisions of the Agreement have a number of important effects, the most significant of which are:

– the recognition by Israel of the existence of 'Palestinian water rights in the West Bank';

– the postponement of negotiations on these rights to final-status talks (due to begin in May 1996 at the latest);

– the provision of an additional 28.6 mcm. of water a year to the Palestinian population of the West Bank and Gaza Strip; and

– the establishment of a Joint Water Committee (JWC) to coordinate management of water and waste-water in the West Bank, during the interim period.

The recognition of Palestinian water rights – the first such recognition by Israel in a formal document – represented a fundamental advance in the Palestinian position. That the discussion of those rights was to be added to the list of issues postponed to final-status negotiations would have been a disappointment to many Palestinians, but must have been seen as a necessary sacrifice to avoid further delay to the conclusion of the Interim Agreement and the greater good that it brought in terms of a major extension of Palestinian control in the West Bank. While important, water was far from being the most important thing at stake.

Of the additional 28.6 mcm. of water a year for the Palestinians, 5 mcm. is to be supplied by Israel to the Gaza Strip via the National Water Carrier. The rest is intended for the West Bank Palestinians, and is to come largely from the Eastern Aquifer (thus avoiding any major impact on water supplied to Israelis on the other side of the Green Line).

More water for the Palestinians. The Interim Agreement puts existing Palestinian abstractions from the Mountain Aquifer at 118 mcm. a year.[79] The additional volume of water to which West Bank Palestinians are entitled under the terms of the Agreement amount to 23.6 mcm. a year. This represents an increase of some 20%. While this is a significant increase in relative terms, the new total allowed to the West Bank Palestinians will not do more than provide them with some relief from the constraints on domestic water. It will only slightly narrow the gap

---

[78] The water provisions of the Agreement are set out in Annex III, Article 40 and Appendix I, Schedules 8-11.

[79] Annex II, Appendix I, Schedule 10.

between themselves and the Israelis in terms of water per capita: overall consumption per capita by West Bank Palestinians will be some 89 cubic metres per person per year (instead of around 74 at present), compared with 365 cubic metres per person per year for Israelis.[80]

The additional 5 mcm. a year for Palestinians in the Gaza Strip represents between five and seven percent of present consumption. However, given the serious over-exploitation of the Gazan aquifer, sound management would require that there be no increase in the consumption of water: the main effect of the additional water would then be to reduce slightly the rate at which the aquifer is being over-exploited. The Agreement is also helpful in this regard in specifying that use of water by Israeli settlements and military installations in the Strip shall be held at present levels.[81]

In the Interim Agreement, the Israelis and Palestinians also agreed that 'the future needs of the Palestinians in the West Bank are estimated to be between 70-80 mcm. year'.[82] Curiously, the wording does not specify the time period involved. However, a later paragraph makes it clear that this will not prejudice the negotiation of Palestinian water rights in the final-status talks.[83]

Water purchases. The Agreement recognises the possibility of purchases of water by one side from the other. Such purchases are to take place at 'the full real cost incurred by the supplier'. This is a provision with important potential implications: in the future, the Palestinians may find it more profitable to sell water to Israel rather than to use it themselves; equally, they might find it makes better economic sense in some areas to buy water from the Israeli system rather than to abstract it themselves by drilling wells directly into the Mountain Aquifer below the West Bank (where the water lies at a much greater depth than it does on the Israeli side of the 1949 line).

Data. In the Interim Agreement, the Israelis made a formal commitment to exchange water data with the Palestinians. Sharing data (almost entirely a one-way street, as the Palestinians have very little data-collecting capacity of their own) will be vital if the Palestinians are to manage effectively water supplies to the communities for which they have become responsible, and to play a full part in the JWC. That the

---

[80] This calculation assumes a population of 1.6 million Palestinians in the West Bank. It also assumes that Israel's annual water consumption (all users) is around 2,000 mcm., including recycled and brackish water.

[81] Annex III, Appendix I, Schedule 10.

[82] Paragraph 6 of Article 40.

[83] Paragraph 8 of Article 40.

Israelis are now ready to provide their data to the Palestinians is some indication of the trust which has been established between the two sides.

Cooperative management. The Agreement sets out the JWC's main areas of responsibility, which cover all questions relating to the management of water and waste-water, in terms of quality as well as quantity. Among the most important of these responsibilities are approving the drilling of new wells or increased abstraction from existing wells, determining changes in abstraction rates in response to natural variations in the volume of ground-water available and approving the construction of new water and waste-water systems.

The establishment of the JWC is probably the most important aspect of the water provision of the Agreement, in that it gives practical expression to the principle of joint management of shared water resources. The Agreement sets up the JWC 'for the interim period', but the continued existence of the JWC (or something similar) is likely to be an important element of any final-status agreement on water.

Water in the final-status negotiations. The water provisions of the Interim Agreement represent a major step towards a permanent Israeli-Palestinian accommodation over water. That this step has been taken should not obscure the fact that the Palestinians continue to regard the present division of the water resources which they share with the Israelis as being heavily and unfairly weighted in favour of the latter: Palestinian spokesmen have asserted that they have a right to abstract 500 mcm. a year from the West Bank aquifers, more than twice their level of consumption agreed in the Interim Agreement. Moreover, the Agreement makes no reference to the surface waters of the basin of the River Jordan, to which the Palestinians believe they have a right as a result of their riparian position in the West Bank.

International law has not advanced sufficiently to offer more than the most general guidance on the division of shared water resources.[84] As far as the West Bank aquifers and the Jordan are concerned, the Israelis may be expected to argue that the principle to be applied is that of 'established rights' – that they have for many years used a certain volume of water from both sources, and must therefore be allowed to continue to do so. Indeed, some Israeli commentators have drawn a parallel between the Israeli use of the shared West Bank aquifers and the Egyptian use of the Nile, both being existing and long-standing

---

[84] For a fuller discussion of the state of international law on shared water resources, see Chapter 7.

uses of water downstream of the country in which the source of the water lies.

For their part, the Palestinians are likely to prefer the principle of 'equitable and reasonable use', whereby any division of the shared sources of water would take into account many factors in addition to existing uses. Since Israelis use three to four times as much water per head as do Palestinians, there seems little doubt that any neutral adjudication based on equitable and reasonable use would award the Palestinians much larger volumes of water than those which they currently take.[85]

For this very reason, there seems very little likelihood of Israel's agreeing to any such adjudication. Indeed, Israeli proposals, in emphasising ways of increasing supply for the area as a whole, seem designed to suggest that such an adjudication is unnecessary: Palestinians can have more water without Israel having to make do with less. Israelis also stress the need to control demand: in addition to its inherent merits, this approach would reduce the volumes of water needed by the Palestinians, again reducing the scale of the sacrifice in terms of water which Israel may have to make for peace.

Nonetheless, it is hard to avoid the conclusion that Israel will have to adjust to taking a smaller proportion of the shared ground-water resources of the Mountain Aquifer as a necessary condition for peace, or perhaps concede Palestinian 'ownership' of a larger proportion of these resources, continuing to use the same amount in exchange for payments to the Palestinians, or some combination of both.[86] Whatever arrangements are made with respect to volumes of water, Israel will also want guarantees that Palestinian provisions for the handling of waste-water will be adequate to protect the shared aquifers from contamination.[87] Again, Israel might consider compensating the Palestinians for refraining from economic activities (such as intensive agriculture or polluting industries) that it believes could damage the quality of the water in the shared aquifers.

The dispute between Israel and the Palestinians over ground-water is connected with the question of the location of the permanent boundary between Israel and the Palestinian-controlled West Bank, which has also been held over to final-status talks. When the negotiators get to grips with the boundary question, the Palestinians will press for a full

---

[85] The comparison between Israeli and Palestinian consumption takes into account agricultural and industrial as well as domestic uses.

[86] It is in this context that the significance of the Interim Agreement's provisions on water purchases becomes fully apparent.

[87] See *Mideast Mirror*, 21 July 1995 ('No immediate solution on tap'), quoting Israel's Agriculture Minister, Tzur.

Israeli withdrawal to the line delimited in 1949 by the Armistice Agreement between Israel and Jordan. For their part, the Israelis are likely to seek a line further to the east, at least in some places, in order to avoid a return to the vulnerable situation which pertained before June 1967, when the narrowness of Israel's 'waist' along the coastal plain made it vulnerable to a military advance that could cut the country into two. A broader Israel in this area could also encompass a substantial number of Jewish settlements (which are particularly dense in the western and north-western portions of the West Bank), reducing the scale of the problem which the government will have to face in dealing with settlements in territory that is transferred to Palestinian control.

A boundary to the east of the 1949 line would enable Israel to maintain sole control of a larger portion of the Western Aquifer than would be the case if the 1949 line became the permanent boundary. Indeed, there have been suggestions that a desire to achieve such a situation has led the Israelis to consider a line well to the east of the 1949 line and close to the ground-water divide between the Western and the Eastern Aquifers.[88]

Wherever the line drawn and whatever agreement is reached on the apportionment of water between Israel and the Palestinians of the West Bank, the two sides will find some kind of cooperative management essential. Given the variations in the rainfall which recharges the shared aquifers, a joint decision-making mechanism on how much water can safely be abstracted will be required. The JWC will provide valuable lessons for the permanent body which will almost inevitably be established to provide the necessary cooperative management. Indeed, it seems probable that the JWC will itself evolve into such a permanent body.

The Palestinians have also made plain their wish to assert their rights as a riparian to the waters of the Jordan basin.[89] They may base their claim on the Johnston Plan. While it made no separate apportionment for the West Bank (only suggesting an overall share for the Kingdom of Jordan, which then included the West Bank), it assumed that about 30% of the irrigable land in the valley of the lower Jordan basin lay in the West Bank. Some of this land was to have been supplied with water from side-wadis and wells, but most of it would have used water drawn from the Yarmuk or the Jordan. The amount intended to be

---

[88] To the best of the present author's knowledge, no specific territorial claim to parts of the West Bank beyond the 1949 line has ever been made by the current Israeli government. Academic studies (e.g. Alpher, 1994) have shown what such claims could look like.

[89] See *Mideast Mirror*, 21 July 1995 ('No immediate solution on tap'), quoting al-Khoudary, head of the Palestinian delegation to the Multilateral Water Resources Working Group. See also Rodan (1995).

taken from these rivers could have been as high as 140-150 mcm. a year.[90]

That Israel has, in its treaty with Jordan, limited its use of the waters of the Yarmuk to its apportionment under the Johnston Plan could be seen as a helpful precedent for the Palestinians in their attempts to obtain for themselves a share of the surface waters of the Jordan basin. However, the likelihood that the Israelis will have to make concessions to the Palestinians over West Bank water will probably make them less willing to do so over surface waters. Moreover, the fact that the Israelis have (as they see it) had to pay in concessions over water the price of their treaty with Jordan will almost certainly make them less willing to do the same for the Palestinians. Their reluctance will be reinforced by the sharp domestic criticism of other aspects of the Palestinian track of the peace process (e.g. security): the Israeli government will not want to add water to this list.

Final-status negotiations are due to begin simultaneously on several issues. According to the timetable set out in the Declaration of Principles of September 1993, final-status negotiations will begin by May 1996 at the latest, and will be concluded by 1999. Despite the wide gap between the two parties on water, other questions such as borders, settlements and Jerusalem will be more difficult to resolve. The experience of working together through the JWC will help water negotiators find solutions, an advantage that does not apply to other issues.

Indeed, it is more likely that deadlock over other issues will hold up the achievement of an accord on water than vice versa. This would not necessarily happen through the explicit linkage of negotiations over the various issues: it might simply be that ill-feeling in the negotiations over one issue might spread to others, creating a general atmosphere of non-cooperation.

The Syrian and Lebanese tracks

As far as water is concerned, Israel's aim on the Syrian and Lebanese tracks must be to preserve (as much as possible) the status quo. For Israel, in its negotiations with Syria, there are significant water interests at stake: in July 1995, the late Israeli Prime Minister Yitzhak Rabin was reported to have remarked that the greatest danger Israel faced in the negotiations with Syria was the possibility of losing control over

---

[90] Elmusa (1993), Hillel (1994). According to one source, Arafat rejected an Israeli draft for the Interim Agreement on the ground that it made no mention of Palestinian rights to water from the River Jordan. At this stage (according to the same source), the Palestinians were demanding the right to 130 mcm a year from the Jordan: see Rodan (1995).

Water in the Madrid Peace Process 39

the water resources of the Golan.[91]

The most important of these resources is the Banias, and Israel would undoubtedly wish to make a deal that ensured that its flow was not drastically reduced. The same would probably be true for the many smaller streams which flow off the Golan into the Upper Jordan (although, even in total, the volume of water in these streams is less than that in the Banias). However, the Israelis are not just concerned about volumes of water, but also that return flows from Syrian agriculture and other activities on the Golan could lead to a significant deterioration in the quality of water in Lake Tiberias: it would be surprising if they did not require guarantees, in a treaty with Syria, that this would not occur.[92] Israeli negotiators will also resist Syrian demands for a withdrawal to the 'line of the 4th of June 1967', which would not only give Syria a position astride the Upper Jordan in the central area of the DMZ but also a shoreline on the eastern side of Lake Tiberias. Given the sensitivity of Lake Tiberias as the country's main reservoir, it is hard to see Israel accepting any proposal that would allow these areas to come under Syrian control. In January 1996, Shimon Peres, who succeeded as Israel's Prime Minister after the death of Yitzhak Rabin, remarked that it would be 'suicide' to relinquish Lake Tiberias. His Foreign Minister, Ehud Barak, put the Israeli position equally bluntly: 'We don't want to see Syrian feet in the Kinneret'.[93]

One possibility that has been mooted is an arrangement under which Syria would not reduce the flow of water to Israel and would be compensated by water from Turkey.[94] This could take the form of additional flow down the Euphrates, in which case Turkey could either charge Syria an agreed rate, or supply the water free of charge as a contribution to the peace process or in return for inducements provided by the international community. Alternatively, Turkey could supply water by pipeline from other rivers, such as the Ceyhan or Seyhan. The initial Turkish reaction to this suggestion has, however, been discouraging.[95] Moreover, these proposals presuppose the achievement of a degree of cooperation between Turkey and Syria that does not seem possible in the present atmosphere (or indeed in the foreseeable future). It also appears unlikely that Syria would accept the notion that it should pay

[91] Qol Yisrael radio report, 19 July 1995, translated by Foreign Broadcast Information Service (FBIS).
[92] For an example of Israeli fears, see *Mideast Mirror*, 18 January 1994: 'Knesset panel calls for continued control of area's water sources.'
[93] Both quotations are from *Mideast Mirror*, 15 January 1996.
[94] See the *Jerusalem Post International Edition*, 17 February 1996: 'Talks with Syria resume this month.'
[95] See the comments by a senior Turkish foreign ministry official quoted in the *Financial Times*, 15 February 1996: 'Euphrates power plant generates new tension.'

for water from Turkey, as this would undermine Syrian claims to a larger share of the flow of the Euphrates, as of right.[96]

As in the case of the Palestinian track, water is only one of the issues to be negotiated by Israel and Syria. In another sense, however, water negotiations on the two tracks will be very different. On the Palestinian track, the water resources at stake are of major importance for both sides. On the Syrian track, the water resources involved are of major importance only for Israel: for Syria, they may be valuable on a local scale but – being less than one percent of the flow of the Euphrates – are not of national significance. Syria's main goal appears to be the recovery of the territory occupied by Israel in 1967 for reasons of national pride, regardless of the resources contained within that territory. But the same desire to re-establish sovereignty over occupied territory may also lead Syria to insist on unfettered control of water resources within the territory. Negotiations over water could prove difficult and protracted.

The Hasbani, which rises in Lebanon, is a significant contributor of water to the Upper Jordan river (about a quarter of the average flow at the confluence with the Dan and the Banias). As in the case of the Banias, Israel would want any peace agreement with Lebanon to include provisions ensuring the continued flow of the Hasbani. For its part, Lebanon is likely to want to secure a share of the flow, perhaps in line with its 'Johnston share' of 35 mcm a year. This volume of water might be used to develop the country's southern border areas. Alternatively, having gained recognition of its 'ownership' of an annual quota of Hasbani water in a treaty, the Lebanese might find it more profitable to sell this water to Israel rather than use it within Lebanon's own boundaries. For Lebanon, as for Syria, water is a secondary issue in its dispute with Israel, ranking much lower in importance than the withdrawal of Israeli forces.

Bilateral versus comprehensive

Ideally, the apportionment of the waters of the whole basin should be agreed by all five parties (Israel, Jordan, the Palestinians, Syria and Lebanon) in a single, comprehensive agreement, providing for the management of the basin as a unit. However, Israel has made a bilateral agreement with Jordan over water, and another (albeit temporary) with the Palestinians. It seems likely that Israel will eventually also sign separate bilateral agreements with Syria and Lebanon that will include provisions on shared water resources. Any treaty between all five

---

[96] See Chapter 4: 'The Tigris-Euphrates Basin'.

Water in the Arab-Israel Dispute

countries which share the Jordan basin is likely to come only much later.

The Challenge of the Future

In the present peace process, the leaders of Israel and its Arab neighbours are facing the challenge of making peace. Reaching compromises over water is part of that process. A bigger challenge may still lie ahead. Growing populations and their aspirations to higher living standards mean greater demand for water, the existing supply of which is already fully utilised. Failure to find a solution to this problem could be a cause of internal instability, or undermine international agreements that have been achieved by the countries of the area.

Population growth

The West Bank and Gaza Strip, Israel, Jordan, Syria and Lebanon are areas of rapid population growth, the result of both natural increase and (for Israel and Jordan) immigration. This growth translates into increased demand for water on the part of domestic consumers. It also means greater demand for food, which – if higher imports are to be avoided – must be met by higher production at home, something that can only be accomplished by the use of more water for irrigation. The desire for better living standards means a greater increase in demand for water in both the domestic and agricultural sectors.

The Palestinian population of the West Bank is growing through natural increase at a rate of over 3% a year; for the Gaza Strip, the figure is probably higher.[97] Although the annual rate of natural increase in Israel is low, below 2%, the high level of immigration in recent years (mainly of Jews from the former Soviet Union) pushes this figure up to 2.3%.[98] For its part, Jordan has had to cope with both a high rate of natural increase (3.4% p.a.) and a sudden influx of 300,000 Jordanian émigré workers from the Gulf, following the Iraqi invasion of Kuwait. As a result of this influx alone, Jordan's population was

---

[97] There is little agreement among the sources. For example, the Statistical Abstract of Israel (1992) gives a figure of 4% for the West Bank, but only 3.3% for the Gaza Strip. Omran and Roudi (1993) also give 4% for the West Bank, but 5% for the Gaza Strip; Abdulhadi, quoted by Gruen (1992), gives 3% and 3.5% respectively.

[98] The figure for the overall rate of increase is from the Israeli Central Bureau of Statistics, quoted by Voice of Israel: see BBC *SWB*, 6 September 1994: 'Population reaches 5.4 million according to government statistics.'

10% higher after the Gulf crisis than it was before. Syria's population is growing at about 3.8% a year, Lebanon's at 2.1%.[99]

Table 2. POPULATION GROWTH IN ISRAEL AND NEIGHBOURING COUNTRIES

	Population in 1993 (× 1,000)	Natural increase (% p.a.)	Projected population in 2025 (× 1,000)
Israel	5,270	1.5	7,994
West Bank	1,600	4	2,980
Gaza Strip	694	5	1,889
Jordan	3,824	3.6	8,281
Syria	13,463	3.8	36,529
Lebanon	3,552	2.1	6,134

The return to Jordan of *émigré* workers was an isolated event; the immigration to Israel of Jews from the Soviet Union will inevitably peter out.[100] And rates of natural increase are declining in Jordan and Israel, at least. But this decline is far too slow to have much of an impact on rising demand for water. Moreover, assuming that the Palestinians acquire a 'right of return' at some future time, there may be substantial immigration to the West Bank and Gaza Strip on the part of those at present in the 'diaspora'. Even ignoring this factor, on present population forecasts, and assuming *domestic* consumption of 100 cubic metres of water per person per year by Israelis, Palestinians Jordanians and those Syrians and Lebanese who live in the Jordan basin, there will be no fresh-water left for any other purpose within a couple of decades.[101]

Balancing supply and demand

Proposals that aim to find a balance between supply and demand, whether in the area as a whole, or in individual countries, are addressing problems common to most arid lands. Nonetheless, there are implications for the international disputes over water within the area, since increased supplies

---

[99] Omran and Roudi (1993).

[100] According to a survey by the Jewish Agency, there are only 1,434,000 Jews left in the states which once formed part of the Soviet Union. The survey is quoted in *The Washington Report on Middle East Affairs*, Feb/Mar 1994: 'Survey indicates only 1.4 million Jews remain in former USSR.'

[101] Author's interview with Ben Meir, former Israeli Water Commissioner, June 1993, and Ben Meir (1995). Domestic consumption of one hundred cubic metres per person per year is, by world standards, a low figure.

The Challenge of the Future

of water, or measures to reduce demand, should have the effect of blunting competition for existing sources. Proposed solutions fall into six main categories:

- Increasing supply through conventional methods;
- Increasing supply through the importation of water;
- Increasing supply through non-conventional methods;
- conserving water;
- managing demand to keep it in line with supply; and
- managing the area's water resources in a cooperative manner.

Increasing supply through conventional methods

The traditional ways of dealing with the demand for more water have been to build more dams, dig deeper wells, and move water by pipeline or canal from one part of the country to another. In the West Bank and Gaza Strip, Israel, Jordan and adjoining parts of Syria, opportunities for further development along these lines are very limited.

The only significant surface water-course which is not yet fully developed is the Yarmuk. As we have seen, Syria is continuing to increase its exploitation of the Yarmuk basin by the construction of small dams.[102] It is not clear whether Syria has much scope for further activity of this kind.

The treaty between jordan and israel will, without solving Jordan's water problems, make a valuable contribution towards easing them. If all the measures set out in the treaty are implemented, Jordan should have between 150 and 200 mcm. more water available each year than it has now, an increase of some 20-25%. Now that the Jordanians, as a result of the treaty, are willing to engage in cooperative ventures with Israel, further joint projects not specified in the treaty may well emerge in the future to provide more water for both countries.

The signature of the treaty, although it makes no mention of the Unity Dam, may mean that the Israelis would have no further objection to the project. However, given the scale of present Syrian use, and the abstractions and works provided for in the Jordan-Israel peace treaty, the project may well not be viable. Even if it were, it would probably have to be on a much smaller scale than the original conception.

The Jordanians are proceeding with plans to build or enlarge dams on smaller water-courses, particularly the wadis on the eastern side of the Jordan valley. These projects should provide useful additions to

[102] See above p. 18.

Jordan's water stock, especially in years of heavy winter rainfall, when storage capacity has proved inadequate and water has been lost.[103] According to a senior Jordanian official, these projects will enable nearly 350 mcm of water to be impounded each year.[104]

To meet the increasing demand for water in Amman and surrounding urban areas, Jordan has looked to the Qa Disi aquifer, which lies beneath both Jordan and Saudi Arabia. The water has the advantage of being of good quality, but the disadvantage of being located over 300 km. from Amman. Taking all the costs into account, water from Qa Disi would probably cost between 80 and 90 US cents per cubic metre, delivered to the consumer – an acceptable price for domestic consumption and many industrial purposes. Another possible use for Qa Disi water would be to mix it with brackish water to produce water of adequate quality for irrigation. A pipeline that would bring up to 80 mcm. of water a year to the Amman area is projected; at this rate, Qa Disi could probably supply water for 100 years.[105]

Israel has already developed all the sources of water within its pre-1967 boundaries that can be exploited by conventional means. As far as the Gaza Strip is concerned, there are no opportunities for further exploitation of the aquifer by drilling new wells: any such activity would only accelerate the deterioration of the aquifer. In the West Bank, the limitations are political as much as hydrological. There is no doubt that the Palestinians could make use of substantially greater volumes of water from the Mountain Aquifer beyond those specified in the Interim Agreement, if an accord could be reached with the Israelis. Agreement will be much easier to achieve in the case of the Eastern Aquifer than in the case of the Western and North-eastern Aquifers, where increased Palestinian use would mean equivalent reductions in the volume available to Israel. But some such such sacrifice will probably be unavoidable if an overall settlement is to be reached.

---

[103] Interview with the Jordanian Minister of Water and Irrigation, published in *Al-Aswaq* (Jordanian periodical, in Arabic), 12 May 1992. According to the Minister, 1,700 mcm. of rainfall had been 'wasted', 10 times the quantity which had been stored in the Kingdom's reservoirs.

[104] Dr. Abdul Aziz Wishah, Secretary General of the Jordan Valley Authority, quoted by the *Jordan Times*, 30 April/1 May 1992: 'Record rainfall amounts reported for past winter.' One of the largest of these projects will be the Karameh dam, with a capacity of 55 mcm. Part of this capacity will be used to store winter flow from the Yarmuk, conveyed via the King Abdullah Canal: see the *Jordan Times*, 24 June 1995: 'Karameh dam to make benefits of peace visible.'

[105] The longevity of Qa Disi depends on other factors as well, especially local use for irrigation, and abstractions by Saudi Arabia from the other side of the border. The dispute between Jordan and Saudi Arabia over this aquifer is examined in Chapter 6.

Importing water

Bringing water from one river basin to another in order to balance supply and demand is a well-established practice. It is, for example, highly developed in Canada, where water is conveyed across provincial boundaries as well as across watersheds.[106] Zionist and Israeli plans for the development of the region's water resources have included the conveyance of water from the Litani. This idea continues to surface from time to time. The volume of water involved would not be large: 100 mcm. a year has been mentioned by an Israeli study as the upper limit.[107] Selling water from the Litani to Israel is an option for the Lebanese, as water sold to Israel would probably bring much higher returns than any use within Lebanon's own boundaries. To be satisfactory to the Lebanese, such an arrangement would need to affirm clearly their sovereignty over the river. Nonetheless, the Lebanese would have to balance their own needs against the commercial attractions of such an idea. The choice would not be an easy one, as the country may find itself facing a deficit in its overall water budget by the turn of the century.[108]

The possibility of bringing water from larger and more distant rivers has also been considered. These include the Nile, the Euphrates, and a number of wholly Turkish rivers.

Proposals to bring water from the Nile to the Gaza Strip and the Negev, and possibly also to the West Bank and Jordan, are tempting, given the huge size of the Nile relative to the water resources to Israel, Jordan and the West Bank and Gaza Strip at present. These proposals are, however, based on two assumptions: that there is surplus water in the Nile, and that the governments of the Nile basin would agree to the transfer of water to non-riparian states.

The first assumption is undoubtedly mistaken, and the second one almost certainly so. When President Sadat offered to sell water to Israel in 1979, he appears to have believed that the fact that a quantity of Nile water flowed into the Mediterranean meant that there was an exportable surplus. In fact, this flow is vital to flush return flows from irrigation and other uses into the sea. As for the second assumption, a rejection by Sudan's Islamic regime is a foregone conclusion, and it is hard to imagine the Ethiopian government being much more sympathetic to the idea: these states would be likely to seize on such a suggestion as evidence that there was no reason why they should not themselves make more use of Nile water. Probably with such con-

---

[106] Newson (1992).
[107] Merhav (1989).
[108] Comair (1993).

siderations in mind, the Egyptian government continues to rule out the provision of water to Israel.[109]

In the early 1980s, Jordan examined the feasibility of bringing 160 mcm. of water a year to Amman from the Euphrates in Iraq.[110] However, the estimated cost per unit of water delivered to Amman was discouragingly high, at $2 per cubic metre (even before the cost of distribution within Amman was added). Moreover, Iraq's supply of Euphrates water has fallen since 1982 as a result of increased use by Turkey. It is likely to fall still further in coming years, both in quantity and in quality. Iraq will probably become increasingly reluctant to share the Euphrates with Jordan.

In 1987, Turkey proposed the construction of the 'Peace Pipeline'. The idea was to draw surplus water from two wholly Turkish rivers, the Seyhan and Ceyhan, and convey it to a number of Arab countries through two huge pipelines. One pipeline was to supply Kuwait, eastern Saudi Arab and the other GCC states.[111] The quality of the water would be high and, according to a study carried out by engineering consultants Brown and Root, would cost only one-third as much as desalinated sea-water.[112] This would make it competitive with new water from other sources, such as Qa Disi.

Despite energetic promotion by the late Turgut Özal, both as President and Prime Minister of Turkey, the scheme was not received with enthusiasm by its proposed customers.[113] The Arab states seemed to fear the dependence on other states, especially a resurgent Turkey, that use of the pipeline would have created. Moreover, Turkey has now itself ceased to promote the peace pipeline.

Similar difficulties appear to apply to proposals to bring water to Syria, Jordan, the West Bank and Gaza Strip and Israel from the reservoir behind the Atatürk Dam, or from Turkish rivers that flow into the

---

[109] Radi, the Egyptian Minister of Public Works and Water Resources, told a seminar in June 1994 that the question of transferring Nile water to Israel was 'definitely not on the table', and that the Salam Canal (which conveys water to Sinai from the Nile) had nothing to do with this idea. See BBC Monitoring *SWB*, 21 June 1994: 'Minister denies plan to transfer Nile water to Israel.'

[110] See *Financial Times*, 24 September 1982: 'UK group set to design Iraq-Jordan water plan'.

[111] GCC: Gulf Co-operation Council: Saudi Arabia, Kuwait, Bahrain, Qatar, the United Arab Emirates and Oman.

[112] Kolars (1991).

[113] The Israeli attitude was more positive, but Turkish spokesmen were generally reluctant to say openly that Turkey was prepared to supply Israel as well as Arab states. However, such a possibility was revealed from time to time: for example, see *The Times*, 10 April 1991: 'Turkey is ready to pipe water to Israel.'

Black Sea.[114] The first of these proposals would have the additional drawback that one of the major customers, Syria, would be asked to pay for water drawn from the Euphrates that it believes it is entitled to receive for nothing.

Israel continues to consider the possibility of increasing its own water supply by bringing water from the Manavgat River in Turkey by sea, in giant bags.[115] The primary purpose of this project would be to mitigate Israel's water shortages, rather than those of the area as a whole. If if proved capable of enhancing Israel's water supply to a significant extent, however, it would make it easier for Israel to make do with less water from the sources which it shares with the Arabs. Such a scheme has also been considered as a short-term way of increasing the water supply of the Gaza Strip.

Non-conventional methods

There are many ways of increasing a country's water supply, apart from building more dams digging more wells, or bringing water from other river basins.

Desalination. Desalination of sea-water makes economic sense for uses of water that require high quality and bring high returns, such as domestic consumption – provided that energy is available at low cost. In such circumstances and with the latest technologies, water can be produced at around $1 per cubic metre. Low-cost energy is of course available in the oil-producing countries of the Persian Gulf, but not in Jordan, Israel or the West Bank and Gaza Strip. In these areas, large-scale desalination of sea-water is only likely to be introduced if a major new source of cheap energy can be found.

There are two main possibilities. The first is a breakthrough in energy economics, perhaps through solar power, or nuclear fusion. This cannot be predicted with confidence at the moment. The second possibility is one of a number of schemes designed to generate hydro-power by exploiting the difference between the level of the Dead Sea or the

---

[114] These schemes have been put forward by Wachtel, an Israeli consultant, and Haddadin, the chief Jordanian water negotiator, respectively: see Wachtel (1994) and Haddadin (1992).

[115] *MEED (Middle East Economic Digest)* for 25 November 1994 reported that Israel was discussing the purchase of 180 mcm. a year from Turkey, at a price of $0.45 per cubic metre. Avraham Katz-Oz, head of the Israeli delegation to the Multilateral Water Resources Working Group (see pp. 28 ff.) has been quoted as saying that Turkey would be ready to sell Israel 200 mcm. of water a year at a price he believes would be about half the cost of desalinated water: see Rodan (1995).

lower Jordan valley and that of the Mediterranean or Red Seas.[116] A 'Med-Dead' canal has been proposed that would begin in the Gaza Strip and pass south of Beersheba. A canal connecting the Mediterranean with the Jordan valley would begin south of Haifa and follow the Vale of Esdraelon. A 'Red-Dead' canal would follow the course of the Wadi Araba. All of these schemes would generate electricity that would in turn power desalination plants, or make use of the difference in height between the highest point of the canal and the Dead Sea to produce desalinated water by the 'reverse osmosis' technique.[117]

Water of acceptable quality might also be produced by the desalination of brackish ground-water. There are drawbacks: reserves of brackish ground-water are finite, and there are pumping costs to be met as well as the costs of the desalination process itself. However, as such water is less saline than sea-water, the process is less costly.

Desalination of brackish ground-water may be particularly attractive for Jordan. Not only does Jordan lack cheap energy, but also its main concentrations of population are at a much higher elevation than the places at which desalinated sea-water could be produced – on the Red Sea coast, or below sea-level in the Wadi Araba if the 'Red-Dead' project went ahead. Additional costs would be involved in pumping the water to where it was to be consumed.

Re-use. Israel and Jordan have been using waste water for irrigation for many years. In the 1970s. Israel embarked on the Dan Region Waste-water Reclamation Project. This treats water collected from the Tel Aviv urban area and conveys it south to the Negev for use in irrigation. A similar scheme is in operation in the Haifa area, and there are smaller-scale facilities elsewhere. Reclaimed waste-water now accounts for about 20% of irrigation water. In Jordan, about 8% of irrigation water comes from waste-water.

It seems certain that waste-water will become increasingly important in maintaining supplies of water for agriculture in both countries. Tahal, Israel's water planning organisation, has prepared a national programme for effluent reclamation that aims to double the volume of effluent re-used in agriculture from around 200 mcm. per year in 1990 to about 410 mcm. in the year 2005.[118] This will be made possible not so much

---

[116] The Dead Sea is now 404 metres below sea level, having fallen 13 metres since 1946: see *Middle East Monitor*, May 1994, quoting a presentation by Gideon Biger of Tel Aviv University to a conference at the University of Durham.

[117] The three proposals are reviewed in Richard Morris & Associates (1994). A feasibility study by Israel's National Planning Authority concluded that these proposals would be uneconomic unless finance could be arranged at extremely low interest rates.

[118] Harrosh (1993).

by using a higher proportion of the effluent produced by urban areas (three-quarters is used already), but mainly by the greater production of raw effluent as a result of population growth and higher use of water *per capita*. Eventually, crops in Israel will be irrigated almost entirely with recycled water, as all fresh water supplies are needed for domestic and industrial consumption.[119]

Jordan also plans to make more use of effluent in agriculture: it could provide some 70 mcm. more water per year for irrigation by 2005.[120] This would represent some 13% of current agricultural consumption. However, the potential for reclaiming water for irrigation is not as great in Jordan as it is in Israel, because Jordan has fewer people, who also consume less water per person (at only 43 cubic metres per year, *per capita* domestic consumption is among the lowest in the world). Moreover, it may prove more difficult for Jordanian farmers, on the whole less well-trained than their Israeli counterparts, to use waste-water safely.

While at first sight the cost of water supplied for irrigation in this way may seem high, one must remember that urban effluent requires a degree of treatment before it can be disposed of, even if no use is to be made of it.[121] The true cost of re-using effluent for irrigation is thus the difference between the cost of treatment and conveyance for disposal, and the combined cost of treatment for irrigation and conveyance to the field. As far as investment is concerned, the Tahal programme mentioned above involves investments of $550 million, compared with investments of $350 million if the effluent were treated to the degree necessary for its safe disposal alone.

Cloud-seeding. Cloud-seeding has been carried out over northern Israel since 1976, producing perhaps 5% more rainfall than would occur naturally. On a large scale, and with improved techniques, it might increase the replenishment of Israel's sources of water by between 50 and 100 mcm. a year.[122] Jordan has also been running a cloud-seeding programme, but very little information on its effects is available.

Irrigation with brackish water. Brackish water is already used on a significant scale in Israel to irrigate salt-tolerant crops. It could probably

---

[119] See, for example, remarks made by Agriculture Minister Tzur to a Voice of Israel interviewer on 10 July 1995, translated by BBC Monitoring *SWB* and published on 12 July 1995.

[120] Fataftah and Abu-Taleb (1992).

[121] No accurate figure is available, but the cost of providing water for irrigation from this source probably works out at about 50-70 US cents per cubic metre.

[122] Tahal (1990).

be developed further in Israel and elsewhere. Other techniques, such as recharging aquifers and trapping storm-water in normally dry wadis, may make some addition to the water stock of the countries of the area.

The wide range of methods of increasing water supplies should not hide the fact that most of them are expensive (in terms of cost per cubic metre) or capable of making only a marginal addition to water stocks, or both. The gains that they offer are being cancelled out by the rapidity with which the population of the area is growing. No solutions can be found to the area's water problems unless wastage is reduced and demand contained as well as supplies increased.

Conserving water

Both the Israeli and Jordanian governments have shown enthusiasm for reducing wastage in water use. Given the position of agriculture as the dominant user of water, it is improvements in irrigation techniques that have had most impact. How much room is left in Israel for further water-saving by such improvements is open to question. In Jordan, the possibilities are greater: in the Jordan valley, half the irrigated area is still supplied with water by surface flow rather than drip or sprinkler methods.

While the proportion of total water supplies consumed by domestic users is relatively low, there are opportunities to make savings by reducing losses in urban distribution networks. Some of these losses are due to illegal connections, other to leaks in ageing pipes. Such losses may be high: for the Amman and Zerqa Governorates in Jordan, more than half of the water entering the networks is unaccounted for; similar figures are reported from the Gaza Strip.[123] There are further ways of saving water in urban areas, such as the use of 'minimum-flow' fixtures for toilets and showers.

Managing demand

Given the limited opportunities for increasing supply in the region, and their high cost, demand management offers the most promising means of preventing the imbalance between supply and demand from growing still further.

There is little scope for finding alternatives to water in domestic or industrial activities. In any case these uses not only consume relatively

---

[123] Jordanian Government (1992a), and *Jerusalem Post* 2 July 1987: 'Territories' water supply drying up with overuse.'

small volumes of water, but also bring high returns per cubic metre. These observations do not apply to irrigation. The agricultural sector uses large volumes of water and generally brings low returns per cubic metre – in some cases, less that the cost of the water used. (In Israel, the press has from time to time complained that Israeli taxpayers are subsiding European consumers of Israeli produce, because of the below-cost price for water paid by farmers.[124]) Moreover, food imports provide an alternative to food grown at home by irrigated agriculture – and hence an alternative to water in that use.

Nonetheless, until recently, no government in the area had adopted a policy of reducing the size of the irrigated agricultural sector. The reasons for this very from one country to another.

For Israel, agriculture (and therefore irrigation) was fundamental to Zionist ideology, as representing redemption of the land and rootedness in it. It was also a vital part of its policy of spreading Jewish settlement throughout the territory of the state, for defensive purposes.

The importance of these factors has undoubtedly fallen with time. Questioning the ideological aspects of agriculture is no longer regarded as heresy.[125] In an age of ballistic missiles and nuclear weapons, the distribution of population has little to do with the defence of the state. Meanwhile, however, a strong agricultural lobby has developed and entrenched itself in the institutions of government. Water policy-making is the province of the Minister of Agriculture, who also sits on the board of directors of Mekorot, the national water company. A controlling share of Mekorot's stock is held by the Jewish Agency (the business of which is the settlement of Jews on the land) and the government. The Water Commissioner, who manages Israel's water affairs, operates from the Ministry of Agriculture. The structure of policy-making and management of water in Israel is complicated, but it is clear that the interests of domestic and industrial consumers are much less well represented than those of farmers.

Despite these obstacles, Israel has for some years shown itself ready to address the need to adjust the allocation of water between economic sectors. A policy of steadily reducing the proportion of the total water budget allocated to agriculture was adopted in 1989.[126] In early 1991, in response to drought conditions, the Ministry of Agriculture announced

---

[124] See the example the *Jerusalem Post*, 11 April 1990 (editorial).

[125] See for example the editorial in the *Jerusalem Post*, 1 April 1991, entitled 'What to do about water', which described the ideology of redemption as 'anachronistic' and 'irrelevant in a sovereign state'.

[126] Lonergan and Brooks (1995). In July 1995, Tzur, Israel's Agriculture Minister, remarked that about 60 mcm. of water were transferred each year from agriculture to domestic use.

that water quotas for farmers would be cut back by around 60%, while water for domestic consumption would be reduced by only 15%.[127] From 1991/2, this measure was strengthened by water pricing, which 'became a powerful mechanism to cut water demand'.[128] Israeli farmers now pay about $0.20 per cubic metre of water, one of the highest rates in the world. Moreover, most of them now seem to accept that agriculture is the 'reserve water sector': that is, it will be agriculture that will endure the most severe cutbacks in drought periods.[129]

Peace with Egypt has enabled Israel to benefit from the Nile, not directly in the form of imports of water but indirectly in the form of imports of agricultural products that require large quantities of water. By importing cucumbers and tomatoes from Egypt rather than growing them at home, Israel can free its own water supplies for other sectors.[130]

In the West Bank and Gaza Strip, the Israeli authorities were able to prevent increased use of water for irrigation.[131] However, even with its use of water constrained in this way, the sector is still one of the most important in the West Bank economy, especially in employment terms.[132] The PNA will therefore want to develop agriculture rather than curtail it. One particular factor will be a desire to reduce the dependence on the Israeli labour market: until the imposition of Israeli restrictions on security grounds, about one in three Palestinians worked in Israel.[133] Frequent and protracted closures of the West Bank and Gaza Strip have highlighted the disadvantages of such dependence.

The additional 28.6 mcm. of water stipulated in the Interim Agreement is to meet the immediate domestic needs of the Palestinians. At the same time, the Agreement recognises that the Palestinians can use the rest of the 70-80 mcm. a year (the 'future needs' of the Palestinians in the West Bank) for either domestic or agricultural purposes.[134]

---

[127] 'Voice of Israel, 27 January 1991, translated by BBC Monitoring *SWB*, 5 February 1991: 'Agriculture Ministry announces reduction in water quotas.'

[128] Saul Arlosoroff, a former Deputy Water Commissioner, addressing the conference 'Water in the Jordan catchment countries' at the School of Oriental and African Studies on 15 May 1995 (and reported by *MEED*, 26 May 1995; 'Running on empty').

[129] Allan (1995).

[130] See 'Peace with Israel: as cool as a cucumber', in Special Report on Egypt, *MEED*, 3 June 1994.

[131] See the section entitled 'Disputing the waters – from June 1967 to the Madrid Peace Process'.

[132] According to Aboudi (1994), quoting Israeli statistics for 1991/2, agriculture contributed 35% of Palestinian GDP and provided jobs for 26% of the Palestinian workforce.

[133] Fischer (1993/4).

[134] Paragraph 6 of Article 40 refers to the 'future needs' of the West Bank Palestinians; sub-paragraph 7b(6) of Article 40 refers to the Palestinians' right to use the remainder of this for agriculture.

As has already been noted, the transfer of control of water in the Gaza Strip from the occupying Israeli authorities to the PNA has resulted in a relaxation of restrictions. Nevertheless, the PNA will need to tighten controls in future if an unplanned contraction of agriculture is not to be forced upon it by a continued and unsustainable fall in the water table or a deterioration in the quality of the water, or both.

Jordan has wished to expand its irrigated agriculture for a number of reasons. Obtaining foreign exchange by exporting agricultural produce, saving foreign exchange by growing food for domestic consumption, maintaining a degree of food security, avoiding dependence on aid from abroad, preventing rural depopulation and providing employment at lower capital cost than in industry are some of the most frequently cited factors.[135]

Unlike the situation in Israel, there is no institutionalised 'water lobby' in Jordan. However, the fact that members of the Jordanian elite have significant farming interests may make the government less willing to consider cutting back on the supply of water for irrigation as a possible solution to the country's water problems. Whether this is the case or not, the Jordanian government has continued to stress the importance of agriculture. In January 1993, the Minister of Agriculture told an interviewer: 'We as a country want to push agriculture on all fronts ... The purpose is to increase our relative self-sufficiency.'[136]

Syria too has shown every sign of aiming to develop its irrigated agriculture.[137] This is a national policy rather than one related specifically to those parts of the country bordering Israel and Jordan, but there is no indication of any Syrian readiness to use less water from the Yarmuk basin in irrigation, in order to spare it for other purposes.

Despite the reluctance of governments in the area to adopt clear policies to reduce the allocation of water to agriculture, the importance of the sector has shown a continuous decline. It now accounts for a small percentage of GDP, foreign exchange earnings and employment in Israel and Jordan; it remains a very important part of the economy in Syria (see Table 3). None of these countries is self-sufficient in food.[138]

Further contraction of agriculture would represent the continuation

---

[135] See for example *Jordan Times*, 10 May 1992: 'Jordan's agricultural sector – achievements and obstacles', and *Jordan Times*, 16 October 1991: 'Food production up but problems remain in making Jordan self-sufficient, minister says'.

[136] *ICARDA News*, 12 January 1993.

[137] See for example the policy statement made by Syria's Prime Minister on 14 November 1994, reported by BBC *SWB*, 22 November 1944: 'Prime minister delivers government policy statement on economic issues'.

[138] Israel, which has an approximate balance in its agricultural trade, comes closest, but is nevertheless far from self-sufficient in the crucial area of cereals.

of an existing trend, rather than a national catastrophe. Moreover, both the Israeli and Jordanian governments have shown themselves willing to restrict the allocation of water to agriculture in times of shortage. For Israel, a cut-back in irrigation sufficient to allow the Palestinians an equitable share of the ground-water under the West Bank could be a sacrifice worth making for the over-riding goal of achieving peace, if the other conditions were right. And over the long-term, for all countries in the region, peace should lessen the emphasis placed on food security – and therefore domestic production – as a strategic requirement.

Table 3. AGRICULTURAL SECTOR AS % OF TOTAL ECONOMIES IN ISRAEL AND NEIGHBOURING COUNTRIES

	GDP	Exports	Employment
Israel	2	3	5
Jordan	7	13	7*
Syria	27	4	21

* The figure for agricultural employment in Jordan relates only to Jordanian nationals: it would be roughly twice as much if foreign workers were included.
Sources: *Statistical Abstract of Israel* (1992); *Monthly Statistical Bulletin* (Central Bank of Jordan); *UNCTAD Trade Statistics Yearbook* (1992).

Cooperative management

All the people of the area would benefit from cooperation over water. The ideal situation would be the management of each shared source – whether a river basin or an aquifer – as a unit, by a single authority, along the lines of the Tennessee Valley Authority in the United States. For sovereign states, the degree of sovereignty which would have to be given up makes such arrangements seem utopian, even in parts of the world where relationships between the states involved are as harmonious as they could be. In the Middle East, where lack of trust is likely to endure long after the relationships between the countries of the region are regulated by peace treaties, any supra-national water authority will probably remain an impossible dream for many years to come.

Nevertheless, less ambitious forms of cooperation are now being instituted in the context of the peace settlements between Israel and its Arab neighbours. This has already happened between Israel and Jordan, and Israel and the Palestinians. Both these agreements provide for joint committees to promote cooperation over water. In the case of the Israeli-Jordanian committee, the emphasis is likely to be mainly on the implementation of the projects listed in the treaty between the two countries. As well as this function, the Israeli-Palestinian JWC will also be managing the day-to-day exploitation of a shared resource, the Mountain Aquifer. A permanent equivalent of the JWC with more extensive responsibilities (e.g. relating to all uses of the Mountain Aquifer) would be a positive outcome of final-status negotiations.

Cooperative arrangements would also be necessary to implement and manage some of the projects which would create new water for the area, such as the proposals for linking the Dead Sea to the Red Sea or the Mediterranean, or the various schemes for pipelines from Turkey. Exchanges of technical information should make some of the non-conventional techniques, such as the use of brackish water for irrigation, and cloud-seeding, more successful.

Water, War and Peace

Israel and its Arab neighbours have all made a strategic choice in favour of peace. In the case of Egypt, Jordan and the Palestinians, this choice is now embodied in peace agreements, while Syria and Israel are negotiating seriously. Even if the process that is still ongoing at the time of writing were to be abandoned, Israel's military superiority should for the foreseeable future ensure that armed conflict does not break out, whether over water or any other issue.

Given this superiority, it is hard to think of any water project that Israel might undertake that would tempt the Arab states to attack: even in the early 1960s, before the shortcomings of the Arab armed forces had been so spectacularly revealed by the war of June 1967, Arab leaders declined to take military action to prevent Israel going ahead with its National Water Carrier.[139]

Equally, it is doubtful if the Arab states would take the risk of proceeding with any water projects that would affect Israel's supply of water, without Israel's tacit consent at least. In the highly improbable event of the Arab states going ahead with a project such as the Unity Dam without Israeli agreement, the most likely outcome would be an Israeli strike followed by an abandonment of the project: the near-certainty of full-scale military defeat would surely dissuade Arab leaders from retaliating.

There is another question. If the present peace process were to fail, and the Israelis were faced with a situation in which they found it increasingly difficult to balance water supply and demand, would they be tempted to use military means to secure sources of water lying beyond the existing limits of their control?

Such action would be extremely hard to justify to the international

---

[139] See the section above entitled 'Disputing the waters – up to June 1967.'

community, unless it took place in the context of an external threat, in which Israel could present its actions as those of defence rather than aggression (as it did in 1967). Another consideration, of at least equal importance, is the lack of any significant water resources within exploitable distance: Israel could not make the same hydrological gains as it made in June 1967. The only possibilities within reach are the Yarmuk and the Litani. In the case of the former, Israel would have to block the diversion into the King Abdullah Canal in Jordan, or destroy a large number of small dams in Syria, or both, to secure a worthwhile increase in water supply. In the case of the Litani, the volume of water in the lower part of the river is hardly sufficient to justify the cost of the storage and diversion works which Israel would have to install in order to make use of the waters, let along the costs and risks of military action. The only way of increasing the volume of water in the lower Litani would be to destroy the works upstream which divert part of the flow into the Awali.

Israeli decision-makers would be far more likely to take tough measures within their own boundaries, to bring demand into line with supply (as they have indeed done in recent years). The limited advantages that would accrue from military action could not outweigh the international opprobrium that Israel would incur by taking it.

Such scenarios have a rather dated ring in the context of the achievements of the peace process since Madrid. Even if there were to be no further progress in the peace process, their relevance would still be questionable. Only a reversal of the process would make them worthy of deeper consideration. In the foreseeable future, war between Israel and its Arab neighbours over water seems out of the question.

3

THE NILE

The Geopolitics of the Nile Basin

With a length of 6,825 km. from its most distant source in Burundi in central Africa to the Mediterranean coast of Egypt, the Nile is one of the world's longest rivers. Its drainage basin covers over 3 million square km., a tenth of the area of the African continent. In terms of the *volume* of water it carries, however, the Nile occupies a much lowlier position among the world's rivers. The Amazon carries thirty-five times as much water, the Mississippi seven times as much.[1]

The average annual flow of the Nile is normally given as 84 bcm. (billion cubic metres). This figure, the average for the years 1900 to 1959, measured at Aswan, was accepted as the basis for the 1959 Nile Waters Agreement between Egypt and Sudan.[2] In the period since then, this average has seemed first too small, and then too large.[3]

The Nile shows substantial variations in flow from year to year the full dimensions of which may not be revealed by any particular series of years. Within the last quarter of a century the flow of the Nile has been as low as 50 bcm. at Aswan (in 1971-2) and as high as 100 bcm. (in 1975-6). The impact of these annual variations has been the greater because years of low flow tend to occur consecutively; so do years of high flow.[4] Heavy rains over the upper basin of the White Nile produced high flows in the 1960s; by contrast, there was a particularly long period of low flows in the Nile during the 1980s.

The waters of the Nile are derived essentially from rainfall on the Ethiopian highlands and the catchment areas of the Equatorial lakes (see Map 3). The contribution from rainfall further downstream is slight. As these two regions have different rainfall regimes, there is no correlation between annual variations in the flow of the Blue and White Niles: in some years, both rivers may be low or high; in others, one may carry more water that the average and the other river may carry

---

[1] Waterbury (1979).
[2] See the section of this chapter entitled 'Treaties and disputes'.
[3] Waterbury (1979) and Abu-Zeid and Biswas (1991).
[4] Evans (1990).

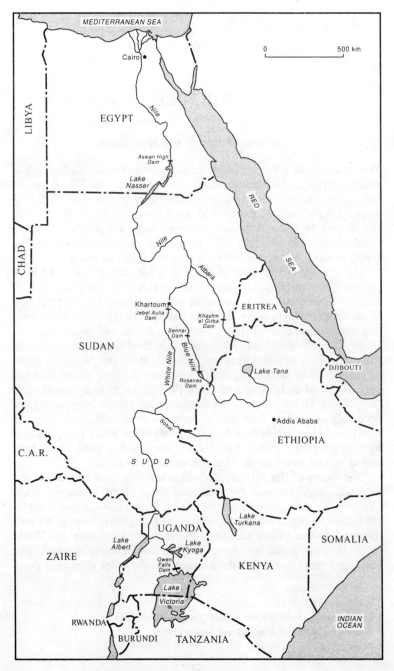

Map 3. THE NILE BASIN

less. In the 1970s, higher-than-average flows in the White Nile made up for low flows in the Blue Nile. For most of the 1980s, both rivers carried less water than average, with almost disastrous consequences for Egypt.[5]

The basin of the Blue Nile is much smaller than that of the White Nile. However, its contribution to the flow of the 'main' Nile – the river formed by the confluence of the two Niles at Khartoum – is greater, being on average 59% of the total. The White Nile contributes only 28% of the water in the main Nile (the remaining 13% is accounted for by the Atbara, which flows directly into the main Nile below Khartoum). The principal reason for this is the enormous evaporation losses from the Sudd, the vast marshes of southern Sudan.[6] When it leaves the Sudd, the White Nile carries less than half as much water as it had when it entered: in an average year, some 17 bcm. of water are lost through evaporation.[7]

The flow of the main Nile is very unevenly distributed over the year: four-fifths occurs between August and October, when the Blue Nile is in flood, following the monsoon rains over the Ethiopian highlands. At this time, there may be sixty times as much water pouring down the Blue Nile as there is during the low season. The main Nile is at its lowest in August (just before the arrival of the Blue Nile flood). When the Blue Nile is in flood it may account for 90% of the water in the main Nile; at other times of the year it may provide only 20%, with the bulk of the flow in the main Nile coming from the White Nile. The latter exhibits much less seasonal variation than the Blue Nile, its flow in flood being generally no more than three times that of the low season.[8] This is partly due to smaller seasonal differences in rainfall over the White Nile catchment. The effect of the Sudd is also important as, rather than flowing directly downstream, the floodwaters of the White Nile spread out over the swamp; some of this water returns to the river as it falls, while some is evaporated.

The contribution of the states of the basin

Ten states share some portion of the Nile basin. They are Egypt, Sudan, Ethiopia, Eritrea, Zaire, Uganda, Kenya, Tanzania, Rwanda, and Burundi.[9] There are enormous differences in terms of the contribution of

---

[5] See the section of this chapter entitled 'Regulating the Nile'.

[6] Sudd means 'barrier' in Arabic.

[7] Between 1905 and 1980 the average annual inflow into the Sudd (at Mongalla) was 33 bcm., while outflow was 16 bcm.; see Collins (1990).

[8] Waterbury (1979).

[9] The Central African Republic (CAR) could also be said to occupy part of the basin

each state in the basin to the flow of the river. We have already noted the important contribution of Ethiopia to the supply of water to Egypt and Sudan through the Blue Nile. Ethiopia's crucial role emerges even more clearly when the Sobat and Atbara rivers are taken into account. The former, a tributary of the White Nile, provides some 14% of the total flow of the main Nile, the latter, which flows directly into the main Nile below Khartoum, about 13%. Around 86% of the water in the main Nile therefore comes from the Ethiopian highlands, 'Africa's water tower'.[10] At the other extreme is Egypt, which adds no water whatsoever to the Nile. While water is added to the Nile in Sudan by rainfall (almost entirely in the South), this is out-weighed by the losses in the Sudd. The contribution of the black African states of the upper White Nile basin to the flow of the main Nile is relatively small: in total, they provide only 14% of its flow.

Regulating the Nile

The use of the Nile for agriculture dates back some 7,000 years. At this time the inhabitants of Egypt started to plant seeds on the land from which the flood-waters of the river had retreated. The first attempts to control the river were made about 5,000 years ago with the introduction of 'basin' irrigation, involving the deliberate diversion and retention of water by dikes. The same technique was employed at roughly the same time in what is now northern Sudan. The first mechanised irrigation was made possible by the development of the *shadoof* during the 18th Dynasty (1550-1307 BC) and the *saqia* in early Ptolemaic times (323-30 BC). Both these devices enabled water to be raised in years of low flood and in summer to fields that would have been too high for irrigation by the basin method.[11]

From that time until the middle of the nineteenth century, there was essentially no change in the irrigation techniques practised in Egypt and northern Sudan. Their prosperity remained dependent on the level of the Nile flood. In years when the flood was very low, the area which could be cultivated might be halved; the result would be famine. At the other extreme, very high floods would destroy the basins and leave pestilential swamps.

---

in that, according to Waterbury (1991), seasonal torrents on its border with Sudan empty into the Bahr al-Arab river which drains into the western Sudd. But since both the area and the volume of water concerned are tiny, it seems more sensible to consider the CAR as lying outside the basin.

[10] Wolde-Mariam (1972). A very small part of the flow of the Atbara comes from Eritrea.

[11] Chesworth (1990).

Egypt

Muhammad Ali Pasha, who ruled Egypt from 1805 to 1848, was responsible for the introduction of the first modern regulatory works on the Nile. As well as excavating new canals, Muhammad Ali began the construction of two barrages north of Cairo, where the river divides into the Damietta and Rosetta branches of the Delta. They were completed in 1861, but only functioned properly after they had been repaired and renovated under the supervision of British engineers with experience from India.[12]

The barrages raised the water-level in the Damietta and Rosetta branches of the Delta in summer, so that it would flow into canals that could previously only be used in winter, when the water level was naturally higher. They could not store water from winter for use in summer (nor, of course, could they supply the valley above the Delta). This degree of control only became possible when the first Aswan dam was completed in 1902. The reservoir behind the dam provided water for year-round ('perennial') irrigation in most parts of the Nile valley below Aswan, making it possible for farmers to grow more than one crop per year on each field. Over the next half-century further works were installed downstream to enable better use to be made of its water (see Table 4). The construction of the Jebel Auliya Dam on the White Nile south of Khartoum provided additional storage of water for use in Egypt from January to July, when the Blue Nile flood had passed and the natural level of the main Nile was low.

While the Aswan and Jebel Auliya Dams had sufficient capacity to store water from one season to another, they could not protect Egypt from the effects of variations in the flow of the Nile from year to year – flooding in years of high floods and insufficient water for agriculture in low years. It was to eliminate this uncertainty that the High Aswan Dam was built.

The same function could have been fulfilled by dams elsewhere in the basin. Indeed, the idea of using the Equatorial lakes, Lake Tana on the Blue Nile and reservoirs in Sudan for such over-year storage had been proposed as early as 1920.[13] A fully elaborated plan to achieve this goal was produced just after the Second World War by H.E. Hurst, a senior British official in the Egyptian Ministry of Public Works, and 'the Nile's most authoritative twentieth-century student'.[14] It was based on a new concept called 'century storage'. This meant that the reservoirs

---

[12] The British occupied Egypt in 1882.

[13] The 1920 proposal was made by Sir Murdoch MacDonald, the founder of the British consulting firm Sir Murdoch MacDonald & Partners, now Mott MacDonald. See Collins (1990).

[14] Waterbury (1979).

constructed under the plan would have sufficient capacity to maintain a steady outflow, even in years of the lowest rainfall which mathematical probabilities suggested would occur in the basin in any 100 years. Egypt adopted Hurst's plan in the late 1940s, but the only one of its projects to be implemented was the Owen Falls Dam in Uganda, at the point where the White Nile leaves Lake Victoria. Before other projects could be carried out, Nasser had taken power in Cairo. He and the other members of the Revolutionary Command Council soon became convinced that the construction of a single, massive dam at Aswan was a better prospect than storage in a number of reservoirs upstream. The great appeal of the High Dam project was strategic rather than technical: the 'century storage' which it would provide would be under wholly Egyptian control. Enough water could be stored in Lake Nasser in years of high flood to ensure that Egypt would not be at the mercy of upstream states in years of low flood.

Table 4. CHRONOLOGY OF MAJOR WORKS ON THE NILE

1843-61	Construction of Delta barrages
1890	Repair and renovation of Delta barrages by the British
1902	First Aswan Dam
1902	Assiut Dam
1903	Zifta Barrage
1909	Isna Barrage
1912	Aswan Dam raised
1925	Sennar Dam on the Blue Nile (to irrigate Gezira Cotton Scheme)
1930	Nag Hammadi Barrage
1933	Aswan Dam raised again
1937	Jebel Auliya Dam (on the White Nile, south of Khartoum)
1951	Edfina Barrage
1954	Owen Falls Dam, Uganda (at the outflow from Lake Victoria), completed
1958	Sennar Dam raised
late 1950s	Hydro-power station installed at Aswan Dam

The High Dam project had other advantages as well. It would give a major boost to Egypt's industrial development and modernisation by generating large quantities of hydro-power: the Dam was to have an installed capacity of 10 billion kWh. per year. Moreover, the time taken to build it would be half that required for Hurst's scheme. And the Dam would serve as a 'massive symbol of a resurgent Egypt', a demonstration of the new regime's commitment to the country's independence and prosperity.[15]

Since the construction of the High Dam the annual Nile flood which determined Egypt's prosperity for some 7,000 years has become a thing of the past: it goes no further than Lake Nasser, the reservoir impounded by the Dam. The flow of the Nile downstream of Aswan can now be managed from day to day and from year to year to meet the needs of irrigation, hydro-power generation and navigation (for tourism). The river in Egypt has become, 'for all intents and purposes, an enormous irrigation ditch'.[16]

While the High Dam enables Egypt to exercise complete control over the water which flows into Lake Nasser, Egypt cannot determine the size of this inflow. Even the enormous storage capacity of the Lake cannot afford the country total protection against an exceptionally long run of low floods – such as occurred during the 1980s.[17] By 1988 the level of the Lake had fallen to the point where there was insufficient water available to meet all the demands for it: the area of land under rice had to be cut back; less than two-thirds of the electricity-generating capacity at the Dam could be used; and the level of the river could not be kept high enough to permit the unrestricted operation of large tourist boats. Another low flood would have caused serious difficulties for Egypt: the Lake would have fallen to the point where no electricity at all could have been generated at the High Dam, and more severe cut-backs in irrigation would have been necessary. As it turned out, the long run of low floods came to an end with the 1988-9 flood; since then, floods have been average or above.

The development of modern hydraulic works has permitted a remarkable increase in agricultural production in Egypt. In part, this has occurred through an extension of the cultivated area, which is now 2.83 million hectares, roughly twice what it was in the days of Muhammad Ali Pasha.[18] This 'horizontal expansion' is still in progress, with Egypt planning to reclaim a further 650,000 hectares by the end of the century.[19] It is a controversial policy. Land brought under cultivation in recent decades has been mainly on the desert margins of the Delta. The soils of these 'New Lands' are not so fertile as the 'Old Lands', which have

---

[15] Collins (1990).

[16] Waterbury (1979).

[17] The live storage capacity of Lake Nasser is 90,000 mcm., making it one of the largest reservoirs in the world.

[18] Abu-Zeid (1992).

[19] Abu-Zeid (1992).

benefited from the annual deposition of Nile silt for millenia. The New Lands are higher, and water cannot be supplied without pumping, increasing costs considerably.

There has been a long and fierce debate about the economics of the reclamation programme. Egyptian officials have produced figures to demonstrate that the value of the crops grown justifies both the capital costs of bringing desert land under cultivation and the continuing costs of producing crops (including the cost of the fuel used to raise the water to the fields). Outside observers have sometimes come to the opposite conclusion: for example, USAID has criticised the programme as representing a poor return on investment, even without considering the value of the water used if it were put to another use (in economists' parlance, its 'opportunity cost').[20] However, the Egyptian government's justifications for proceeding with reclamation are not purely economic. The programme has social and internal political dimensions, being projected by the government as a response to the country's rapid population growth and consequent over-crowding and unemployment in the cities.[21] There may be a strategic aspect too (although this does not seem to be referred to publicly by official spokesmen), in so far as reclamation in Sinai and the Western Desert offers an opportunity to establish substantial communities in remote areas that were previously very thinly populated.

A further reason for pressing ahead with reclamation may be a desire on the part of Egypt's rulers to reinforce their country's claim to its existing 'share' of Nile water. To do so, Egypt has to be able to demonstrate that it is presently using all the water which it receives – and that any savings made by increases if efficiency could easily be absorbed in bringing new land into production. The capital used in reclamation may thus represent an investment in a negotiating position as much as an investment in productive agriculture.

Just as important as horizontal expansion (and less controversial in economic terms) has been 'vertical expansion' – the cultivation of two or even three crops on the same field during the same year. In effect, because of this double-cropping on much of its cultivated area, Egypt has almost twice as much land available for agriculture in any given year as the figure for cultivated area suggests.

The impact of modern hydraulic works on Egypt's industrial development through the generation of hydro-power began much later. The first hydro-power station was not installed until the late 1950s (at the old Aswan Dam). By the mid-1970s, the picture had been transformed,

---

[20] Pacific Consultants (1980).
[21] Assen (1986).

with the High Dam producing half of the country's electricity.[22] Since that time, however, Egypt has met its growing demand for electricity from non-hydraulic sources (recently, increasingly from gas), to the extent that, by the mid-1990s, the High Dam was generating less than one-fifth of Egypt's energy consumption. This proportion is still falling rapidly: it may not be long before it is below a tenth.[23]

The High Dam has been the subject of long-running controversies because of its harmful side-effects downstream. Most of these have been connected with the loss of the fertile silt which was previously deposited on Egyptian farmland by the annual flood, or fed (with the algae which it carried) the sardines off the Mediterranean coast which sustained an important fishing industry. Because the river below Aswan is no longer burdened with a heavy load of silt, it flows faster, scouring its banks (and bridges, embankments and other installations). Now that the coast-line of the Delta is no longer being built up by deposits of silt, erosion is causing it slowly to recede.

These side-effects are internal to Egypt, and thus fall outside the scope of this book.[24] Another effect of the Dam – the loss of water to evaporation from the vast surface area of Lake Nasser – *does* have international implications, because it 'consumes' water that could have been used elsewhere if storage had been provided in a cooler and more humid location. As the area in which the lake is situated is situated is intensely hot and dry, surface evaporation is about 2.7 metres of depth a year – one of the highest rates on the Earth's surface.[25]

How much water is *actually* lost in any given year depends on the surface area of the lake, which varies in turn with its level. In 1967-8, when the level was 151 metres above sea level, the surface area was 2,200 km.^{2}, while in 1970-1, the level was 165 metres, and the surface area 3,500 km.^{2} In the first case, evaporation has been estimated at 5.9 bcm., in the second at 9.4 bcm.[26] To these losses must be added the escape of water through seepage into the ground below the lake. Egypt's 1959 agreement with Sudan allowed for a loss from Lake Nasser of 10 bcm. a year to evaporation and seepage.[27] This was too small an

---

[22] Waterbury (1979).

[23] Allan (1993b). In January 1995, al-Banbi, Egypt's Petroleum Minister, said that the proportion of electricity generated from natural gas had risen from 20% in 1984 to 80% in 1994.

[24] For recent attempts to put the environmental impact of the High Dam is perspective, see Abu-Zeid, in Thanh and Biswas (1991), and Hunt (1987).

[25] Waterbury (1979).

[26] Waterbury (1979).

[27] On the 1959 Agreement, see the section below entitled 'Treaties and disputes'.

allowance for much of the 1970s, when lake levels were high; the opposite was true in the 1980s.

The 1959 Agreement allocated to Egypt 55.5 bcm. of Nile water a year. With the agreement of Sudan (which has been unable to use its full share), Egypt has used slightly more. Over the first twenty-year period of the operation of the High Dam, the average annual water release was 56.269 bcm.[28]

In fact, Egypt has had more water available than this figure suggests, since water applied to Egyptian fields can often be used a second and sometimes even a third time. This is a result of the unique hydrology of the Nile basin in Egypt, which ensures that excess irrigation water either returns to the river or canals, or remains in the ground from which it can be retrieved by pumping. The volume of drainage water re-used in this way is presently 4.7 bcm. a year. Smaller but still significant quantities of water for irrigation come from urban waste-water (sometimes treated, sometimes not). The Greater Cairo Sewerage Project provided 0.9 bcm. of treated water for agricultural use in 1990.[29]

Agriculture accounts for the lion's share of Egyptian water consumption – some 84% in 1990. Industry takes 8%, while domestic and other municipal uses take 5%. The remaining 3% is allowed to flow down the river in winter to keep the Nile high enough for the operation of tourist boats. This must be counted as a separate use, as the releases of water which would be required for irrigation purposes alone, between October and January, would not keep the level of the river high enough for navigation.[30] A further volume of water – not counted here as 'consumption' – has to be allowed to flow to the sea to carry drainage water and other waste-water away. This is variously quoted as between 12 and 15 bcm. per year.

Sudan

Upstream in Sudan, the first modern irrigation schemes were introduced in the early years of the present century. They drew water for cotton plantations by pump, mainly from the Blue Nile. The development of irrigation on a much larger scale was made possible in the 1920s by the construction of the Sennar Dam on the Blue Nile, which provided water to the Gezira cotton scheme. Since becoming independent in 1956, Sudan has built the Roseires Dam (also on the Blue Nile), which

---

[28] Gasser and Abdou (1989). M.M. Gasser and Mohammed Ibrahim Abdou are Director and Research Engineer respectively at the Hydraulics and Sediment Research Institute, Delta Barrage, Cairo: their figures can presumably be regarded as having official sanction.
[29] Abu-Zeid (1992).
[30] Abu-Zeid (1992).

supplies water to an extension of the Gezira scheme, and the Khashm el-Girba Dam on the Atbara. Water impounded by the Khashm el-Girba Dam irrigates land on which were settled Sudanese citizens displaced by the encroachment into Sudan of Lake Nasser (known in Sudan as Lake Nubia).

The area to which irrigation water can be supplied from the Blue and White Niles and the Atbara is around 1.9 million hectares, but the area cropped in recent years has been much less, probably under 1.2 million hectares (mainly because some of the pump schemes have fallen into disuse).[31] All three dams also produce hydro-power (although the generating capacity of the Sennar and Khashm el-Girba stations is very small). Together they account for over half of Sudan's generating capacity.

Domestic consumers in Sudan use very little water per head, and there are few industries of any size. Consumption in these sectors together amounts to no more than 2% of total consumption of water: agriculture accounts for 98% of Sudan's abstractions of Nile water.

Different sources give different figures for the volume of Nile water taken by Sudan annually for all uses. Three published sources give roughly similar figures of 12.6, 13 and 'just over' 14 bcm.; a fourth gives 16.12 bcm. for irrigation alone.[32] Although the last figure is in the most recent source, there is no reason to believe that it is more accurate than the others, since there has been no major expansion of the irrigated area in recent years that could account for such an increase. It is impossible to be at all precise about this, as the Sudanese themselves do not know accurately how much water they are using. For example, the volume of water taken by pumps from the White Nile is not measured.[33] For the purposes of this study, 14 bcm. per year seems a reasonable approximation.

Since the early years of this century, a number of schemes have been proposed which would reduce the enormous loss of water to evaporation in southern Sudan.[34] The central element of all these proposals has been the cutting of a canal or canals to allow some part of the waters of the White Nile to pass through the Sudd without overflowing into the swamps. The only one of these schemes to have gone beyond the drawing-board was the Jonglei Canal (Phase I of a much larger scheme), which was to have saved 4.7 bcm. of water a year (see

---

[31] Chesworth (1990), and Knott and Hewett (1990).

[32] The sources are Chesworth (1990), Zaki (1991), Knott and Hewett (1990) and Adam (1993).

[33] Author's interview with Dr Bayoumi Attia, Ministry of Public Works and Water Resources, Cairo, June 1993.

[34] See the preceding section of this chapter, 'The geopolitics of the Nile basin'.

Map 4). Excavation began in 1978. Some two-thirds of the canal had been dug before work was brought to a halt in 1984 by the civil war in southern Sudan; it has not yet resumed.[35]

Further upstream

Upstream of Sudan, the regulation and use of the Blue and White Niles have been limited. This is a reflection both of the higher rainfall in the upper parts of both basins (which reduces the need for irrigation) and of the less developed nature of those countries.

Ethiopia has done little so far to exploit the Blue Nile and its tributaries. A hydro-power station 25 km. downstream of Lake Tana uses river flow (without storage) to generate electricity. A dam on the Finchaa tributary, completed in 1972, stores water for the generation of electricity and for irrigation. By the late 1980s, barely 25,000 hectares were under irrigation in the Blue Nile basin, with another 6,200 hectares being prepared for irrigation.[36]

The Owen Falls Dam, at the outlet of Lake Victoria, in Uganda, was completed in 1954. Its main function is to generate electricity for Uganda. As originally conceived, it formed part of the much larger scheme to provide 'century storage' in the Equatorial lakes. However, without the other elements of the scheme, and especially the second stage of the Jonglei Canal, the contribution which the Owen Falls Dam can make to such storage is minimal.

Upstream of Uganda, proposals have been made for the utilisation of the waters of the basin of the Kagera river (which flows into Lake Victoria), mainly for the generation of hydro-power. None has so far gone any further than a feasibility study.

The quality of the Nile waters

The water in the Nile basin is mostly of high quality, in terms of levels of salinity and pollution from agri-chemicals, and domestic and industrial uses. This is partly because very little use is made of the Nile upstream of Sudan, and partly because, in the areas where Nile water *is* used for irrigation, the soils are of types that either do not seriously reduce the quality of the water as it passes through them, or do not permit return flows. The only significant problems in this regard are in Egypt, where upstream uses *within* Egypt cause a deterioration in water quality that is felt when that water is re-used downstream. Drainage water in

---

[35] On the Jonglei Canal see Howell *et al.* (1988) and Collins (1990).
[36] Abate (1994). The Ethiopian name for the Blue Nile is the Abbai or Abbay.

parts of the Delta has to be blended with fresher water from the Nile itself before it can be used for irrigation. By the time it reaches the Mediterranean, Nile water has a salinity between 1,000 and 7,000 ppm. Egyptian farmers have proved adept at coping with high levels of salinity, and the only area where the quality of water in the Nile system has been so low as to restrict its use is the northern part of the Delta. Here, soil salinity is particularly high because of the presence near the surface of saline ground-water or because of sea-water intrusion into the sub-soil; this exacerbates the effect of the salinity of irrigation water that has already been used once.

Particular difficulties have been experienced in Sudan because of the heavy load of silt carried by the Blue Nile when in flood. Over the years, large quantities of silt have been deposited in the reservoirs behind the Roseires and Sennar Dams, substantially reducing the volume of water which they can store. The Roseires Dam is currently being heightened by 10 metres to increase its storage capacity, a development made necessary partly by increasing demand for water but mainly by the effects of siltation. According to official projections, the work should be completed by 1997.[37] The Sennar reservoir has less than half its original capacity of 0.93 bcm. Siltation has also severely affected the Khashm el-Girba reservoir on the Atbara, where over two-thirds of the original storage capacity of 1.3 bcm. has been lost.[38] The high silt content of Blue Nile water has necessitated the installation of special filters in the Khartoum water-supply system.

Treaties and Disputes

The potential vulnerability of Egypt's supply of Nile water has preoccupied its rulers for centuries. Indeed, according to legend, the sultans of Egypt sent emissaries to Ethiopia with tribute, to persuade the emperor to allow the Blue Nile to continue to flow.[39] The need to ensure that no one would tamper with the Nile was one of the main goals of the British officials who worked in Egypt from 1882.

Agreements from the colonial period

Britain sought to secure the uninterrupted flow of water from the Ethiopian highlands by signing agreements with Ethiopia or with Italy,

---

[37] *Sudan News* (weekly information bulletin published by Sudan Information Office), 2 February 1993: 'Canal and dam projects hailed as example to the Third World.'

[38] Knott and Hewett (1990).

[39] Collins (1990).

whose influence in Ethiopia was recognised by Britain. In 1891, Britain and Italy negotiated a protocol for the demarcation of their respective spheres of influence in Eastern Africa. In Article III of the protocol, Italy undertook not to do anything that would impede the flow of the Atbara, the only tributary of the Nile which arose on territory then under Italian control. In 1902, Ethiopia and Britain (acting for Egypt and Sudan) signed the Addis Ababa Agreement. Ethiopia undertook to seek the prior consent of Britain before initiating any works that might affect the flow of the Blue Nile or Sobat. The principle of non-interference with the flow of the Blue Nile, Sobat and Atbara was recognised by Italy and France in the 1906 tripartite agreement with Britain which defined the three states' interests in Ethiopia, Finally, in 1925, an exchange of notes took place between Britain and Italy.[40] Italy recognised the 'prior hydraulic rights' of Egypt and Sudan, and agreed not to construct any works likely to modify the flow of the Ethiopian tributaries of the Nile.

Britain was also concerned about what might be done in the upper basin of the White Nile. An agreement signed by Britain and the Belgian Congo in 1906 stipulated that the latter would do nothing to diminish the flow of the Semliki and Isango Rivers into Lake Albert.

The first agreement to make an apportionment of the Nile waters was that signed by Britain and Egypt in 1929.[41] In signing the agreement, Britain was acting on behalf of all British-administered territories in the Nile basin.[42] However, the principal effect of the agreement was to ensure Egypt's water supply. Its main provisions were:

– a guarantee that no works would be constructed on the river or any of its tributaries that would prejudice Egyptian interests;
– the definition of Egypt's 'acquired rights' as 48 bcm. a year, and Sudan's as 4 bcm.; and
– the reservation to Egypt of the entire flow of the main Nile during the period from 20 January to 15 July.

The agreement also allowed the Egyptians to build the Jebel Auliya Dam which, despite its location in Sudan, was designed to store water for use in Egypt. The last of the 'colonial' agreements was the exchange of notes between Britain (acting on behalf of Uganda) and Egypt which

---

[40] On the basis of the tripartite agreement of 1906, Britain still recognised much of Ethiopia to be within Italy's sphere of influence.
[41] Its full title was 'Exchange of Notes between His Majesty's Government in the United Kingdom and the Egyptian Government in regard to the Use of the Waters of the River Nile for Irrigation Purposes'.
[42] Sudan, Uganda, Kenya and Tanganyika.

Treaties and Disputes 71

allowed Uganda to construct the Owen Falls Dam.[43] The exchange of notes kept within the terms of the 1929 Agreement by giving Egypt the right to station at the dam an engineer who would regulate the releases through it according to Egyptian needs for water rather than Ugandan needs for electricity.

We now need to look at the extent to which these agreements have been accepted by the independent states of the Nile basin, following the withdrawal of the colonial powers. If the agreements were still regarded as being in force, they would add up to a legal regime covering almost the whole of the basin, and could form the basis for a cooperative approach to the use of the waters of the Nile. In fact, the reverse is the case.

Ethiopia has shown no inclination to accept any of these agreements, whether they were signed by Ethiopia itself, by Italy on behalf of Ethiopia, or by other powers in the basin. The 1891 protocol was signed on Ethiopia's behalf by Italy, acting on the basis of the Treaty of Ucciali between the Italian government and Emperor Menelik of Ethiopia in 1889. According to the Italian version, the Treaty delegated responsibility for all Ethiopia's foreign relations to Italy. This version was accepted by other European states and the 1891 protocol was concluded with that understanding. However, the only version of the Treaty recognised by Menelik was that in Amharic (the official language of Ethiopia), and this stated merely that Ethiopia *could* make a delegation of its responsibility for foreign relations, while Ethiopia does not appear to have made such a delegation for the purposes of the 1891 protocol. A further reason for Ethiopia to reject the protocol is the annulment of the Treaty of Ucciali in 1896, following the Italian defeat by Ethiopian forces at the battle of Adawa.

It seems equally unlikely that Ethiopia should regard itself as bound by the Addis Ababa Agreement of 1902, as Ethiopia did not ratify it.[44] As for the 1925 agreement between Italy and Britain, Ethiopia (whose independent status was demonstrable by its membership of the League of Nations) contested Italy's right to sign on Ethiopia's behalf at the time. Ethiopia was not a signatory of the 1929 Agreement, and has not accepted Egypt's claim to 'acquired' or 'historic' rights to a certain volume of Nile water.

Agreements signed by colonial powers pose the question of the obligations of the independent states which succeed those powers. This is a

---

[43] The formal title of the agreement was 'Exchange of Notes between the Government of the United Kingdom of Great Britain and Northern Ireland and the Government of Egypt regarding the construction of the Owen Falls Dam in Uganda, Cairo, 30 May 1949'. There were further exchanges of notes on 16 July 1952 and 5 January 1953, dealing with the contracts for the dam and its financing and maintenance.

[44] Waterbury (1987).

matter on which international law offers no clear guidance. It is not surprising that Egypt has asserted the principle that treaties concluded before independence remain binding, as these accords were designed to protect Egyptian interests.

For Ethiopia, the question is an academic one as far as the agreements relating to the Nile are concerned, since it has other reasons for not regarding them as valid. Sudan rejected the 1929 Agreement upon its accession to independence in 1956, on the ground that it had not been a party to the Agreement. For their part, upstream states on the White Nile have adopted a similar stance by embracing the 'Nyerere doctrine', which argues that states that were formerly colonies should not be assumed to be bound automatically by treaties signed by colonial powers, as the new states had no role in the negotiation of those treaties.[45] This position certainly serves the interest of the states upstream, by eliminating possible constraints on their freedom of action. Tanzania, Uganda and Kenya all repudiated the 1929 Agreement after they became independent in the early 1960s.[46]

The only agreement signed by a colonial power which appears to remain in force is that concerning the Owen Falls Dam. Since an Egyptian engineer is still permitted to regulate the releases of water through the Dam, it can be assumed that Uganda continues to recognise the agreement.

The 1959 agreement between Egypt and Sudan

In December 1952, five months after it had taken power in Cairo, the Egyptian Revolutionary Command Council (RCC) announced that it planned to build the High Aswan Dam. Meanwhile, Sudan, still under British rule, was already considering the possibility of a dam at Roseires. Each state needed the agreement of the other in order to proceed with its plans. Egypt needed Sudanese agreement because the vast reservoir to be impounded by the Dam would flood Sudanese territory. Less immediate but more important in the long term was the Egyptian desire to ensure that Sudan would not do anything that would reduce the flow of the Nile into Egypt to an extent that would jeopardise the operation of the High Dam. For its part, Sudan needed international finance for Roseires, and this money was not likely to be forthcoming as long as Egypt raised objections to the project.

Negotiations dragged on far a number of years, the principal stumbling

---

[45] The doctrine is named after the former president of Tanzania, Julius Nyerere.

[46] For an example of the Egyptian attitude, see Ahmed (1990); for an example of the attitude of upstream states (in this case Kenya), see Okidi (1990). Tanzania became independent in 1961, but continued to be known as Tanganyika until 1964.

Treaties and Disputes 73

block being Sudanese unwillingness to agree to the High Dam (a project that would bring no benefits and indeed do some damage to Sudan) without a substantial increase in the paltry 4 bcm a year of Nile water allocated to Sudan by the 1929 Agreement.

The deadlock was eventually broken. In 1958, Egypt had received a promise of funding for the High Dam from the Soviet Union – a promise that was not conditional on Sudanese agreement to the project. The Sudanese found themselves in a less favourable position as regards Roseires: they asked the World Bank for finance but were told in March 1959 that this would only be forthcoming if they were to sign an accord with Egypt. Probably more compelling was the eagerness of the military regime which had taken over in Khartoum in November 1958 to improve Sudan's relations with its powerful and by that time rather threatening northern neighbour. Reaching agreement on the Nile was its top priority, and the Sudanese negotiators quickly came to terms with the Egyptians.[47]

The result was the Agreement for the Full Utilization of the Nile Waters, signed on 8 November 1959. The Agreement took the annual flow of the Nile at Aswan to be 84 bcm. and allocated 55.5 bcm. to Egypt and 18.5 bcm. to Sudan; the remaining 10 bcm. was written off to evaporation and seepage from Lake Nasser. While Sudan agreed to Egypt's High Dam, Egypt agreed to Sudan's Roseires, as well as 'any other works which the Republic of the Sudan considers necessary for making use of her share.'[48] Egypt was to pay Sudan 15 million Egyptian pounds in compensation for the displacement of some 50,000 Nubians from the Wadi Halfa district and the flooding of around 8,700 hectares of their land.

The figure of 84 bcm. a year used by the Agreement was the average for the years 1900 to 1959. The Agreement recognised that this average might rise: if it did so, then the two countries would divide the additional water equally between them. Any increase in the volume of water resulting from the implementation of projects in southern Sudan would be divided in the same way. The Agreement also recognised that there might be periods when there was not enough water to satisfy the full requirements of both countries. The responsibility for devising a system of apportioning the available water between the two countries during such periods was given to a body created by the Agreement, the Permanent Joint Technical Commission (PJTC). The PJTC's functions were,

---

[47] For a Sudanese account of the political background to the negotiations, see Abdalla (1971).

[48] Agreement for the Full Utilization of the Nile Waters, Second Article (2), quoted by Collins (1990).

however, much wider than this: it was made responsible for the implementation and supervision of the Agreement as a whole.

The 1959 Agreement was a success in permitting both Egypt and Sudan to carry out projects that they regarded as vital to their development, and in removing a cause of tension that had soured relations between them for most of the 1950s. Moreover, it 'has been faithfully applied, the PJTC has regularly met whatever the political climate between the two countries, and both have, without exception, received their designated share.'[49] This assessment still holds good, although it is equally true to say that the PJTC has never been really put to the test. It is impossible to say how well it would have performed if the run of low floods in the 1980s had not come to an end in 1988: the strain would certainly have been severe.

For Egypt in particular, the Agreement also brought the benefit of the enhanced security of water supplies. There were two elements. The first was the removal of the Sudanese 'threat' in that the maximum volume of water which Sudan could take was defined: as long as the Sudanese respected the terms of the Agreement by taking no more than their designated share, Egypt would be assured of sufficient water. The second element (probably the more important) was the Agreement allowed the High Dam to go ahead, enabling Egypt to store water from year to year on its own territory, and thereby to have complete control over the timing of its release.

The attitude of other riparians

The great shortcoming of the 1959 Agreement was that it was signed by only two of the states in the Nile basin. While it removed a potential Sudanese 'threat' to Egypt over the Nile, it did nothing to secure the flow *into* Sudan of the waters which fed the main Nile. The Agreement did recognise that, at some point in the future, other states in the basin would make claims to a share in the waters. When such a claim was made, Egypt and Sudan would reach 'one unified view' regarding it; if they accepted that a volume of Nile water could be allotted to the state making the claim, that volume would be taken equally from the Egyptian and Sudanese shares.[50] The approach adopted by Egypt and Sudan in the 1959 Agreement – that other riparians might make use of Nile water if the Egyptians and Sudanese agreed that they could – has not found favour with the upstream states.

---

[49] Waterbury (1979).

[50] Agreement for the Full Utilization of the Nile Waters, Fifth Article (2), quoted by Collins (1990).

The states of the upper White Nile basin

For the six states upstream from Sudan on the White Nile and its tributaries, the use of Nile water is a much less urgent question than it is for their neighbours downstream. Because rainfall in these six states is higher, in most areas irrigation is not essential to cultivation, as it is in northern Sudan and Egypt. Moreover, for all the upstream states, capital is difficult to come by: they are too poor to generate it from their own resources, and political instability has made most of them unattractive for international lenders. When capital *can* be obtained, it may well yield greater returns in projects that do not involve the use of the Nile. Further, nearly all these states have suffered prolonged periods of unrest and sometimes civil wars that have compelled regimes to concentrate on day-to-day survival, rather than on planning the development of their countries' water resources.

Because the exploitation of the Nile waters is a much lower priority for them, the White Nile states have resisted attempts by the Egyptians (formerly abetted by the Sudanese) to draw them into agreements that would constrain their future freedom of action. Moreover, they have yet to train a large enough cadre of experts in hydrology and related disciplines to enable them to assess their likely future water needs. In the absence of such a cadre, a further reason for their reticence has been the fear that they might be outsmarted in negotiations by superior Egyptian expertise and knowledge. Egypt's greater international clout and military strength have also made the White Nile states feel that they might be intimidated into giving undertakings that they would later regret.

With these considerations in mind, the six have preferred to limit their cooperation with Egypt and Sudan to the collection and analysis of hydrological and meteorological data. This function has been fulfilled since the late 1960s by the Hydrometeorological Survey of the Equatorial Catchment – Hydromet for short.[51] While the area covered does not extend into their territory, Egypt and Sudan have been members of Hydromet since its formation. Ethiopia joined as an observer in 1971. While Hydromet's activities demonstrate that technical cooperation between Nile riparians is possible, the organisation itself has not been able to expand its functions to become an institution that could co-ordinate the exploitation of the waters of the Nile basin as a whole.

In the late 1970s, the White Nile states rebuffed a joint Egyptian-Sudanese attempt to create, through Hydromet, a Nile Basin Commission embracing all the riparians.[52] The proposed Commission was intended

---

[51] For the creation and development of Hydromet, see Collins (1990).
[52] Ethiopia did so too: see below.

to serve as a framework for negotiations on the apportionment of the Nile waters and their development. There was every reason for Egypt and Sudan to want to see such a Commission set up, but the other riparians had no incentive to agree to its establishment. They had nothing to gain, and might well have lost valuable water rights by making premature commitments.

This reversal led the Egyptians to look for a vehicle for the discussion of the Nile that would also serve to convince the states of the upper White Nile basin that they could profit from being on good terms with Egypt. Given the lack of trade and other forms of interaction between Egypt and these states, this was bound to be an uphill struggle, but one that the Egyptians evidently believed was unavoidable. As a result, the Undugu Group was set up in 1983, on Egyptian initiative. It is a loose grouping of most of the Nile basin states, plus the Central African Republic, with the common denominator being similar positions on regional issues. Kenya has only ever attended as an observer.[53]

The Undugu Group has met regularly, but has made no noticeable progress on the water issue. Communiqués issued after its meetings have made very little mention of the Nile. Apart from platitudinous statements on African and Middle Eastern political questions, these communiques have tended to focus on closer cooperation in developmental matters unrelated to the use of the Nile waters, such as transport and telecommunications.

Undugu's lack of progress on water issues may not be particularly worrying for the Egyptians. It is clear that any significant consumption of Nile water by the upper White Nile states is many years away. Moreover, Egypt cannot benefit from water storage projects in the Equatorial catchment until a *second* Jonglei canal has been cut through the Sudd: with the first canal still unfinished, this is also a distant prospect. It may therefore suit Egypt to spend the coming years demonstrating to the states upstream that there is something to be gained from a cooperative relationship, for example by engaging in joint research projects under the auspices of international organisations, or offering training programmes through the Egyptian Fund for Technical Cooperation in Africa, leaving the nitty-gritty of international water management and apportionment until they are ready.[54]

Although the White Nile states have shown little enthusiasm for discussion of the use of the waters of the Nile basin as a whole, they

---

[53] Undugu means 'brotherhood' in Swahili. Ethiopia was not invited to the early meetings of the Group and – until the Ethiopia-Sudan declaration of December 1991 (see below) – responded to invitations to more recent gatherings by attending only as an observer.

[54] Information on Egyptian assistance to the White Nile states from author's interview with Dr Mahmoud Abu-Zeid, Chairman of the Water Resources Centre, Ministry of Public Works and Water Resources, Cairo, June 1993.

have been ready to prepare the ground for cooperation over part of the basin which lies within their territory. In the late 1970s, Rwanda, Burundi and Tanzania set up the Organisation for the Management and Development of the Kagera River Basin, commonly known as the Kagera Basin Organisation (KBO); Uganda became a member in 1981.[55] The KBO's terms of reference include the use of the waters of the basin (which provide a quarter of the inflow into Lake Victoria) but extend beyond water use to the development of agriculture, transportation, communications, training and energy in the area as a whole. Constrained by political instability in member states but even more by a lack of money, the KBO's activities in exploiting water resources have so far gone no further than planning and carrying out feasibility studies.

While the major disputes over the apportionment of Nile water are to be found downstream, the White Nile states have not always been able to agree among each other on the use of shared water resources. Tanzania has investigated the feasibility of using the water of the Mara river (60% of which comes across the border from Kenya) for hydropower and irrigation. The two countries have met only once to discuss Tanzanian plans, and failed to reach agreement.[56]

Ethiopia

Ethiopia has repeatedly made strongly worded assertions of its right to use the waters of the Blue Nile basin. In 1956, while its neighbours downstream were talking about how they would divide the Nile waters between them, Ethiopia formally declared that it 'reserved its right to utilise the water resources of the Nile for the benefit of its people, whatever might be the measure of utilisation of such waters sought by riparian States.'[57] The declaration was particularly forceful in that it made no reference to the desirability of achieving an apportionment of the waters of the Nile through negotiations, let alone to the co-operative development of the basin as a whole.

This shadow-boxing on the Nile drew in the superpowers. While Egypt had obtained Soviet support for the High Aswan Dam, Ethiopia sought the assistance of the United States in demonstrating that its right to the Nile waters was more than theoretical. In 1957, Ethiopia commissioned the US Bureau of Reclamation to investigate the irrigation

---

[55] The reason why Uganda joined late was a political one: Tanzania refused to have any dealings with Uganda while Idi Amin remained in power. He was overthrown in 1981.

[56] Matondo (1986).

[57] The declaration took the form of official notes to diplomatic missions in Cairo. The extract is quoted by Collins (1990).

and hydro-power potential of the Blue Nile basin in Ethiopia. The Bureau's study, completed in 1963, recommended four major hydro-power dams on the Blue Nile, and twenty-nine irrigation and hydro-power projects on its tributaries. The study concluded that if all the projects which it proposed were implemented, irrigation withdrawals and losses from evaporation from reservoirs would reduce total annual flows of the Blue Nile into Sudan by 8.5%.[58]

However, Ethiopia was too poor to implement the recommendations of the study itself, and unable to get assistance from outside on the necessary scale, especially in the teeth of determined opposition from Egypt and Sudan. The World Bank lent funds for the Finchaa hydro-power plant, which started producing electricity in 1972 (presumably on the ground that the generation of power did not consume water and therefore could not be regarded as harmful to states downstream).[59] But when Ethiopia tried to obtain funds to install an irrigation network for sugar plantations with water drawn from the Finchaa Dam, its application to the African Development Bank was opposed by the Egyptians and Sudanese, on the ground that they had not been consulted about the Dam's construction.[60]

By the mid-1970s, the Ethiopian revolution and the decision by President Sadat of Egypt to break with the Soviet Union in favour of a closer relationship with the USA had produced a switch in international alliances.[61] Sadat's move turned out to be a successful one; Ethiopia's revolution and its association with the superpower which collapsed was not. If the new regime in Addis Ababa entertained hopes that the Soviet Union would show the same generosity to Ethiopia in the 1970s that it had shown to Egypt in the late 1950s, it was to be disappointed.[62]

Perhaps because of their lack of progress in staking a claim to the waters of the Nile by building dams, the Ethiopians continued to make verbal assertions of their rights. At a major UN conference on water in 1977, Ethiopia stated that its policy was to seek international agreement

---

[58] No dams were proposed to impound the water of the Blue Nile itself for irrigation because the Bureau decided that there were no lands suitable for irrigation: for most of its length in Ethiopia, the river flows through a deep and inaccessible gorge. For a detailed account of the study, see Guariso and Whittington (1987).

[59] Waterbury (1982).

[60] The loan was eventually approved. The author has heard two explanations of this. The first is that Egypt and Sudan, having made their point that Ethiopia could not make use of the waters of the Blue Nile basin without their agreement, then withdrew their objections. The second is that the loan was approved by a majority vote of the Bank's board.

[61] Emperor Haile Selassie was overthrown by a military coup in September 1974.

[62] At least in respect of the Nile: the Soviet Union did provide funds for water installations on the Awash.

on the use of shared rivers, a position that represented some evolution with respect to that of 1956. The Ethiopian statement added, however, that the absence of such agreements did 'not in any way diminish the right of one basin state to go along, unilaterally, and develop the waters of the international rivers within its territorial jurisdiction.' At the same time, Ethiopia announced that, in the short term, it intended to irrigate 90,000 hectares of land in the Blue Nile basin, and another 28,000 hectares in the basin of the Baro (a tributary of the Sobat). In the medium term, the total abstraction of Nile water might reach four bcm per year.[63]

By the late 1970s the exchange over the Nile between Ethiopia and Egypt were taking place against a background of hostility in other areas. Not only did the two countries have different superpower backers: they gave support to each other's regional enemies. Ethiopia had drawn close to Libya, with which Egypt had fought a brief border war in July 1977, while Egypt had supported Somalia during its war with Ethiopia over the Ogaden region in 1977-8.

The Egyptians seem to have feared that, with Soviet help, Ethiopia might use the Blue Nile 'for political ends'.[64] In mid-1978, Sadat threatened strong counter measures, even if this led to war, if any step were taken to alter the course of the Blue Nile.[65]

When, in 1980, Egypt announced its intention to irrigate land in Sinai with Nile water, Ethiopia (probably at Soviet instigation) sent a memorandum to the OAU accusing Egypt of misusing the waters of the Blue Nile and infringing the rights of other riparian states (on the ground that Sinai lay outside the Nile basin).[66] The memorandum reserved Ethiopia's right to use the waters of the Blue Nile on its territory as it wished. Sadat responded with public threats of war, on one occasion advising an audience of army officers to prepare a plan to foil any attempt by Ethiopia to impede the flow of the Nile.[67]

Since then, Ethiopian and Egyptian statements on the division of the waters of the Nile have been less bellicose. President Mubarak, who succeeded Sadat after his assassination in 1981, has not repeated Sadat's threats. However, Egyptian ministers continued to allude to their country's vital interest. In 1985, Boutros-Ghali, then Minister of

[63] Ethiopian paper at the UN Water Conference, Mar del Plata, Argentina, March 1977, quoted by Waterbury (1982).
[64] *Al-Ahram*, 5 October 1991.
[65] Voice of Revolutionary Ethiopia, 1 June 1978, translated by BBC Monitoring *SWB*, 3 June 1978.
[66] The Ethiopian note of 1980 made no reference (for reasons that are not clear to the author) to Sadat's offer of 1979 to supply water to Israel in exchange for concessions on the Occupied Territories and Jerusalem.
[67] See *The Guardian*, 6 June 1980: 'Sadat warns Ethiopia.'

State for Foreign Affairs, told an interviewer that the 'next war in our region will be over the waters of the Nile, not politics.'[68] In October 1991, General Tantawi, the Minister of Defence, told an interviewer that Egypt might use force to protect Egypt's supply of Nile water. He made clear, however, that this would be a last resort, should all other means fail: 'We are not ruling out the possibility of using some acts of deterrence after exhausting peaceful means in case any party tries to control the River Nile.'[69] If these statements were intended as a warning to Ethiopia that what Tantawi called 'Egypt's lifeline' could not be interrupted with impunity, it was a rather gentle one compared to Sadat's dramatic threats of over a decade before.

Throughout the 1980s and into the early years of the present decade, Ethiopia remained aloof from regional discussions touching on the Nile waters. Ethiopian representatives attended meetings of Hydromet and the Undugu Group, but only as observers.[70] Meanwhile, Ethiopian spokesmen continued to insist that their country had a right to make use of the waters of the Blue Nile basin.

The Ethiopian case was based on the principle of international law known as 'equitable use', which entitles all states in the basin to a fair (but not necessarily equal) portion of the water of a shared river. This position was balanced by Ethiopian recognition of the other major legal principle, namely that such use should not result in any 'appreciable harm' to other riparians. At the same time, Ethiopian spokesmen made it clear that they believed that such harm could be done by states downstream to those upstream, and that Egypt's reclamation programme fell into this category by pre-empting water that Ethiopia would wish to use as its equitable share when it had the means to do so.[71]

Recent statements of Ethiopia's position have shown a further evolution, going beyond the question of the apportionment of the Nile to the notion of its 'integrated management' through cooperation on the part of the states of the basin. However, Ethiopia has continued to reject the 1959 Agreement between Egypt and Sudan, as being 'in conflict with the present-day international principles and conduct on water allocation'.[72] Meanwhile, Egypt maintained that it possessed 'ac-

---

[68] See the *International Herald Tribune*, 22 February 1985: 'Egypt is African and its principal problem is water.'

[69] *Al-Ahram*, 5 October 1991.

[70] Waterbury (1991).

[71] For a discussion of international legal principles relating to shared water resources, see Chapter 7, 'Some common themes'. For an example of the Ethiopian attitude, see Abate (1991).

[72] Ethiopia (1993).

quired rights' to Nile waters, and that those rights amounted to the 55.5 bcm. a year allocated to Egypt by that very same Agreement. Like Egypt, Sudan had its quarrels with revolutionary Ethiopia. Ethiopian provision of bases for the southern Sudanese rebel movement, the Sudanese People's Liberation Army (SPLA), was paralleled by Sudanese support for a range of Ethiopian opposition movements. In the 'downstream/upstream' wrangling over the Blue Nile, Sudan had long before made common cause with Egypt through the 1959 Agreement. Since the military coup of 1989 in Khartoum, however, Egyptian-Sudanese relations have deteriorated badly, and a crack has appeared in the hitherto united front on the Nile waters.

With the fall of Mengistu in May 1991 and the withdrawal of Ethiopian support for the SPLA, Sudan and Ethiopia were quickly on much better terms. In December 1991, ministers of the two states signed a peace and friendship declaration that included statements relating to the Nile that were apparently made without Sudan's having consulted Egypt in advance. According to the declaration, the two states believed in the principle of 'equitable entitlements to the uses of the Nile waters without causing appreciable harm to one another', deemed it 'essential to establish a joint technical committee' that would hold consultations, exchange data and explore areas of co-operation, and committed themselves to work towards the establishment of a Nile Basin Organisation that would include all riparian countries. The declaration also signalled a more forthcoming Ethiopian attitude to existing Nile basin organisations: Ethiopia would now participate as a full member.[73]

A rapprochement between Egypt and Ethiopia had begun before Mengistu's fall; it gathered pace with the change of regime. In July 1993, the two states signed a 'Framework for General Cooperation' that included clauses relating to the Nile. The agreement left the details of the use of the use of the Nile waters to be worked out by experts from both countries, 'on the basis of the rules and principles of international law'. It did, however, specify that neither country would do anything with the Nile that would cause 'appreciable harm' to the other. Further, Egypt and Ethiopia undertook 'to consult and cooperate in projects that are mutually advantageous, such as projects that would enhance the volume of flow and reduce the loss of Nile waters through comprehensive and integrated development schemes.'

The agreement safeguards Egypt's supply of Nile water from Ethiopia by giving prominence to the principle of the avoidance of appreciable harm: the Egyptians would almost certainly argue that any reduction of flow in the Blue Nile caused by works in Ethiopia would constitute

---

[73] Declaration of peace and friendship between Ethiopia and Sudan, Khartoum, 23 December 1991.

such harm. The concomitant gain for Ethiopia is Egyptian cooperation in developing the Blue Nile basin for Ethiopia's benefit (as well as for Egypt's).

Both the 1991 declaration by Ethiopia and Sudan and the 1993 agreement between Ethiopia and Egypt were statements of general principles. The former appeared to concede more to Ethiopia's position than the latter, since Ethiopia had for some years argued that the guiding principle of the international law of shared rivers was that of equitable entitlement. The wording of Ethiopia's agreement with Egypt, in making no explicit mention of equity, still allows the Egyptians to insist (as they would probably wish to do) that the guiding legal principle should rather be the avoidance of appreciable harm.[74]

In November 1993, Ethiopia reached a similar agreement in principle with Uganda, to the effect that usage of the Nile should be 'fair'.[75] None of these agreements gave any indication of what volume of water Ethiopia might use. The 1959 Agreement between Egypt and Sudan remains the only accord which makes any apportionment of the waters of the Nile.

Questions of quality

As we have seen in a previous section, the only country in the Nile basin which has experienced a significant deterioration in water quality is Egypt. Since these problems are derived almost entirely from activities on Egyptian soil, there have so far been no international disputes over water quality.

Meeting New Demands

The populations of all the Nile basin states are growing rapidly, at between 2.4 and 3.4% (see Table 5). This growth will translate into increased demand for water – for direct consumption, for irrigated agriculture (to meet greater demands for food) and for industry (to provide new jobs). Moreover, most of these states are among the poorest in the world and, although their development is proceeding only slowly, they will inevitably consume more water per head in future.

---

[74] Comment in the Ethiopian opposition press has portrayed the agreement as a 'victory' for Egypt, and has claimed that the Tana-Beles project, 'a large agricultural scheme right at the gates of the Nile', has been frozen as a result of Egyptian pressure. See *Tobbia*, 4 August 1994.

[75] President Meles Zenawi, quoted by the Voice of Ethiopia, 7 November 1993, and translated by BBC Monitoring *SWB*, 9 November 1993.

Table 5. POPULATION GROWTH IN THE NILE BASIN

	Population in 1992 (mid-year estimate, × 1,000)	Rate of growth (% p.a.)	Population in 2025 (× 1,000)
Egypt	54,842	2.4	93,536
Sudan	26,656	2.9	60,602
Ethiopia and Eritrea*	52,981	2.9	130,674
Uganda	18,674	3.1	45,933
Kenya	25,230	3.4	63,826
Tanzania	27,829	3.4	74,172
Zaire	39,882	3.3	104,530
Rwanda	7,526	3.3	20,595
Burundi	5,823	2.9	13,392

* Separate figures for Eritrea not available.
Sources: (for 1992 figures) *Population and Vital Statistics Report* (UN, 1992); for other figures *World Population Report 1992* (wall-chart, UN Department of Economic and Social Development, Population Division, 1992).

For the states of the Nile basin upstream of Egypt and Sudan, shortages of water could act as a constraint on economic development. This would be essentially the result of an incapacity to exploit water resources to the full (in turn, mainly due to a lack of investment capital) rather than reductions in flow caused by consumption on the part of upstream neighbours. (Indeed, for Ethiopia, Kenya, Rwanda, Burundi and Eritrea there are no states further upstream on the Nile or its tributaries.)

For Egypt and Sudan, the situation is different. Both countries already make extensive use of Nile water, and could find existing economic activities and their plans for development, especially in agriculture, curtailed by increased consumption in Ethiopia or the upper White Nile basin. In addition, Egypt could suffer from higher consumption by Sudan, if the latter failed to keep below the ceiling imposed by the 1959 Agreement. Egypt is particularly vulnerable. It has no significant sources of water apart from the Nile. Moreover, it has been using the whole of its quota under that Agreement: there is no slack to be taken up. Indeed, it has had to 'borrow' water from Sudan's quota. A re-negotiation of the Agreement to give Egypt *more* water is out of the question: assuming that no major increase in supply can be engineered, 55.5 bcm. a year is the most Egypt can hope to have from the Nile. With a population that grows by one million every nine months, that volume is getting smaller in *per capita* terms all the time.

Higher consumption upstream would only add new pressures to the existing strain on Egypt's water supplies. In order to determine how serious those pressures could become, we now need to look at how great the increases in consumption upstream might be, and how soon they might occur. In this context, the states of the upper White

84   *The Nile*

Map 4. THE NILE BASIN: SUDAN AND ETHIOPIA

Nile basin fall into a different category from Ethiopia. Until the Jonglei Canal is completed, the effect of greater use of water in the upper White Nile basin would be dampened by the effect of the Sudd: as half of the flow of the White Nile is lost to evaporation, any reduction in flow would also be halved. Moreover, as we have seen earlier, the White Nile as it leaves the Sudd (and before it is joined by the Sobat from Ethiopia) only accounts for 14% of the flow of the Nile at the Sudan-Egypt border.[76] In the case of Ethiopia, an increase in consumption of water from the Sobat, the Blue Nile, the Rahad, the Dinder and the Atbara would be felt directly and would affect a dominant proportion of the flow of the main Nile.

The upper White Nile basin

Despite these remarks, the White Nile's contribution to the water supply of both Egypt and Sudan is not insignificant, especially given the great seasonal and annual variations in the flow of the Blue Nile. Completion of the Jonglei Canal and the other projects designed to reduce losses in the swamps of southern Sudan would greatly enhance the importance of the White Nile. It is therefore necessary to try to determine how much water the states of the upper White Nile basin might use in future.

Such an assessment is difficult, because these states have yet to produce detailed plans. Nevertheless, some general statements can be made with confidence. First, it is unlikely that either Rwanda or Burundi will ever make use of such quantities of Nile water that the effect is noticeable downstream. Both states have plentiful rainfall and irrigation would only be needed locally for certain crops.[77] Average rainfall in Rwanda is 1250 mm. a year.[78] Together with the other members of the Kagera Basin Organisation, Rwanda and Burundi plan to generate electricity from the river (at Rusumo), but this would not be on a very large scale, so that the losses to evaporation from the reservoir would be minimal, especially as evaporation rates at that high altitude are very low. In any case, 'political instability, ideology, and the failure of the regional governments to meet their financial pledges to the organisation appear to have postponed this project far into the future.'[79] For its part, Zaire does not seem to have made any statement of its future water needs from the Nile.

As for Kenya, Tanzania and Uganda, the only quantitative assessments

---

[76] See the section above entitled 'The geopolitics of the Nile basin'.

[77] The part of Burundi which lies within the Nile basin has an average annual rainfall of 1200 mm; see Bigirimana and Ndorimana (1991).

[78] Nkurunziza and Rushemeza (1991).

[79] Collins (1990).

of their needs for Nile water appear to have been made towards the end of the colonial period. In the summer of 1959, Britain officially informed Egypt and Sudan that its East African territories would reserve 1.75 bcm. of Nile water per year for their irrigation requirements.[80] In 1961, however, in negotiations with the PJTC, representatives of the three territories put their existing needs at 0.7 bcm. of water a year, and estimated their future needs at five bcm. This figure does not seem to have been based on precise projections of likely use, and indeed was rejected by the PJTC for lack of supporting data.[81]

It is doubtful whether any more precise estimate could be made now. No water master plans have been produced by any of the White Nile states. This is partly because there is no urgent need to do but also because the resources are not available: these states have neither the expertise to prepare such plans themselves nor the funds to pay outside experts to do for them. For example, a paper prepared by a senior Ugandan official for a conference in 1993 bemoans the lack of 'adequate manpower in the water sector [as being] one of the major constraints affecting ... water resources planning'.[82] Kenya has stated that 'in the long term', it intends to introduce irrigated agriculture in the area around Lake Victoria, but has not quantified the likely water demand.[83]

The present plans of the White Nile states would not cause a reduction in the volume of water flowing into Sudan by more than two or three bcm. a year.[84] Since roughly half of any flow into the Sudd is lost to evaporation anyway, the effect of these plans on the White Nile as it emerged from the Sudd would not be more than one or 1.5 bcm. a year. And it will be well into the next century before such a reduction in the flow of the White Nile is felt, given that finance has still to be found before the implementation of these plans can begin.

Given the modest nature of the likely use of White Nile water upstream of Sudan, the effect on water quality will almost certainly be slight, at worst. Increased salinity and pollution with agri-chemicals will result from the introduction of irrigation, but given the relatively small areas involved, the effect will not be great. Kenya has indicated its concern about pollution from industry and municipal sources in the area around Lake Victoria, as well as form irrigated agriculture, but it seems highly improbable that this will cause a noticeable deterioration in water quality in the Nile system as a whole.[85]

[80] Waterbury (1982).
[81] Ibid.
[82] Kahangire (1993).
[83] Kenya (1993).
[84] Allan (1991).
[85] Kenya (1993).

Ethiopia

The existence of the comprehensive study of the Blue Nile basin by the US Bureau of Reclamation makes it possible to see the potential for its development – and the likely impact downstream – more clearly than is the case regarding the White Nile. While at first sight the consequences for Egypt and Sudan of the realisation of the Bureau's recommendations seem alarming, a closer examination suggests that the net effect would not necessarily be very harmful, and might possibly be beneficial.

One of the main elements in the Bureau's recommendations was the construction of four large hydro-power dams on the Blue Nile. Since electricity demand is relatively stable from season to season and year to year, these dams would release a generally steady flow of water, ending the river's flood, which at the moment reaches as far downstream as Lake Nasser. The High Aswan Dam would no longer be required to fulfil this function of evening-out the flow of the Nile, and Lake Nasser could be kept at a much lower level. The result would be a massive saving of water that is lost to evaporation through keeping the lake high. The range of losses already experienced gives some idea of how great this saving could be: in the late 1970s when the lake was full, some 13 bcm. of water were lost each year, compared with about 6 bcm. per year in the late 1980s, when the level was exceptionally low.[86] Of course, there would be evaporation from the reservoirs in Ethiopia, but this would be much less than from Lake Nasser. Evaporation rates in the Ethiopian highlands are barely one-third of that at Aswan for each square metre of water surface. Moreover, the ratio of surface area to volume would be lower for reservoirs in the deep valley of the Blue Nile in Ethiopia than it is for the broad and rather shallow expanse of Lake Nasser: in other words, in Ethiopia, a smaller area of surface would be exposed to evaporation for every cubic metre of water stored.

An academic study of the Bureau's recommendations for the development of hydro-power on the Blue Nile has shown, using mathematical models, that even if Ethiopia were to manage its reservoirs with the sole objective of producing as much electricity as possible, without considering the interests of Egypt and Sudan in any way, 'the amount of water available to those two states would not be substantially affected.'[87] By taking advantage of the storage of water in Ethiopia and operating Lake Nasser at a lower level, and thereby reducing evaporation

---

[86] Allan (1991).
[87] Guariso and Whittington (1987).

losses from its surface, they would enjoy a large net gain in terms of available water.

Under the terms of the 1959 Agreement, Egypt and Sudan would share that net gain equally. But in other ways, Sudan would benefit more than Egypt. Large-scale storage of Blue Nile water in Ethiopia would eliminate or at least reduce many of the problems of operating the Roseires reservoir.[88] By contrast, Egypt would lose much of its hydro-power generating capacity at Aswan which, though a declining proportion of its total capacity, remains important.

Moreover, the picture looks different when Ethiopian irrigation potential is considered, especially if irrigation schemes are implemented before hydro-power projects. It is hard to imagine the Ethiopians not giving a higher priority to irrigation than to electricity: their country has experienced disastrous famines when the rains have failed, the famine of 1984-5 being only the most recent and well-publicised occurrence. Electricity is much less a matter of life and death. It will be many years before Ethiopia can use the huge amounts of power that could be generated on the Blue Nile, and Ethiopia's neighbours are not likely to provide a promising export market for electricity in either the short or medium terms. Even official targets (which usually turn out to be optimistic) for the construction of hydro-power dams stagger the implementation of the priority projects over a period of half a century.[89]

If Ethiopia were to implement the irrigation projects recommended by the Bureau of Reclamation study, it would require a large volume of water. Irrigation of land in the Blue Nile basin in Ethiopia might need four or 4.25 bcm. a year; irrigation schemes using water from the Rahad and Dinder (which join the Blue Nile in Sudan) could require an additional one bcm a year from each river. Allowing for the return of water draining back into these rivers from irrigated fields, the total net loss of flow into Sudan would be of the order of three bcm.[90] This would still be enough to do serious damage to Sudanese irrigation potential, particularly on the Rahad. The total net loss to Egypt and Sudan might be around 4.4 bcm. a year.

This reduction in quantity could be more than offset if the Egyptians were to operate Lake Nasser at a lower level to cut evaporation losses. This presupposes, however, that Egypt would be prepared to entrust the security of its water supplies to another state. To outsiders, there might appear to be relatively little risk involved. After all, even the

---

[88] Ibid.
[89] Abate (1991).
[90] This calculation assumes that 30% of the water applied to the fields would drain back (as 'return flow') into the rivers from which it had come, an assumption that is in line with observations made in irrigation schemes elsewhere in the region.

possibility of impounding water behind big hydro-power dams on the Blue Nile as a means of damaging Egypt would only be available to Ethiopia in a drought (since in years of high flood, the reservoirs would not have sufficient spare capacity). Assuming that the Ethiopians acted according to economic rather than strategic criteria and sought to produce as much electricity as possible from the reduced volume of water available, they would not wish to impede the passage of water through their turbines. Moreover, Ethiopia would pay a heavy penalty in terms of its relations with the West and the Arab world if it were to use water as a weapon against Egypt.

These arguments by themselves are not likely to reassure the Egyptians. Nasser opted for the High Aswan Dam rather than storage in the Equatorial lakes precisely because he was not prepared to take what he saw as the strategic risk of allowing others to control the flow of the Nile. Despite the improvement in relations between Egypt and Ethiopia in recent years, there is no sign of the fundamental change of heart which would be necessary on the part of the Egyptians for them to contemplate such an arrangement. At present, there is no reason for Ethiopia to wish to damage or put pressure on Egypt, but this happy state of affairs may not last for ever. The two countries have opposed each other in the recent past, and there have been enough about-turns of foreign policy in both Cairo and Addis Ababa in recent decades for it to be impossible to say that they will not again be adversaries.

Another reason for Egypt and Sudan to be concerned at the possibility of large-scale use of water for irrigation in Ethiopia is the likely effect on water quality. Water used to irrigate Ethiopian fields would, on draining back to the Nile, have a higher content of salts and agri-chemicals than it does at the moment. Until Ethiopian plans are formulated in more detail, it is impossible to predict how harmful this would be to the downstream riparians. Nevertheless, it is difficult to avoid the conclusion that some damage would be done, particularly in areas such as the Delta where water quality has already fallen to the point where further deterioration would impose stricter limitations on its use or even render it useless.

Sudan

The most recent comprehensive plan for the exploitation of water resources in Sudan is the Master Plan of the Nile Waters (1979). The Plan lists four projects for the Blue Nile with a total water requirement of around four bcm per year, and two for the White Nile with a requirement of 1.25 bcm. As well as these major proposals, modernisation of the smaller pump schemes, a project on the upper Atbara, irrigation upstream of Malakal (to supplement rainfall) and increasing cropping intensities on existing irrigated areas along the main Nile would, if implemented, add up to a further additional water requirement of some 4.5 bcm. a year.

On top of this increased consumption in agriculture, heavier evaporation losses will be incurred through the heightening of the Roseires Dam (because the reservoir behind it will have a greater surface area) and will also be incurred if the proposed hydro-power dam at Merowe (for which a feasibility study is under way) is built: annual evaporation at Roseires will increase by 0.45 bcm. while 1.75 bcm. would be lost from the Merowe reservoir.[91] It seems inevitable that the very low consumption of Nile water by domestic users will rise, partly as a result of population growth and partly through higher standards of living. A net loss of water of 0.6 bcm. a year to urban consumption alone can be envisaged in the next century.[92]

At present, Sudan may be consuming about 14 bcm. of Nile water a year, and possibly quite a lot more. Whatever the true figure, the unused portion of Sudan's annual quota under the 1959 Agreement (18.5 bcm.) is insufficient to meet all these possible extra demands, which add up to over 12.5 bcm. As is the case for Ethiopia, political pre-occupations and shortages of funds mean that few of these Sudanese projects will be implemented in the near future. It will therefore be some years into the next century before Sudan is faced with the choice of breaching the terms of the 1959 Agreement or accepting limitations on the development of its water resources.

Climatic change

Potential demand in the Nile basin as a whole is clearly much greater than the existing supply. The implications of this situation for the future would be even more daunting if that supply were to be drastically reduced by lower rainfall resulting from climatic change, induced in turn by greenhouse gases.

The long drought of the 1980s led to suggestions that such change was already under way over the Nile basin. In the present state of scientific knowledge, however, it is impossible to say whether this so, or whether there will be any effect of this kind in future. Different models of the effects of climatic changes produce very different outcomes. Two such models applied to the Blue Nile basin suggested reductions in its flow of 8% and 0.4% by 2025; a third suggested an *increase* by the same date of 22%.[93] With this degree of uncertainty,

---

[91] The proposed dam at Merowe is sometimes referred to as the Hamdab Dam.
[92] Knott and Hewett (1990).
[93] Conway (1993).

'it is not possible to predict the onset of climatic changes, including their magnitude and spatial distribution, with any degree of confidence.'[94] Climatic change perhaps appears the more threatening because it is so difficult to predict, but it is to some extent comforting that even the wide range of outcomes referred to above falls within the normal variation in Blue Nile flows recorded in the past.

Making more water available

It would be much more comforting if we were able to identify ways of substantially enhancing the supply of water to meet the certainty of increasing demand and the possibility of falling supply caused by climatic change. We have already mentioned two of the main ways in which losses of water could be cut and more water therefore made available, namely, storage of Blue Nile water in Ethiopia and the concomitant operation of Lake Nasser at a lower level, and the reduction of losses in the Sudd via the excavation of the Jonglei Canal.

A lower Lake Nasser. The full benefit to Sudan and Egypt of storage in Ethiopia could only be gained through continuous cooperation between the three countries, to co-ordinate the operation of their respective reservoirs. At the moment, such an arrangement seems only a distant prospect at best. In any case, given the time-span needed to construct the dams which would be required in Ethiopia to exploit the lower evaporation there, no increase in supply can be sought from its source in the short or medium terms. Moreover, if Ethiopia were to implement all the irrigation schemes proposed by the US Bureau of Reclamation study, as well as those designed to produce to produce hydro-power, the additional volume of water might not be very great.

Nevertheless, Egypt could save water in the short term by operating Lake Nasser at lower levels than originally envisaged, through the introduction of modern computer techniques. This would not require any new storage upstream.[95]

Cutting losses in southern Sudan. Two-thirds of the Jonglei Canal have been dug. But no work has been done on the project for a decade. The giant excavator which was digging it has received no maintenance since it had to be abandoned by its expatriate operators in 1984, while the section of the canal which has been dug may by now have degraded to the point where it will need to be dug again. However much work

---

[94] Abu-Zeid and Biswas (1991).
[95] Author's interview with Dr Bayoumi Attia, Ministry of Public Works and Water Resources, Cairo, June 1993.

turns out to be necessary to complete the project, nothing can be done while southern Sudan continues to be racked by the civil war, to which there are no signs of an early end. When that conflict is settled, the Jonglei Canal may be further delayed by southern Sudanese insistence on modifications designed to protect their interests, since southern resentment at the imposition of the project by Khartoum was one of the causes of the conflict. It is also hard to see the present governments in Cairo and Khartoum, divided as they are by both ideology and practical issued, working together on a major project. Moreover, in the years since work ceased, the global environmental lobby has gained greatly in strength: it could well mount effective opposition to international funding for the Canal, on the ground that it threatened one of the last great wetlands on Earth.

The Jonglei Canal was designed to make an extra 3.8 bcm. of White Nile water available to Egypt and Sudan.[96] Under the terms of the 1959 Agreement, this would be shared equally between them.[97] Egypt's supply of Nile water would be increased by 3.4%, Sudan's by 10%. But it will be many years before this water becomes available to them, if indeed the project is ever completed at all.

Still further in the future are the other schemes which would reduce water losses in the marshes of southern Sudan. 'Jonglei Phase II' would involve doubling the size of the canal, so that it could convey a volume of water sufficient for it to be worthwhile to increase the storage capacity of the Equatorial lakes. Other schemes would reduce losses in the Machar marshes and the Bahr el Ghazal area. A total of 15.25 bcm. of water a year would be added to the flow of the White Nile.[98]

Dam-busting. Fortunately, there are steps that could be taken that would increase supply in quicker time. The most immediate results would be obtained from the destruction of the Jebel Auliya Dam.[99] Until the completion of the High Aswan Dam, White Nile water was impounded at Jebel Auliya for release between January and July, to supply Egyptian agriculture when the level of the Blue Nile flood had fallen. The High Dam rendered this seasonal storage unnecessary. Since then, the only function which Jebel Auliya has performed is to maintain the level of water upstream high enough to be within reach of the pumps which supply irrigation schemes along the river. There is thus

---

[96] This would be the figure as measured at Aswan, allowing for transmission losses between the end of the Canal and Aswan: see Collins (1990).

[97] Third Article (I).

[98] Figures are from Knott and Hewett (1990).

[99] Details of this proposal come from the author's interview with Dr Bayoumi Attia, Ministry of Public Works and Water Resources, Cairo, June 1993.

some economic benefit from the continued existence of the dam, but the cost in terms of water lost to evaporation is disproportionately high. The reservoir's total capacity is only 5.5 bcm. but because it is very shallow the exposed surface is very large, and loses about 2.3 bcm. a year to the atmosphere. (This is almost a quarter of the average evaporation loss from Lake Nasser, the capacity of which is nearly thirty times that of Jebel Auliya.)

The pump schemes are in any case in poor shape. From April to September, the pumps cannot lift water as the level of the White Nile is below their intakes. Moreover, less than a quarter of the original area now receives water. Using modern electric pumps, it would be possible to draw water from the White Nile at any time of year. According to a study by British consultants Sir Alexander Gibb & Partners, a comprehensive rehabilitation programme would cost some $280 million, but would pay for itself in increased yields, even if no value were placed on the water saved by reduced evaporation losses. The rehabilitated pump schemes would use 1.25 bcm. more water than is being used at the moment (1.6 bcm. a year as opposed to the present 0.35 bcm.), an extra consumption of 1.25 bcm. The net saving of water from the demolition of the Dam would therefore be 1.05 bcm.[100]

Another way of reducing the evaporation losses from Jebel Auliya would be to embank the sides of the reservoir, to increase the ratio of volume to surface area. This solution might have more appeal for Sudan than the demolition of the Dam, as it would probably not require an investment of capital on the same scale as that which would be needed for the pump rehabilitation scheme.

Using ground-water. Both Sudan and Egypt lack major sources of surface water outside the Nile basin. But supply could be increased by exploiting reserves of ground-water. In both countries, aquifers that are re-charged from the Nile (either directly or through drainage from irrigated fields) are tapped. This is especially so in Egypt, where 2.6 bcm. are extracted from such aquifers. There is scope for more extensive use of these aquifers: according to official projections, the annual extraction rate could be increased by the year 2000 by almost 90%, to 4.9 bcm.[101]

Aquifers outside the Nile basin (mostly 'fossil' water that is not replenished significantly by present-day rainfall, if at all) are less fully

---

[100] Because of the nature of the heavy clay soils of Sudan's irrigated areas, there is little or no return flow to be taken into account (Allan, personal communication).

[101] Abu-Zeid (1992). Estimates put Sudanese use of ground-water at between 300 and 400 mcm. per year, but figures for the use of aquifers associated with the Nile are not available separately: see Knott and Hewett (1990).

used. The extent of these ground-water resources has not been so well investigated as have surface waters. In Sudan, the potential does not appear to be great, possibly around 2 bcm. annually.[102] This would make a worthwhile addition to Sudan's water supply (it would be the equivalent of more than 10% of the Sudanese quota of 18.5 bcm. of Nile water under the 1959 Agreement) if the costs of extraction and conveyance turned out to be acceptable. However, even if the whole of this volume turned out to be economically exploitable, it would not be enough to keep Sudan's supply of water ahead of demand for many years.

The same is almost certainly true for Egypt, which has huge fossil aquifers beneath the Western Desert. Most of this water is at such great depths that the cost of pumping would render its use uneconomic. Around 0.5 bcm. of this water is already being tapped each year, mainly to irrigate lands in the New Valley project in the Western Desert. Official Egyptian projections suggest that use of desert ground-water could rise to 2.5 bcm. a year by the end of the century.[103]

Other methods of increasing supply. Given that Egypt has substantial reserves of oil and gas, desalination of sea-water or saline ground-water might appear to be an option for the supply of domestic and industrial consumers, many of whom can afford the necessarily higher prices from this source.[104] For the time being, however, conservation measures are much cheaper per additional cubic metre of water. This is even more true in Sudan, whose oil and gas reserves in the South remain undeveloped because of the civil war.

Importation of water has been proposed as a way of increasing the supply of water to Israel and its neighbours. As far as the Nile basin is concerned, this is simply a non-starter, there being no sources of fresh water within economic reach that could make any real difference. (Indeed, the Nile was one of the sources considered for Israel and its neighbours.)

Conservation measures. There are many opportunities for greater efficiency in Egypt and Sudan, in all existing uses. Since agriculture is the dominant user of water, it is here that the biggest savings can be made by reducing waste. Egyptian and Sudanese farmers mostly use traditional methods of irrigation, and sprinkler and drip systems would make more efficient use of water at the farm level. As far as Egypt is

[102] Knott and Hewett (1990).
[103] Abu-Zeid (1992).
[104] In March 1994, Egypt's proven reserves of gas stood at 21 trillion cubic feet, with annual production at over 400 billion cubic feet (Mohammed al-Tawila, vice-chairman for gas at the Egyptian Petroleum Corporation, quoted by Reuters, 15 March 1994).

Meeting New Demands 95

concerned, however, the gain at the national level would be much less, since water that is not used by plants drains back to canals or the river itself, or sinks into the sub-soil. It can then be recovered for use. Because of this, the overall efficiency of irrigation from the Nile may already be as high as 75%.[105]

Nevertheless, greater benefit could be obtained from the water available for irrigation in Egypt by better management practices throughout the system, and by reducing the volume of Nile water which is lost to the Mediterranean to the absolute minimum necessary to flush salts and pollutants out of the system. Further savings could be made by substituting other, less thirsty crops for rice and sugar-cane.[106] Charging farmers for water according to the volume they use would discourage waste: at present farmers receive water free of charge and have no incentive to use it sparingly. However, this would be a difficult step in terms of domestic politics, and it would no doubt prove necessary to find some way of increasing farmer's incomes (for the most part, very low) to compensate for any charges for water.

Measures are being taken to reduce the volume of water which is released through the High Aswan Dam in winter to keep the level of the Nile high enough during the winter for tourist boats, without impending their operation. The present 'loss' of 1.8 bcm. in this use could be cut to 0.3 bcm.'[107]

In both Egypt and Sudan, the maintenance and modernisation of urban water-supply systems would prevent the loss of substantial quantities of water. Improvements to the system in Cairo are already under way, and Egyptian planners aim to reduce the present loss of half the water entering the system to 20% by the year 2000. Enough water should be saved by improvements in Cairo and other urban areas in Egypt to meet increased demand for domestic and industrial use.[108] In Khartoum, over 60% of the water entering the system is lost.[109]

Using water twice. Egyptian agriculture already makes considerable use of re-cycled water.[110] Official projections suggest that this will rise

---

[105] Author's interview with Dr Mahmoud Abu-Zeid, Chairman of the Water Resources Centre, Ministry of Public Works and Water Resources, Cairo, June 1993. Stoner (1990) puts the overall efficiency at 65%. Surplus irrigation water applied to reclaimed land does not return to the Nile system, but sprinkler and drip irrigation are much more widely used in these areas.

[106] Stoner (1990).
[107] Abu-Zeid (1992).
[108] Ibid.
[109] Zaki (1991).
[110] See above, p. 66.

to 8.7 bcm. a year by the turn of the century, an increase of over one-third. By this time, nearly 15% of irrigation water will have been used before. Of the total, 7 bcm. will be water that has already been used at least once before in agriculture; the remaining 1.7 bcm. will be treated waste-water from Cairo.[111] It seems inevitable that, as Egypt's population grows and becomes more concentrated in the capital and other cities, urban waste-water will become an ever-larger proportion of the supply of irrigation water.

Probably because the pressure on water resources is not so great as in Egypt, there seems to be little or no deliberate re-cycling of water in Sudan. There is undoubtedly scope for the treatment and re-use of waste-water from Khartoum and other urban areas, although this will not be on the same scale as in Egypt. Moreover, Sudan does not have the same opportunities as Egypt for the natural re-use of irrigation water: surplus water applied to Sudanese crops cannot pass through the heavy 'black cotton' clay soils to emerge as 'return flows', but rather evaporates *in situ*.

One authoritative source has estimated the potential gains from all kinds of conservation measures (including re-use) throughout the Nile basin at a staggering 45 bcm.[112]

Re-allocation

Irrigated agriculture generally yields low returns per cubic metre *vis-à-vis* other uses (e.g. industry), particularly where hot and dry climatic conditions mean very high annual water requirements per hectare.[113] Where there is growing pressure on water supplies and all needs cannot be met, as is the case in the Nile basin, economic logic suggests that other users of water be given priority and that agriculture be made to bear the brunt of any reductions. Insofar as domestic use is concerned, governments can hardly avoid this course of action if they are to prevent a fall in living standards in the face of an ever-increasing population.

A reduction in the supply of irrigation water in Egypt and Sudan may well be necessary if the demands of other riparians for a larger share of Nile waters are to be accommodated. Given the position of agriculture as by far the largest user of water in both states, it is only from that sector that sufficiently large volumes of water can be taken.

Nonetheless, Egypt and Sudan have not been exceptions to the general rule that Middle Eastern states have been unwilling to admit the pos-

---

[111] Figures derived from Abu-Zeid (1992).

[112] Author's interview with Dr Bayoumi Attia, Ministry of Public Works and Water Resources, Cairo, June 1993.

[113] These are often over 20,000 cubic metres per hectare: see e.g. Allan (1993a).

sibility that their agricultural sectors will contract rather than expand. Like other states in the region (and beyond), Egypt and Sudan have sought such expansion as a way of achieving a certain level of self-sufficiency in food as a contribution to national security.[114] Moreover, exports of agricultural produce earn foreign exchange. The sector also provides employment. For Egypt, it is a means of demonstrating that the government has an answer to population growth and overcrowding in the cities.

For Sudan, the contraction of agriculture does not appear to make any sense at the moment. It currently provides 95% of foreign exchange earnings, and occupies 61% of the work-force; it also contributes 34% of GDP.[115] But this situation is the result less of the success of Sudanese farming as it is of the failure of other sectors to make progress. Political stability and improved economic management (when they can be achieved) should result in a lessening of the dominance of the agricultural sector in the national economy.

In Egypt, the output of agriculture has grown continuously, but the sector has been in relative (but not absolute) decline as other areas of economic activity (especially manufacturing and oil and gas) have grown in importance. Although the sector still provides a third of all jobs, it only contributes one-fifth of GDP and 14% of foreign exchange earnings.[116] Moreover, in spite of the time, effort and money devoted to both reclamation of new land and 'vertical' expansion on existing land, production has not managed to keep pace with population growth and changing consumption patterns. Egypt has not had a balance in its trade in agricultural goods since 1970; it currently imports the greater part of certain basic foodstuffs.[117] A reduction in the volume of irrigation water would merely reinforce existing trends to which Egyptians have been accommodating themselves for a long time, rather than plunge the country into an unfamiliar and frightening situation.

Enough water for all?

The question which remains to be answered is whether the countries

---

[114] In 1994, the government of Egypt urged the country's farmers to aim for 60% self-sufficiency in wheat. See *MEED*, 25 November 1994: 'Egyptian wheat: closing the supply gap.'

[115] Figures from a variety of sources.

[116] Statistics on employment from Ministry of Planning, Five-Year Plan for Economic and Social Development, 1992/3-1996/7: those on GDP from Central Bank of Egypt, Annual Report, 1990/1.

[117] In 1994, despite improvements in wheat production, Egypt was still importing 54% of its wheat requirements. See *MEED*, 25 November 1994: 'Egyptian wheat: closing the supply gap.'

of the Nile basin will be able to find ways of living within their collective water means. That demand will increase (both within the two main existing 'user' states and elsewhere in the basin) is certain, even if the rate of increase in consumption cannot be accurately predicted.

Much less certain is the time which will be required to implement the major projects which aim to increase supply; indeed in some cases, such as the Jonglei Canal, it cannot be said with confidence that they ever will be implemented. Measures designed to make better use of existing supplies of water hold more promise. Not only are they much less disruptive of the environment than major supply-side projects, they do not require the mobilisation of enormous capital sums at one time, or depend on co-operation between governments that have often shown themselves unwilling to work together. Moreover, they do not arouse opposition from vested interests in the way that planned shifts in allocation between sectors would.

Even the progressive realisation of such measures at an expeditious pace may not save enough water to permit Egypt and Sudan to embark upon major new water-using projects, if aspiring users (Ethiopia in particular) are not to be deprived of a share of Nile water. The most obvious targets for further savings are the Egyptian reclamation programme and Sudan's Merowe Dam project (because of the heavy evaporation losses). If these sacrifices prove insufficient, a gradual reduction in the supply of water to agriculture should enable Egypt and Sudan to keep within smaller water budgets. These steps might appear to be difficult to sell to the public, especially in Egypt after so many years of official promotion of agriculture in general and reclamation in particular. However, similar adjustments have been made over the past two decades, without their existence having been admitted in public: the likelihood is that the government can go on making them without feeling the need to announce any change of policy.

The outlook

Predicting the outcome of the intensifying competition for Nile water is fraught with risk, because of the plethora of factors involved. Moreover, each of these individual factors has its own uncertainties. For example, the models of climatic change might give the wrong answers (some of them, at least, must be doing so), or renewed political instability in Ethiopia might postpone still further that country's plans for the development of its water resources.

A crucial 'unknown' is the further relationship with each other of the two main consumer states, and of those two states with Ethiopia, the main supplier and the main potential consumer. These relationships may be good enough to encourage co-operation in the exploitation of the shared water resource; or they may be so poor that the degree of trust necessary for such cooperation cannot develop. The marked deterioration in relations between Egypt and Sudan in recent years illustrates just how quickly a tradition of cooperation can be undermined by a change of regime [118]

A dismal scenario. If cooperation does not materialise, the future is likely to be dominated by increasing competition for water between Ethiopia and Egypt, with Ethiopia seeking international funding for water projects and Egypt trying to obstruct Ethiopia's efforts on the grounds that its proposals would deprive Egypt of its 'acquired rights' and cause it 'appreciable harm'. (Because of its lesser international importance, Sudan would be a much less prominent player than Egypt. Under its present regime, Sudan would be unlikely to side with Egypt, but a successor regime might see its interests as lying in supporting Egyptian attempts to prevent funding for Ethiopian projects.) Given Egypt's significant international role and its privileged access in Western capitals, its opposition to Ethiopian applications for funds would probably be successful, at least initially. In turn, this would thwart Ethiopian plans to dam the rivers on its territory to pay for large-scale water projects.

International lending agencies might offer Ethiopia loans for projects on rivers that are not shared with other countries. However, the scope for such 'consolation prizes' is small: only 10% of the country's surface water resources are not shared in this way. Moreover, over two-thirds of Ethiopia's surface water resources are in the Nile basin. It seems unlikely, therefore, that Egyptian objections could block international funding indefinitely, in the face of Ethiopia's obvious need for more reliable food supplies (which only irrigation could ensure, at least in the absence of substantial new sources of foreign exchange with which Ethiopia could pay for imported food).

If Ethiopia *were* to obtain money for a major water project against Egyptian opposition, Egypt might consider other action. Its options in this respect are few. It has no economic leverage over Ethiopia, trade between the two countries being minimal. The existence in Ethiopia of a situation in which a minority monopolises power to the exclusion of large ethnic groups could provide opportunities for subversion, enabling Egypt to demonstrate that there was a price to be paid for harming its interests.

---

[118] In July 1989, Sudan's parliamentary system was overthrown by a military-Islamist coup. Within two years, relations with Egypt had begun to deteriorate; they were seriously damaged by the Sudanese refusal to condemn the Iraqi invasion of Kuwait, by the Egyptian government's perception that Sudan was supporting its Islamist opponents, and by the territorial dispute over the Halaib Triangle.

The final option is the use of direct military action. The use of military force would require a reversal of policy for the Egyptian government, President Mubarak having made it clear that Egyptian forces will not be used in foreign adventures. If such a change of policy did take place, military action would presumably take the form of attack from the air. Such action would probably only be possible if relations between Egypt and Sudan were such that the Egyptian air force were to be permitted the use of Sudan's air bases. Even limited aerial bombardment of Ethiopian construction sites could be quite effective if it scared away expatriate experts, without whose services Ethiopia would not be able to complete its projects; more sustained bombing would clearly be necessary to destroy dams once they had been built.

In their present enfeebled condition, the Ethiopian armed forces would not be capable of retaliating. But military action against Ethiopia could be costly for Egypt in other ways. It would endanger its image in the international community as a peace-loving (indeed, as a peace-making) state, particularly if the safety of expatriate experts from major powers was put at risk. Egypt would find great difficulty in convincing the rest of the world that it was justified in attacking a development project in a country with a per capita GDP less than a fifth of its own. The aid on which the Egyptian economy has come to depend might be put at risk.

Somewhat similar considerations would govern Egyptian reactions to increased Sudanese use of the Nile. But there are differences. For one thing, Sudan still does not use all the water to which it is entitled under the 1959 Agreement: Egypt would be in no position to object to increased Sudanese consumption until the 'ceiling' of 18.5 bcm. a year had been reached.[119] At that point, the Sudanese would almost certainly seek to prevent any further rise in consumption rather than breach an accord with a powerful neighbour. Sudan is much more vulnerable to Egyptian retribution than Ethiopia. It might find itself subjected to a boycott of Sudanese exports, subversive activity (Egypt has long played a role in Sudanese politics and would find it much easier to operate there than in non-Arab Ethiopia), or pressure over the disputed territory of Halaib. And Sudan is within reach of Egyptian land as well as air forces in a way that Ethiopia is not.

Following the assassination attempt on President Mubarak in Addis Ababa in June 1995, and Egyptian accusations of Sudanese involvement, the Sudanese leader Turabi made veiled threats against the 1959 Agreement.

---

[119] Indeed, the Egyptian Minister of Public Works and Water Resources, Radi, was reported (by *Al-Ahram Weekly* 6-12 July 1995: 'War of words and water') to have said that 'Egypt is not against Sudan using its full quota of water.' The same report said that Radi's Ministry agreed in 1982 to the Merowe (or Hamdab) project.

Although Sudanese Vice-President Saleh subsequently denied that Turabi was speaking for the Sudanese government, Mubarak warned the Sudanese not to encroach on the waters of the Nile in forceful terms: 'Any step taken to this end will force us into confrontation to defend our rights and life. Our response will be beyond anything they can imagine.'[120] The forceful nature of Mubarak's response to even the hint of a possible unilateral renunciation of the Agreement by Sudan shows what a risk the Sudanese would run if they chose this course of action.

Grounds for optimism. Egypt's public emphasis on agriculture, food self-sufficiency and the defence of 'its' annual quota of 55.5 bcm. of Nile water suggests a readiness to resist the attempts of upstream states to increase their use of the Nile. Such increased use would undoubtedly make life more difficult for Egypt, but would not create a new situation: as a result of the growth in Egypt's population, the country has not been able to feed itself (in the sense of producing all its food needs) for a quarter of a century. Like many other countries, it has coped with this situation in a pragmatic manner by importing a growing volume of food.

A calculation of the additional volume of water which Egypt would need each year in order to produce all the food which it now imports produce a figure of around 20 bcm.[121] It would be much easier for Egypt to continue to find ways of dealing with this 'water gap' by importing whatever quantities of food are required by its citizens, rather than pushing disputes with other states in the basin to the point of armed conflict. An essential part of this unannounced strategy has been aid from another state (the United States), a dependence that many Egyptians have found uncomfortable. However, the development of other sectors of the economy should enable Egypt to generate the foreign exchange necessary to pay for a greater proportion of its food imports.

The accords signed by Ethiopia and Sudan in 1991 and by Ethiopia and Egypt in 1993 also suggest that discussion and negotiation are more likely than war. Of course, there is a great distance to travel between these general declarations of intent and a new apportionment of the Nile waters that takes Ethiopian requirements into account, let alone the cooperative management of the basin as a whole (or at least the Blue Nile basin). The current hostility between Egypt and Sudan is a major obstacle to progress.

Nevertheless, these agreements seem to be informed by a realisation on the part of both upstream and downstream states that the costs of conflict are too great to be borne. Ethiopia needs the consent of Egypt

---

[120] See *Al-Ahram Weekly* 6-12 July 1995: 'War of words and water.'
[121] Allan (personal communication).

and Sudan if it is not to find that its applications for international funding for the development of its water resources are met by stiff resistance. For their part, Egypt and Sudan need the co-operation of Ethiopia in ensuring that the development of its water resources takes place in a way that does not harm their interests and perhaps even enhances their supply of Nile water. The three key states in the basin may be driven towards cooperation by a hard-headed assessment of their own self-interest. But we may expect each to defend its interests with vigour, and their negotiations may be difficult and protracted, and marked by periods of acrimony.

4

THE TIGRIS–EUPHRATES BASIN

The Geopolitics of the Tigris-Euphrates Basin

The Euphrates and Tigris, the two longest rivers of southwest Asia, rise in the mountains of eastern Turkey (see Map 5).

The Euphrates

The Euphrates is formed in Turkey by the confluence of the Karasu and Murat. A number of substantial tributaries join the Euphrates in the 455 km. between that point and the Syrian border at Jerablus. During its course of 675 km. through Syria, the Euphrates is joined by three main tributaries, the Sajur, the Belikh and the Khabur. Much of the water in all three of these comes from Turkey, whether it crosses the border as rivers on the surface or flows beneath it as ground-water, to emerge in springs on the Syrian side. According to conservative estimates, 88% of the water in the Euphrates as it crosses the border between Syria and Iraq is derived from snow and rain that fall in Turkey, and only 12% from rainfall in Syria. One calculation, however, has produced figures of 98% for Turkey, and only 2% for Syria.[1]

The Euphrates flows for some 1,200 kms in Iraq before reaching the Persian Gulf. After the first third of this distance, near Hit, the river enters the alluvial lowlands of Mesopotamia: it has only a little over 50 metres to fall to the Gulf in 735 km. From Nasiriya, the river divides into a number of channels, some of which flow into Lake Hammar, while the remainder join the Tigris near Qurna to form the Shatt al-Arab. During its passage through Iraq, the Euphrates receives only a negligible amount of water.

Although the longer of the two, the Euphrates is smaller than the Tigris in volume. A 1994 study, drawing together a wide range of available data, calculated that the average annual natural flow of the

---

[1] Kolars and Mitchell (1991). This calculation takes into account the fact that much of the water in the springs which feed the tributaries of the Euphrates which rise in Syria is derived from rainfall in bordering areas of Turkey, and reaches Syria as underground flow through a limestone aquifer.

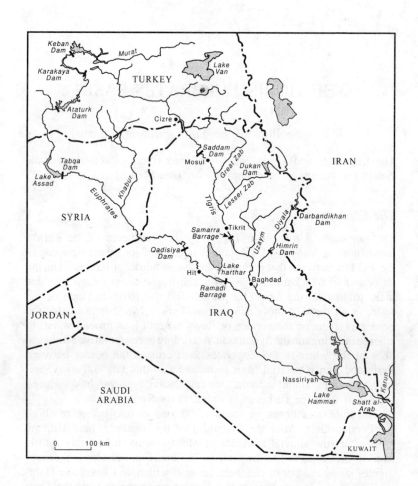

Map 5. THE TIGRIS-EUPHRATES BASIN

Euphrates at the Turkish-Syrian border was 32.5 bcm.[2] From year to year, the volume of water in the Euphrates varies greatly. Since the 1920s the lowest flow recorded at Hit was 10.7 bcm. (in 1929-30), or less than one-third of the average flow. The highest flow was 63.4 bcm. (in 1968-69), not far short of twice the average flow and six times the flow of 1929-30. Runs of years of low flow are not uncommon: there were particularly marked periods of drought from 1958 to 1962, and from 1970 to 1975; the latter may have contributed to the tensions between Syria and Iraq which coincided with Syria's filling of Lake Assad.[3]

The waters of the Euphrates are derived mainly from melting snow in the mountains of eastern Turkey, and the river's peak flow comes in spring and early summer. Low flow is from July to October. Rain over the Turkish mountains during the rest of the year makes for flows closer to the annual average. There is a substantial difference in the volume of water carried by the Euphrates through the year: in April and May the flow is eight times that in August, September and October.

The Tigris

Unlike the Euphrates, the Tigris is divided only between Turkey and Iraq, apart from a stretch of some 80 km. where it forms the boundary first between Turkey and Syria (about 73 km.) and then between Syria and Iraq (about 7 km.) The river enters the Mesopotamian plain between Tikrit and Samarra. Several large tributaries emerge from Iraq's northern mountainous to swell the Tigris, the most notable being the Greater Zab, the Lesser Zab, the Uzayam (Adhaim) and the Diyala.

The average annual flow of the Tigris at Cizre, near the point at which the river becomes the boundary between Turkey and Syria, is around 19.7 bcm.[4] Taken together, the tributaries which join the Tigris in Iraq add 29.5 bcm. to its flow.[5]

In geopolitical terms, the Tigris is therefore strikingly different from the Euphrates. While the latter receives virtually no additional water

---

[2] Manley (1994). Manley's study employs the term 'traditional' rather than 'natural', as the measurements on which it draws were made during a period when there was *some* human use of the rivers, but before the major abstractions caused by the construction of large modern dams; the difference between the 'traditional' and the 'natural' flows are probably negligible. The official Turkish figure for a point on the river near to the Turkish-Syrian border is slightly lower than Manley's figure for a point on the river near to the Turkish-Syrian border, at around 31 bcm. (Bagis, 1989), while the official Syrian figure is lower still, at about 28 bcm. (Abu Daoud, 1990).

[3] See the section below entitled 'Agreeing and disagreeing'.

[4] Manley (1994).

[5] Ubell (1971).

after entering Iraq, the tributaries which join the Tigris in Iraq provide 60% of the water in the Tigris below Baghdad. As a result, Iraq's supply of water from the Tigris is much less vulnerable to developments upstream than is its supply from the Euphrates. It is true that the headwaters of some of these tributaries rise beyond Iraq's borders: in Turkey in the case of the Greater Zab, in Iran in the case of the Lesser Zab and the Diyala. But the proportion of their flow which rises in Turkey and Iran is small. Moreover, the areas of Turkey and Iran in which these rivers rise are remote, and not likely to be seen as promising for major hydraulic developments.

As with the Euphrates, the volume of water in the Tigris varies greatly from year to year. In 1961, its flow at Cizre was less than half the average; in 1969, it was twice the average. Because the flow of the Tigris depends on the same climatic conditions as that of the Euphrates, periods of low flow tend to coincide: there was much less water than usual in the Tigris in the late 1950s and early 1960s, and again in the early 1970s, just as there was in the Euphrates. This may limit Iraq's opportunities for substituting water from the Tigris for that of the Euphrates, or vice-versa, when flow in one river is low.[6] The pattern of seasonal variation in the flow of the Tigris also resembles that of the Euphrates. At Cizre, peak flow comes in April, when it is over two-and-a-half times the monthly average; low flow, in September, is less than a quarter of the average. Further downstream, the coincidence of spring rainfall and melting snow can cause a sudden increase in the flow of the left-bank tributaries, sometimes resulting in destructive flooding where the valleys open out onto the Mesopotamian plains.

The Karun

About 100 km. below Qurna, the Shatt al-Arab is joined at Basra by the Karun, which flows southwards from the Zagros Mountains in Iran. In terms of the volume of water that it carries, the Karun is a major river: it may contribute as much as two-thirds of the natural flow of the Shatt al-Arab.[7] However, because it lies wholly in Iran and joins the combined Tigris and Euphrates only a short distance before they reach the sea, its international significance is much less than that of these other two rivers.

---

[6] Iraq has the physical means to do so, having constructed canals linking the two: see the following section.

[7] Al-Rubaiay (1984), quoted by Schofield (1986).

Using the Rivers

For some 7,500 years, the waters of the Tigris and Euphrates have been diverted by human action to irrigate farmland on the Mesopotamian plain, in what is now Iraq. Centrally-controlled irrigation was practised from the time of the Sumerian civilisation, over 4,000 years ago. However, the system fell increasingly into disrepair during the later years of the Abbasid caliphate, partly because of the declining effectiveness of central government, and partly because of physical causes such as the silting-up of the major canals. Irrigation in Mesopotamia was already close to collapse when it was given the *coup de grâce* by the Mongol invasion of 1258.

A return to large-scale irrigation did not begin until late in the 19th century, when a number of the ancient irrigation canals were cleaned.[8] In the years immediately before the First World War, when Iraq still formed part of the Ottoman Empire, a barrage was constructed on the Euphrates at Hindiya, to divert water for irrigation.

Later, Iraq sought to control the two rivers for other ends as well. Barrages were built on the Tigris to produce hydro-power, and a barrage was constructed on the Euphrates at Ramadi to protect areas further downstream from flooding, by diverting spring flood-waters into Lake Habbaniya and the desert depression of Abu Dibis.

By the mid-1960s, the development of irrigated agriculture in Iraq was far ahead of that in Syria and Turkey: Iraq was irrigating over five times as much land as Syria, and nearly ten times as much as Turkey.[9]

The Haditha Dam on the Euphrates was completed in 1985. It was later renamed the Qadisiya Dam, after the victory of the Arabs over the Persians in AD 636. The dam has substantial hydro-power generating capacity (660 megawatts), and is also designed to store water for the irrigation of 1 million hectares. In 1990, work started on another hydro-power dam at Khan al-Baghdadi, 40 km. downstream from the Qadisiya, but was brought to a halt by the crisis caused by Iraq's invasion of Kuwait in August 1990.

Construction of the Third River – a canal 565 km. long, running from near Baghdad to Basra – began in the 1950s, but was only completed in 1992. Its stated purposes are to provide irrigation water for land between the Euphrates and Tigris, and to carry drainage water from land affected by high salinity and which is to be reclaimed. Since the Kuwait crisis, Saddam has promoted the project as a contribution to his country's efforts to counter United Nations measures against it by

---

[8] Beaumont (1978).
[9] Kienle (1990).

expanding agricultural production.[10] Iraqi opposition sources have asserted that the project has the ulterior motive of draining the marshes of southern Iraq to eliminate the refuge which they have provided for Shi'ite dissidents. This appears to be untrue, although the same deplorable goal is being accomplished by other forms of hydrological engineering.[11]

In the late 1970s, as part of their efforts to prevent flood damage, the Iraqis dug a canal to divert excess water from the Tigris into a vast depression in the desert known as Lake Tharthar. Since then, Iraq has completed other similar canals, linking Lake Tharthar to the Euphrates, and connecting the lake with the Tigris further downstream. While these canals were dug with the primary aim of reducing flooding, they opened up the possibility that water from one river could be used to make up for low flow in the other.

As we have seen in the previous section, the two rivers tend to keep roughly in step in terms of their annual and seasonal variations, and so this facility might be of lesser value than might appear to be the case at first sight. There is the further drawback that high levels of evaporation from Lake Tharthar (of the order of 5 bcm. a year) make its water significantly more saline than the water in the two rivers.[12] By 1990, however, Iraq was already diverting water from the Tigris to the Euphrates via the Lake, the volume varying from 150 to 500 cusecs (cubic metres per second). With these large quantities of fresh water flowing in from the Tigris, the quality of the water in the lake has improved.[13] Iraq has made use of this water for irrigation land in the Euphrates basin.[14] Since, as far as Iraq is concerned, the Euphrates is much more vulnerable to reductions in flow caused by human action, it will probably prove necessary for this facility to be used still more if land currently irrigated from the Euphrates is to be kept in production.

According to government sources, in 1984 Iraq was using 48.3 bcm. of water per year. Irrigation was the dominant use, taking 95% of the

---

[10] The Third River was re-named the Saddam River in 1991; it is sometimes referred to as 'the Leader's River'. The construction of further major canals, with similarly heroic names, has since been started. See *Baghdad Observer* 2 August 1994: 'Giant irrigation projects built since July Revolution.'

[11] Manley (1994). The behaviour of the Iraqi government towards the marsh region and its inhabitants is the subject of considerable international attention. However, as it has no international repercussions in terms of the dispute with Iraq's neighbours over water resources, it lies beyond the scope of this book.

[12] Manley (1994).

[13] AMER (1992), quoted by Medzini (1994).

[14] Iraq also aims to irrigate directly from the Tharthar canal. See Iraqi News Agency report for 3 May 1994, translated by BBC, *SWB* 10 May (MEW/0332): 'Irrigation minister inaugurates Tharthar canal project.'

total. Around 2.2 million hectares, some two-thirds of the irrigated land cultivated in Iraq, receives water from the Tigris or its tributaries. Nearly all the remaining third, around a million hectares, receives water from the Euphrates, with the rest (about 105,000 hectares) irrigated from the Shatt al-Arab. Ground-water is little developed; it supplies less than 3% of Iraq's water.[15]

Over the last two decades, Iraq has put considerable effort and many billions of dollars into costly irrigation and land reclamation schemes. The results have been disappointing; production has not kept pace with the growth of population.[16] The effects of Saddam Hussein's wars have played a part here, but the main reason has been the build-up of salinity on farm-land, with existing irrigated areas going out of production almost as fast as new ones are added.

Salinity has been a major problem in Iraq since the time of the ancient irrigated civilisations of Mesopotamia. Indeed, it appears to have contributed to their collapse.[17] It has attacked modern Iraqi agriculture with equal savagery: according to the Haigh Report in 1951, 60% of the country's irrigated area was affected to some degree by salinity. The situation is at least as bad now: an estimate published in 1992 suggested that approximately 65% of the irrigated area suffered from soil salinity.[18]

Syria

The modern exploitation of the Euphrates by Syria began with the installation of motorised pumps in the 1950s. This was the work of individual farmers, interested mainly in the cultivation of cotton. At this time, Syria's efforts at large-scale river control were directed to the Orontes.[19]

In the following decade, a dam at Tabqa on the Euphrates was proposed. This was to be the centre-piece of a project to develop the whole of the Euphrates region in Syria, including the valley of the Khabur. The dam was financed by a loan on easy terms from the Soviet Union, which provided technical assistance in its construction.[20] The dam was finished in 1973, and the filling of Lake Assad behind it was

---

[15] Nasser (1987).

[16] For example, at-Nasrawi (1992) notes that the country's population grew 38% between 1980 and 1989, while production of cereals per capita declined by almost a half during the decade.

[17] Pearce (1992).

[18] EIU (1992-3).

[19] See Chapter 5.

[20] *MEED* 13 April 1979:'Euphrates Dam begins to pay off'

completed in 1975.[21] This action was the subject of a major dispute with Iraq, as we shall see in the next section.

The Tabqa Dam had two purposes: one was the generation of hydropower, the other was irrigation. In neither respect has it fulfilled Syrian hopes. Lack of maintenance, combined with lower-than-expected volumes of water in the river, has reduced the dam's power-generating capacity from 880 megawatts to 150.[22] This disappointing outcome has led Syria to look to other sources of energy, especially gas, of which large reserves have been discovered in recent years.

The irrigation projects connected with the Tabqa Dam and the other parts of the Euphrates project were to irrigate 640,000 hectares of land.[23] This plan would have doubled the area of irrigated land in Syria, had it been successful. But it has not.

The highly soluble nature of gypsum deposits present in extensive tracts of the areas to be irrigated was in large part responsible. The canals conveying water to the farmland frequently collapsed when water was channelled through them or, where they did not collapse, lost large quantities of water into the ground. By the end of the 1980s, just over 50,000 additional hectares had actually been brought under irrigation by the state since the completion of the Tabqa Dam a decade-and-a-half before. When the loss of farmland flooded by Lake Assad is deducted, the net gain is barely 20,000 hectares. And some 3,000 hectares of this newly irrigated land are already affected by salinity and poor drainage.[24]

As well as providing water for irrigation, Lake Assad also supplies water by pipeline to Aleppo. At the moment, the city takes some 0.08 bcm. each year, virtually its entire consumption, from the lake.

Subsequent Syrian projects on the Euphrates have not been on the same scale as the Tabqa Dam. The Baath Dam was completed in 1986.[25] It is a 're-regulation' dam: in other words, its main purpose is to iron out daily fluctuations in flow below Tabqa caused by variations in the rate at which water is released through the turbines there in response

---

[21] The official name of the dam at Tabqa is al-Thawra (Arabic for 'revolution'), but it is more usually referred to as the Tabqa Dam.

[22] Butter (1993).

[23] Of this area, Lake Assad was to provide water for 420,000 hectares that were to be irrigated for the first time and for 150,000 hectares that were already irrigated but were affected by salinity and needed to be 'reclaimed'; the remaining seventy thousand hectares were to be irrigated from other reservoirs.

[24] Figures in this paragraph are derived from Kolars and Mitchell (1991). According to official figures, 200,000 hectares are irrigated from the Euphrates (Abu Daoud (1990)), although this must include land already under irrigation before the creation of Lake Assad; it presumably excludes land irrigated from the Khabur.

[25] After the ruling party in Syria: Arabic for 'resurgence'.

to peaks and troughs of electricity demand. The Baath Dam also generates a small amount of electricity itself, and provides some water for irrigation. At the time of writing, net Syrian use of the Euphrates and the Khabur, its main tributary within Syria, is probably around 3.6 bcm. a year. (The gross volume used, before allowance is made for return flows, is around 5 bcm.) This is made up of irrigation water for around 240,000 hectares of land, both private and state-run, plus the 0.08 bcm. supplied to Aleppo.[26]

The Tishreen Dam, upstream from Lake Assad, is still under construction. Designed mainly to generate hydro-power, the Tishreen Dam will have six turbines, each with a capacity of 105 megawatts: it should produce 1.6 billion kwh. of electricity each year.

Syrian exploitation of the Tigris has been hampered by the fact that it is nowhere wholly within Syria: the boundary with Turkey runs down the middle of the river.[27] Syria could not, therefore, build works to store or divert water without the cooperation of its neighbour on the other bank. No agreement on this subject has yet been signed and, for the moment, Syrian farmers take water from the Tigris only in small quantities, for local use.

Turkey

While the Euphrates is a major element in Syria's total water supply and the Tigris might become so, Turkey not only has other substantial rivers but also receives rainfall that makes agriculture possible without irrigation over much of the country. Indeed, it was the need for additional electricity-generating capacity, rather than for water irrigation, which first led Turkey to exploit the Euphrates.

At the beginning of the 1970s, Turkey depended heavily on imported oil for energy. The oil-price shocks of that decade added greatly to Turkey's import bill, and caused the government to place even greater emphasis on hydro-power. (Domestic lignite has also been developed to the same end.) The share of hydro-power in Turkey's energy supply rose from 30% in 1970 to 40% in 1990, despite a steady increase in the total supply.

The attention paid to the development of hydro-power probably also owed a great deal to the personalities involved. The late president Turgut Özal graduated in electrical engineering, and worked on the hydro-power potential of the Tigris and Euphrates, becoming prime minister in 1983 and president in 1989, which post he held until his death in 1993. Suleyman Demirel, a hydraulic engineer by training, became head of

---

[26] Figures derived from Kolars and Mitchell (1991).

[27] To be precise, the boundary follows the *thalweg* or line of deepest water.

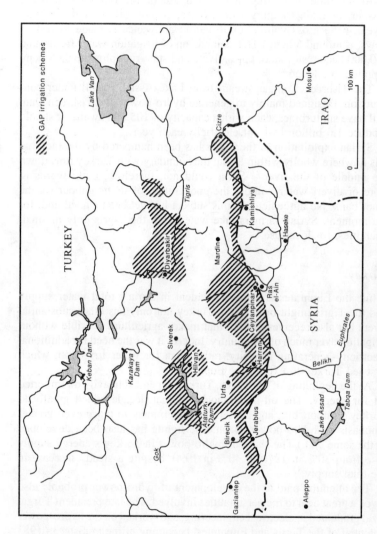

Map 6. THE TIGRIS-EUPHRATES BASIN: SOUTHERN TURKEY AND NORTHERN SYRIA

the Directorate of State Water Works (DSI) in 1955. During his time in that post, he gained the nickname 'the King of Dams'. Demirel was prime minister intermittently during the 1960s and 1970s, and became prime minister again in 1991, holding that position until he became president in 1993 after the death of Özal.

The first major dam on the Euphrates in turkey was the Keban (see Map 6). It has a hydro-power generating capacity of 1,360 megawatts, and is designed to generate almost 6 billion kilowatt-hours of electricity a year (but not to provide water for irrigation). Construction of the Keban Dam began in the mid-1960s; it was producing power by 1974.

The Keban Dam was a large project. It was, however, dwarfed by the schemes which were being drawn up as its construction got under way. These schemes were initially confined to hydro-power generation and the provision of water for irrigation. They were later expanded to cover every aspect of the economic infrastructure of south-eastern Anatolia, and drawn together under the general title of the South-east Anatolia Project, known by its Turkish acronym as GAP.[28] Nevertheless, the central element of the GAP is still water, whether for power-generation or irrigation. The GAP Master Plan envisages the construction of 22 dams and the irrigation of between 1.6 and 1.7 million hectares of land.[29] The schemes on the Euphrates are bigger (both in terms of the power to be generated and the area to be irrigated) and are being implemented first (see Map 6).

The first of the GAP dams to be completed was the Karakaya, in 1988. Like the Keban, its purpose was to produce hydro-power, for which it has a capacity of 1,800 megawatts; it generates around 7.5 billion kilowatt-hours each year. The largest piece in the GAP jigsaw is the Atatürk Dam. It is a huge piece of engineering by any standards. The reservoir which it impounds has a storage capacity of 48.7 bcm. – over four times the volume of Lake Assad. Unlike the Keban and Karakaya Dams, the Ataturk Dam is designed to store water for large-scale irrigation as well as for the generation of hydro-power. For that reason, it is regarded by Syria and Iraq as a more threatening project than its two predecessors on the Euphrates.[30]

The generators at the Atatürk Dam have a capacity of 2,400 megawatts; they began generating power in July 1992. They are intended to produce 8,100 gigawatts of electricity per year, although this will fall to 5,300 gigawatts when all the irrigation projects dependent on the reservoir are complete. These projects, together with others that draw water from smaller reservoirs in the Euphrates basin, envisage the irrigation of as

---

[28] Guneydogu Anadolu Projesi.
[29] GAP Master Plan (1984).
[30] See the section below entitled 'Downstream fears'.

much as a million hectares. In 1994, two giant tunnels began to convey water from the Atatürk reservoir at a rate of 30 cusecs to supply irrigation systems on the Harran plain.[31]

As Turkey's irrigation projects based on Euphrates water are not yet fully developed, Turkish consumption has so far been relatively modest. There is some loss to evaporation from the surface of the three reservoirs but, given the rather cooler and more humid climate, and the generally lower ratio of surface area to volume, these depletions are not as great as from reservoirs downstream in Syria and Iraq. Hydropower installations do not otherwise consume water. They do have an effect on the regime of a river, in the direction of evening-out its seasonal peaks and troughs. As Turkish officials have pointed out, this is beneficial to states downstream in terms of flood reduction, however little gratitude they may feel.[32] More negative is the temporary reduction in river flow which occurs when reservoirs are filled for the first time. In this sense, Turkey may be said to have taken large volumes of Euphrates water over the past two decades (in the sense of having put it into storage), perhaps as much as 90 bcm.[33]

Other schemes on the Euphrates within the GAP framework lie in the future; so do most of those projected for the Tigris. Their impact on Syria and Iraq, the impact of the hydraulic works which Turkey has already built, and the effect of these developments on relations between the three states are taken up in the following three sections.

Iran

The Karun was dammed by Iran at Dezful in the late 1950s, to provide water for irrigation of 125,000 hectares in the Khuzestan lowlands and for the generation of hydro-power. Further dams are bring built on the Karun. Iran's largest dam is under construction on the Karkheh river, which loses itself in the marshes of the lower Tigris in Iraq: it is designed to impound water for the irrigation of 220,000 hectares of farmland, as well as generating hydro-power.[34]

---

[31] See *Financial Times*, 15 February 1996: 'Euphrates power plant generates new tension.' 30 cusecs is the equivalent of 0.93 bcm. a year.

[32] For example, see the statements attributed to Mr Gur of the Turkish Ministry of Foreign Affairs in the *Financial Times* of 15 February 1996: 'Euphrates power plant generates new tension.' The environmental impact may be less favourable: the ecology of the marshes of southern Iraq depends on the marked seasonal variations in the natural flow of the Tigris and Euphrates: see Manley (1994).

[33] The Keban Dam impounds up to 30.7 bcm.. the Karakaya up to 9.5 bcm., and the Atatürk 48.7 bcm: see Manley (1994).

[34] Voice of the Islamic Republic of Iran, 26 September 1994, quoted by BBC, *SWB* 4 October 1994.

The impact of use on water quality

Natural causes may result in variations in water quality. Evaporation in the vast lakes and marshes of southern Iraq makes for a higher concentration of salts; so does the inflow into the Shatt al-Arab of tidal water from the Persian Gulf. For the most part, however, changes in water quality are the result of human activity. In the Tigris-Euphrates basin, where industry is little developed, water quality has deteriorated because of the application of agro-chemicals and the leaching from the soil of salts that have accumulated because of inadequate drainage. In Iraq, the diversion of large volumes of water into extensive shallow depressions has created the same conditions for high evaporation which are found in the southern lakes: the result – higher levels of water salinity – is also same.

Measuring water quality is more complicated and difficult than measuring quantity. In the case of the Tigris and Euphrates, it is not possible to give a reliable picture of the quality of their waters in all parts of the basin. It seems safe to say, however, that the quality of the waters of the waters of the Euphrates is still good in Turkey and Syria, and in Iraq down to Ramadi. At Ramadi, salinity reaches between 250 and 500 mg. of chlorides per litre, a level that is too high for successful cultivation of some crops. It may reach as much as 600 mg. per litre in the south. Below Basra, salinity in the Shatt may be over 5,000 mg. per litre, when high tide combines with low autumn flow.[35]

No equivalent figures are available for the Tigris. However, because the Tigris is less fully developed than the Euphrates, it is reasonable to suppose that the quality of its waters is for the moment higher, at least upstream of the major irrigated areas of Iraq.

Agreeing and Disagreeing

The Tigris and Euphrates did not become international rivers until the break-up of the Ottoman Empire after the First World War. Even after the basins of the two rivers were divided by political boundaries, no disputes over water arose: it was clear that there was more than enough for all.

At the same time, the powers involved were aware that this happy state of affairs might not last for ever. The two rivers featured in a number of agreements, the relevant provisions of which were designed in most cases to protect the interests of Iraq, which was, at the time the agreements were signed, the only state making use of the water on

---

[35] Medzini (1994).

a large scale.[36] The first of these agreements was the Convention of 23 December 1920 between Britain and France (as the respective Mandatory powers for Iraq and Syria). The Convention stated that any plans for irrigation in Syria that might diminish 'in any considerable degree' the flow of the Tigris or Euphrates were to be examined by a commission nominated by the two governments. On becoming independent, Iraq took on Britain's rights and obligations under the Convention by signing the Protocol of 10 October 1932.[37] When, in turn, Syria attained independence, it made no such commitment; the status of the Convention must therefore be in question.

The 1923 Treaty of Lausanne, which of course dealt with many other matters, committed Turkey to consult Iraq before carrying out any hydraulic works on the Tigris or Euphrates.

The 1946 Treaty of Friendship and Good Neighbourliness signed by Iraq and Turkey envisaged a measure of trust and cooperation between the two countries that has not materialised. Turkey agreed to inform Iraq of Turkish plans for the construction of works on the two rivers, 'so that these works may as far as possible, be adapted, by a common agreement, to the interests of both Iraq and Turkey.' Each installation was to be the subject of a special agreement. This clearly offered some protection to Iraq in its vulnerable downstream position. The Treaty also recognised, however, that the best dam sites on the two rivers were probably in Turkey.

In more recent years, this line of reasoning has been unwelcome in Iraq: it is seen as giving Turkey an unacceptable degree of control over a strategic asset. Iraq therefore no longer refers to the Treaty – although it does not appear to have repudiated it.

Almost half a century has passed since the signature of the 1946 Treaty. Since that time, the three riparian states have discussed water in numerous meetings, both bilateral and trilateral, but there has been very little meeting of minds.

In the mid-1960s, the three countries came together to discuss for the first time the possibility of a division of the waters of the Euphrates. For negotiating purposes, each made maximum demands: Iraq for 14 bcm. per year, Syria for 13 bcm. and Turkey for 18 bcm.[38] The sum

---

[36] Only one of these agreements – the 1930 Treaty of Aleppo between Turkey and France (as the Mandatory power for Syria) – seems to have foreseen a need to protect Syrian interests. It referred briefly to Syrian rights on the Tigris, but said nothing about the Euphrates, being concerned with the boundary between Syria and Turkey.

[37] The other signatories were the United Kingdom (as the power relinquishing the Mandate for Iraq) and France (as the power which continued to hold the Mandate for Syria). The commission for which the 1920 Convention made provision does not appear to have ever been formed.

[38] Waterbury (1990).

of these demands is roughly one-and-a-half times the average natural flow of the river.

No agreement was reached. Instead, Iraq and Syria went on to hold bilateral talks about the division of the Euphrates between them. Iraq argued that it deserved a fixed share of the flow on the ground of 'acquired rights': in other words, it was entitled to receive what it had always received. In response, Syria called for this to be balanced by potential needs, a position that reflected the fact that Syria had so far made relatively little use of the Euphrates. While the two countries appear to have come close to agreement, no accord was signed.

By the late 1960s, both Turkey and Syria were embarking on major projects on the Euphrates. Iraq protested to both governments. Iraq objected to Turkey's application for finance from the World Bank for its dam at Keban. In the event, the Bank accepted Turkey's request, but insisted on a guarantee that Turkey would maintain a flow of at least 450 cusecs through the dam.

It was to be Syria which bore the brunt of Iraqi wrath. This may have reflected a realisation on the part of the Iraqis that the Turkish project, would not – once filled – result in any substantial loss of water downstream, and would indeed benefit Iraq by bringing about a more regular flow. By contrast, the Syrian project – the dam at Tabqa – would supply large quantities of water for irrigation and hence reduce the river's flow.

Probably more important in directing Iraqi ire against Syria rather than Turkey was the antagonism between the rival Baathist regimes in Baghdad and Damascus. In the mid-1970s, the two regimes were competitors for influence in the Arab world, only too ready to accuse each other of hostile acts.

In early 1975, Iraq complained that Syria, by filling Lake Assad, had caused it economic damage: while 15.3 bcm. of Euphrates water had crossed the border from Syria in 1973 (the year in which the Tabqa Dam was completed), the flow in 1975 was reduced to 9.4 bcm.[39] Iraq claimed that it had 'established rights' to 16.1 bcm. a year, a figure derived from a 1965 World Bank assessment of water needs based on the extent of existing agricultural land and an estimate of potential.[40] Moreover, Iraq argued that the damage had been deliberate, as Syria had – according to Iraq – impounded more water in Lake Assad than it could use for the generation of electricity or the irrigation of farmland.

In response, Syria contested the Iraqi figure, although it did not deny that Iraq had 'established rights'. For its part, Syria advanced a

---

[39] Iraqi figures, taken from Kienle (1990), who provides a detailed account of the dispute on pp. 96-109.
[40] Kienle (1990).

claim to 13 bcm. from the Euphrates, the same quantity that it had claimed in the talks in the mid-1960s. In support of its claim, Syria argued that its water resources were extremely limited, while Iraq and Turkey both had substantial sources of water in addition to the Euphrates. The dispute became a crisis. The two regimes traded accusations unrelated to the Euphrates. Syria began to give more open support to Iraqi Kurdish dissidents. Both countries sent troops to their common border in March and April 1975 (although it is not clear which side moved first).

It is difficult to know whether Iraq was seriously considering attacking Syria in order to assert the rights which it claimed to the waters of the Euphrates. Given the limited nature of the military movements, it seems unlikely that either side was doing more than posturing. But such situations can develop a dynamic of their own, and deteriorate further than their creators had originally intended. Viewed from that perspective, this was certainly the nearest that the Middle East had come to armed conflict over water since Israel's attacks on the Arab project to divert the headwaters of the Jordan a decade before.

In the event, the situation was contained. The Arab League set up a mediation committee, which appears to have achieved nothing; the Soviet Union and Saudi Arabia also involved themselves. In the end, Saudi mediation successfully defused the crisis by securing the release of additional water by Syria.

Developments since 1980

The 1980s were marked by two developments. The first was the establishment of a tripartite technical committee for the exchange of information on the two rivers; this began work in 1982. The second was the growing feeling on the part of both Syria and Iraq that the likely water demands of Turkey's GAP represented an economic and strategic threat.

Meetings, but not of minds. By 1993 the technical committee had met sixteen times since its formation.[41] These meetings have not, however, led to any real narrowing of the different attitudes of the three states. Even the scope of the committee's functions has not been agreed upon. Syria and Iraq have sought to use it as a vehicle for the discussion of the apportionment of Euphrates water. Turkey has wanted to exclude this issue from the committee's deliberations and have it concentrate on exchanges of information.

---

[41] At the time of writing the committee had not met since 1993.

Nor has there been agreement on the basic nature of the watercourses under discussion. The two Arab states have sought to discuss the Tigris and Euphrates as separate river basins, while Turkey has insisted that the two rivers, meeting in the Shatt al-Arab, form one basin, especially now that Iraq has made physical connections upstream via Lake Tharthar that permit water to be transferred from the Tigris to the Euphrates.[42] This is more than an academic discussion about hydrology: consideration of the two rivers as one basin would weaken Iraq's case for a large share of water from the Euphrates, as it could make up shortages in that river with water from the Tigris and its Iraqi tributaries.

Equally serious is the lack of agreement on the issue to be discussed in any negotiations. Turkey has declared itself ready to discuss its own plan for 'the establishment of principles according to which we would allot the use of cross-border waters to our neighbours.'[43] For their part, the two Arab states felt that their interests would be better served by an agreement that gave them a fixed volume of water, at least for the Euphrates. They laid claim to 700 cusecs (or 21.7 bcm. a year), to divide between them.[44]

The GAP looms. The sheer size of the GAP would have been enough to alarm Turkey's downstream neighbours. The area which Turkey plans to irrigate from the Euphrates under the GAP schemes is just over a million hectares. Even according to Turkish figures, which Syria and Iraq must have assumed to be conservative, these irrigation schemes would reduce the flow of the Euphrates by a third.[45] Moreover, development of these schemes is going ahead before those on the Tigris. And we have already seen that the Euphrates is much the more important of the two rivers to Syria, and the more vulnerable of the two to abstractions upstream as far as Iraq is concerned. It is therefore not surprising to find that the Euphrates has been the focus of the dispute so far.

Until the scale of the GAP dawned on Iraq and Syria, the dispute had been mainly between the two Arab states. It now pitted these two against Turkey. However, because of the hostility between the Baathist regimes in Baghdad and Damascus, which was increased during the

---

[42] See the preceding section entitled 'Using the rivers'.
[43] TRT TV, 31 December 1995, quoting a Turkish diplomatic note of the same date (in Turkish: BBC Monitoring *SWB* translation).
[44] This claim has been recently reiterated by Iraq: see BBC *SWB* 14 February 1996, quoting *al-Hayat* (Arabic newspaper), 12 February 1996.
[45] 10.4 bcm. per annum, according to the GAP Master Plan (1984), quoted by Bagis (1989).

1980s by Syria's support for Iran in the war with Iraq, Turkey's exchanges with its downstream neighbours tended to be on a bilateral basis.

Even during the 1970s, Syria had attempted to prevent GAP schemes from going ahead by objecting to Turkey's application for funding for the Karakaya Dam. Nevertheless, despite Syrian objections, the World Bank provided a large part of the finance for the project: this was a hydro-power project that would have evened-out but not reduced the flow of the river.[46]

Syria and Iraq had more success in opposing Turkey's attempts to secure international funding for the Atatürk Dam. The downstream states had a stronger case than with the Keban and Karakaya Dams: the irrigation works associated with the Dam would clearly reduce the flow of Euphrates. Faced with this situation, and lacking sufficient reserves of hard currency, Turkey was forced to raise funds at home and to award the contracts for the Dam to Turkish companies that would accept payment in Turkish lira. Despite initial scepticism, both within Turkey and abroad, these companies proved themselves capable of carrying out the work.

As a result of Iraq's pre-occupation with its war with Iran and then with the consequences of its invasion of Kuwait, Syria has continued to play the more prominent role in the dispute with Turkey over the Euphrates. A further reason for this was the existence of another issue between Syria and its northern neighbour: the support which Turkey alleged was being provided by Syria for the PKK (Kurdish Workers' Party), an organisation that has used violent means in an attempt to gain independence for the Kurdish population of south-eastern Turkey.

In the mid-1980s, the two issues became linked. This was probably inevitable, as there were both geographical and political connections between the GAP and the Kurdish question. Not only were the GAP schemes being implemented in areas containing some of the largest concentrations of Turkey's Kurdish population, they were also designed to reduce Kurdish discontent (and hence support for the PKK) by bringing prosperity to what was one of the poorest parts of Turkey.

High-level meetings between Turkey and Syria therefore focused on 'border security' (a euphemism for Syrian support for the PKK) and the volume of water which Turkey would allow to flow down the Euphrates into Syria. No formal linkage was ever established, but Turkey appeared to realise that Syria, although at a disadvantage in terms of its downstream position and its weaker armed forces, had in its links with the PKK an asset that Turkey could not ignore.

In 1987, Syria and Turkey signed a Protocol of Economic Co-operation.

---

[46] According to Kolars and Mitchell (1991), the Bank provided $350 million towards estimated costs of $500 million.

Among other matters, this dealt with the allocation of the flow of the Euphrates. However, it did not constitute a permanent settlement of this question. Indeed, the text specified that it related to the period of the filling of the reservoir behind the Atatürk Dam 'and until the final allocation of the waters of the Euphrates among the three riparian countries'. Turkey and Syria agreed to work together with Iraq to achieve an agreement on such an allocation.

Under the 1987 Protocol, Turkey undertook to 'release a yearly average of more than 500 cusecs at the Turkish-Syrian border'.[47] If the flow during any given month fell below 500 cusecs, Turkey was to increase the flow during the following month, to make up the difference.

The filling of the reservoir began in January 1990, when Turkish engineers blocked the flow of the Euphrates through the Atatürk dam with a giant concrete plug. There seems little doubt that Turkey stuck to the letter of the 1987 Protocol, having provided a sufficient volume before this event to make up for the reduction during the filling period, which lasted from 13 January to 12 February 1990.[48]

This was not enough to prevent strident protests downstream. The main cause of the distress expressed in Damascus and Baghdad was probably not the economic damage done, but rather the unwillingness of Turkey to countenance any modification of its plans in the face of their complaints. If Turkey would not listen on this occasion, what grounds had they to hope for better treatment in the future, when the stakes might be higher?

These fears prompted an unprecedented degree of Syrian-Iraqi unity over the Euphrates. In April 1990, the two states signed an agreement that allocated the waters of the Euphrates on a percentage basis: whatever the volume of water which crossed the Turkish-Syrian boundary at Jerablus, Syria would allow 58% of that quantity to cross its border with Iraq.[49] At the same time, the two Arab states made a joint approach

---

[47] Article 6. This rather complicated formulation equates to an annual flow of approximately 15.5 bcm.

[48] It was a reduction rather than a total cessation of flow at the Turkish-Syrian border, because some flow (at least 120 cusecs, according to Turkey) was maintained by tributaries of the Euphrates that join it below the Atatürk Dam.

[49] According to the BBC, Monitoring *SWB* 18 April 1990, the two countries signed the agreement on 16 April 1990 at the Secretariat of the Arab League (then in Tunis). At first sight, this seems to be a poor deal for Syria: if the flow in a given year is 15 bcm. at Jerablus, Iraq would get 8.7 bcm., while Syria would get only 6.3 bcm. However, two factors even up the score. First, the Euphrates in Syria is augmented by water from tributaries such as the Khabour and Belikh, which are not divided under this agreement. Secondly, some of the water that Syria is passing on to Iraq has already been used to irrigate Syrian fields and has returned to the river, whether directly through the sub-soil or through drainage systems.

to Turkey to demand a trilateral agreement that would establish a permanent division of the waters of the river.

The agreement of April 1990 appears to remain in force: it has not been abrogated by Syria or Iraq and there have been no Iraqi complaints that Syria is not applying it. But the united front against Turkey turned out to be very short-lived: it collapsed when Syria opposed Iraq's invasion of Kuwait in August 1990.

The international isolation imposed on Iraq following that event left Syria and Turkey to continue their talks on a bilateral basis. Syria complained in March and December 1991 about temporary reductions in the flow of the Euphrates. A joint communiqué issued in January 1993 declared that the two countries agreed that they would sign a permanent agreement on the question before the end of the year. This goal was not achieved. Indeed, no progress towards it had been made by February 1996, with Turkey arguing that Syria had not done enough to keep its side of the 'bargain' in terms of impeding the movement of PKK fighters across the border. In early 1995, friction between Turkey and Syria increased when, for the first time, the PKK mounted operations in Hatay province, a region of Turkey claimed by Syria.[50] Turkey accused Syria of arming and sponsoring the PKK and providing sanctuary to its leader, Ocalan.[51]

In November 1995, Turkey signed a financial package that will enable it to proceed with the construction of the Birecik Dam on the Euphrates, at a location between the Ataturk Dam and the Syrian border. The project will generate power but also provide water for the irrigation of 70,000 hectares on the Gaziantep and Araban plains. Syria responded by sending diplomatic notes to Turkey, complaining of the likely effect of the dam on the flow of the river, and also of the potential pollution of areas of Syria affected by return flows from irrigation in Turkey. At the same time, there were signs of a revival of the Syrian-Iraqi front on the Euphrates that had been discernible in the months before Iraq's invasion of Kuwait. Syria and Iraq called for a meeting of the Arab League to discuss Turkish actions, Iraq sent diplomatic notes to Turkey along lines similar to those sent by Syria, and an Iraqi technical delegation visited Damascus 'to explore co-ordination between the two countries in relation to Turkey's construction of new dams on the Euphrates'.

Turkey, while reiterating its readiness to discuss the Euphrates, accused Syria of polluting the Orontes and reducing its flow by 90%. It

---

[50] Hatay province, formerly known as Alexandretta, was detached from Syria when that country was part of the French mandate, and given to Turkey.

[51] See *Mideast Mirror* 1 February 1996: 'Syrian-Turkish relations "deteriorating by the day".'

The Tigris-Euphrates Basin

also rejected what it referred to as the 'political pressure' being applied by its two Arab neighbours.[52]

Downstream Fears

The alarm displayed by Syria and Iraq at Turkey's GAP stems from the project's potential impact in economic and strategic terms. The protests made by Syria and Iraq at the filling of the Ataturk reservoir in early 1990 centred on the economic damage that the two states claimed to have suffered as a result of the reduced flow of water, in terms of lost production of irrigated crops and electricity, and (in Syria's case) the interruption of water supply to Aleppo.

Even if the damage suffered was as substantial as claimed, it was temporary. The real economic worries are of the possible permanent effects. Essentially, Syria and Iraq fear that the GAP will consume so much water from the Euphrates and Tigris that they will be unable to complete their own plans to use the rivers for the generation of electricity and for the irrigation of additional large areas of farmland. There is the further anxiety of pollution: that water used by Turkish farms and factories will return to the rivers heavily charged with agri-chemicals and industrial waste, and with a higher salt content, rendering it unfit for domestic consumption, industrial use and irrigation in Syria and Iraq.

Economic concerns are at least to some extent quantifiable, however roughly: estimates can be made of the amount of water likely to be consumed by Turkey, and the degree to which the quality of the water received by the two Arab states will deteriorate. It is far more difficult to put figures to strategic questions. The GAP schemes appear to worry Syria and Iraq for two main reasons. The first is that they will give Turkey a 'water weapon', in terms of the ability to interrupt the flow of the rivers. There is another, less specific, fear: that the economic growth which the GAP will bring about will contribute significantly to the development of Turkey as a major power in the region.

Whether there will be enough water in the Tigris and Euphrates basins for Syria and Iraq as well as Turkey depends essentially on the answers to a number of questions. The first is how much water the GAP irrigation schemes will abstract, bearing in mind that some will reappear as return flow where it can be used again. The second is the volume of water which Turkey will want to release through its dams to generate hydro-power. The third question relates not to Turkish actions

---

[52] See *Asharq Al-Awsat* 8 February 1996: 'Iraq accuses Turkey of polluting the waters of the Euphrates' (in Arabic), and *Mideast Mirror* 1 February 1996: 'Syrian Turkish relations "deteriorating by the day" '.

but concerns the capacity of Syria and Iraq to make use of water from the two rivers.

The issue of water quality – pollution and increased salinity – is connected to that of quantity, since water which falls below certain standards is effectively useless. In other ways, the causes and effects of pollution are different from those which affect the quantity of water available, and so deserve to be treated separately.

Future Turkish consumption

Turkish planners have estimated the likely use of water from the Euphrates at 10.43 bcm. a year, when all the irrigation schemes (covering just over one million hectares) are in operation.[53] This figure does not seem to allow for domestic and industrial use, or evaporation losses from reservoirs. Taking all relevant factors into account, one mathematical model of the Euphrates basin suggests that full development of the GAP schemes would halve the flow of the river at the Atatürk Dam. With further abstractions downstream of Atatürk, the flow at the Turkish-Syrian border would be less than half the natural flow.[54]

One reason why the reduction in flow at the border is so large is the fact that water is conveyed from the Atatürk reservoir and applied to fields in areas along the border with Syria. Any return flows from this irrigation water will not go back to the Euphrates in Turkey, but will instead follow the underground flow into Syria. However, in response to Syrian protests about the likely pollution of ground-water on the Syrian side, the GAP authorities are developing techniques aimed at preventing this flow of drainage water from occurring.[55]

There must be some doubt as to whether *all* such flow can be intercepted: assuming that some of the flow is not, the volume of the flow of the tributaries of the Euphrates in Syria will be increased, but the quality of the water will fall.

Turkish abstractions from the Tigris will be less than from the Euphrates, because the overall area to be irrigated is smaller. Turkish planners have calculated that if all the GAP irrigation schemes in the Tigris basin are realised, the net loss will be 3.7 bcm. or 22% of the

---

[53] Bagis (1989).

[54] Manley (1994). The requirement for a certain volume of water to flow through the turbines of the Ataturk Dam in order to meet Turkish power-generation targets was built into the model.

[55] At the time of writing, the most promising method appears to be to collect water drained from fields in ponds, where it can evaporate. Author's interview with Servet Mutlu, Deputy Director, GAP Administration, June 1993.

flow at Cizre.[56] This level of abstraction will not be achieved for some years. Only some bcm. will be taken for irrigation from the reservoirs which will be impounded by the three dams under construction in the Tigris basin, the Kiralkizi, Dicle and Batman.[57]

For the moment, it is impossible to be more precise about how much water Turkey will abstract from the two rivers for irrigated agriculture (by far the heaviest user of water). There are a number of unknown quantities. Among the most important of these is the type of crops grown, which will determine the amount of water needed per hectare ('the water duty'): the greater the area which is planted with thirsty crops such as cotton, the higher will be the total water consumption. The type of irrigation system used will also make a substantial difference to the volume of water required: since sprinkler and drip systems waste far less water than traditional flood systems, less water is required per hectare for any given crop. The choice of system installed will in turn depend partly on the type of crops and partly on the money available to individual farmers.

Establishing the likely flows of the Tigris and Euphrates after Turkey has completed its GAP schemes has little meaning unless one can also establish the volume of water which Syria and Iraq could use each year. If it turns out that there is insufficient water to enable Syria and Iraq to complete their own development plans, a deterioration in their relations with Turkey can be predicted with some confidence, and the outcome could in fact be much worse. On the other hand, if other constraints prevent Syria and Iraq from using more water than they are likely to receive, there would be no economic motive for tension over water between Turkey and its downstream neighbours. Of course, this would not eliminate the possibility of water's being used as a pretext for the escalation of tension, but the real reason would lie elsewhere.

Syria's needs

Syria's population is growing rapidly, at 3.8% per year. If this rate is maintained, it will lead to doubling of the number of people in the country within twenty years. While the Syrian government does not

---

[56] GAP Master Plan, quoted by Bagis (1989). Bagis's figure for the flow of the Tigris at Cizre – 16.8 bcm. per year – is considerably less than Manley's 19.7 bcm. (Manley (1994). Manley also differs from Bagis in arriving at a much lower figure for the reduction in flow of the Tigris: 1.7 bcm. per year (perhaps because of differences in assumptions about the eventual irrigated area).

[57] Author's interview with Özden Bilen, Deputy Director, DSI, June 1993.

aim to fed all its population with food produced within the country, it does hope to achieve 'relative food security' by the year 2010. This goal is defined as the provision from domestic production of half the international standard in terms of the number of calories per person. Syrian officials calculate that this would require a near doubling of the present total irrigated area in the country, from 800,000 hectares at present to 1.5 million.[58] Such an expansion cannot be brought about without making use of all Syria's main sources of water, including the Euphrates and Tigris.

The setting of targets is one thing, implementation quite another. We have already seen that the results of Syria's attempts to irrigate vast areas of land from the Euphrates have been extremely poor.[59] Although this has not led to a significant downward revision of the original target (Syria still aims to have 630,000 hectares under irrigation with water from the Euphrates and its tributaries by 2010), unofficial calculations suggest that it is unlikely that Syria will be able to bring much more than a total of 400,000 hectares under irrigation.[60] To achieve the latter, more realistic, goal, Syria would probably require about 5 bcm. of water a year. Taking into account losses to evaporation from Lake Assad and other reservoirs and the supply of water to Aleppo, Syria would consume a total of around six bcm of water from the Euphrates basin.[61]

As we have seen, Turkey will probably eventually use some 16 bcm. a year from the Euphrates, which (assuming an average annual flow of 32.5 bcm.) would leave around 16 bcm. for the two downstream states. Such a level of use would permit it to keep to the commitment which it made in 1987 to allow at least 15.5 bcm. (500 cusecs) to flow down the Euphrates into Syria each year. Under their agreement with Iraq of April 1990, the Syrians are obliged to pass on to Iraq a volume of water equivalent to 58% of the flow of the Euphrates which enters

---

[58] Author's interview with Eng. Majid Daoud, Syrian Ministry of Irrigation, June 1993.
[59] See the section above entitled 'Using the rivers'.
[60] The source for the official Syrian goal is Eng. Majid Daoud of the Syrian Ministry of Irrigation, interviewed by the author in June 1993. Kolars and Mitchell (1991) arrive at a lower figure, 411,000 hectares, based on the Syrian government's own downward revisions of the area to be irrigated from individual projects within the Euphrates basin.
[61] These calculations assume that each hectare in Syria requires 12,000 cubic metres of water per year. As regards evaporation losses, Manley (1994) suggests 0.63 bcm. a year for Lake Assad, 0.02 bcm. for the reservoir to be impounded by the Tishreen Dam (still under construction), and 0.013 bcm. for the dams to be built on the Khabur river, making a total of 0.663 bcm. Just over 0.08 bcm. of water are taken from Lake Assad each year for Aleppo. Syria might wish to draw on the lake to supply Damascus as well, but the volume of water would be very small in comparison with Syrian use for irrigation.

Syria from Turkey. On the basis of a flow of 16 bcm. a year, the volume received by Iraq would be 9.3 bcm., leaving 6.7 bcm. for Syria. This quantity appears adequate to meet Syria's needs (although the picture might be different if the assumptions – e.g., about 'water duties' per hectare – are proved wrong). Moreover, Syria would be able to use more than 6.7 bcm. since some of the water applied to Syrian farm-land would return through the soil and sub-soil to the river, and would then flow into Iraq.[62]

Syria also has the flows of the Sajur, Belikh and the Khabur which add just over 2 bcm. a year. The headwaters of all three rivers are across the border in Turkey, and Turkish abstractions will reduce their flow to some extent: for example, around 0.02 bcm. a year will be removed from the Sajur for irrigation in the Gaziantep area. Studies are being carried out to determine the availability of ground-water on the Harran plain, where there appears to be enough ground-water to irrigate between 150,000 and 200,000 hectares.[63] Abstractions at the rate necessary to supply this area would probably reduce the flow of the Belikh, which is fed by the same aquifer.

Nevertheless, the Belikh is a relatively small river, with an average yearly flow of 0.3 bcm. What happens in the upper Khabur basin is much more important, since the Khabur is by far the largest of the three tributaries, with an annual flow of about 1.78 bcm. Over 80% of this quantity comes from Turkey, mostly as underground flow. On present plans, the GAP schemes will probably not have any major impact. Turkey does not appear to have any plans to abstract water from the headwaters of the Khabur, as the irrigation projects intended for that area will use water conveyed from the Atatürk reservoir.[64] Return flows from those projects could increase the underground flow of water into Syria, and therefore of the Khabur: much will depend on how successful Turkish measures to intercept such flows prove to be.

If large-scale pumping of ground-water were to take place in the upper Khabur basin within Turkey, as a means of supplementing the

---

[62] If Syria used no more than 1 bcm. a year for purposes other than irrigation, that would leave 5.7 bcm. for irrigation *assuming no return flow*. If return flow at a rate of 30% is assumed, Syria could use 8.14 bcm. a year for irrigation: the net reduction in flow to Iraq would still be only 5.7 bcm. However, these calculations should be treated with caution, as it is very difficult to estimate how much irrigation water will re-appear as 'return flow': 30% might turn out to be too high (Allan, personal communication). Equally, it might be too low: Kolars and Mitchell (1991) use a 'round figure' of 35%.
[63] Interview with Servet Mutlu, Deputy Director, GAP Administration. At a 'water duty' of 10,000 cubic metres per hectare per year, between 1.5 and two bcm per year would be required to irrigate such an area.
[64] The headwaters of the Khabur within Turkey are not attractive for this purpose as they do not flow all year round: see Kolars and Mitchell (1991).

supply of irrigation water from the Atatürk reservoir, the impact on the Khabur could be serious. So far, Turkey has considered the irrigation of a total of 60,000 hectares in the Mardin-Ceylanpinar plain with ground-water, which would require around 0.6 bcm. a year.[65] It seems likely that the flow of the Khabur will be reduced as a result, although without more detail of Turkish plans one cannot know by how much.

On the basis of present knowledge, the water available to Syria should be more than enough to permit the irrigation of all the areas of the Euphrates basin which Syria appears to be capable of irrigating, even if those areas turn out to be closer to the official target than seems likely at the moment. It should also allow Syria to honour its agreement with Iraq to pass on 58% of the flow of the Euphrates at the Turkish-Syrian border, provided that Turkey maintained that flow at 15.5 bcm. per year.

Despite the many uncertainties involved, this discussion suggests that while some areas may have less water available in future, water should not be a major constraint on the development of irrigated agriculture in the Euphrates basin in Syria as a whole. This conclusion emerges with greater clarity when one takes into account the possible savings of water which could be achieved in Syrian agriculture through the replacement of old-fashioned methods of conveying water and delivering it to crops. Wastage of water by farmers could be greatly reduced by making them pay for it (at present, water is delivered without charge to farmers), although the domestic political obstacles to such a course should not be underestimated. Syria is now starting to improve its irrigation methods, but even according to official predictions, the results will not be apparent until 2010.[66]

Syria has plans to use the Tigris, too, for irrigation. Because only one bank of the river lies in Syrian territory, no storage works to facilitate the exploitation of the river could be built without the agreement of Turkey, and probably that of Iraq as well. In anticipation of such agreement, Syria has drawn up plans for the irrigation of 150,000 hectares, and has laid claim to enough water to increase this later to 372,000 hectares. If this were to take place, Syria would need 5 bcm. a year.[67] There would certainly be enough water in the river as it leaves wholly Turkish territory to allow Syria to take such a volume of water: if Turkey uses no more than 5 bcm. from an annual flow of 19.7 bcm., this would leave 14.7 bcm. to be divided between Syria and Iraq. At

---

[65] Bagis (1989).

[66] Interview with Eng. Majid Daoud, Syrian Ministry of Irrigation, June 1993. That this will take such a long time is not only due to the cost of the investment involved, but also to the need to educate farmers in the use of systems that are new to them.

[67] Interview with Eng. Majid Daoud, Syrian Ministry of Irrigation, June 1993.

the same time, Turkey and Iraq would probably not be happy to see Syria taking almost a third of the volume of a 1,840 km.-long river on which it only has a toehold of some 80 km. on one bank. If Syria does not have enough water from the Tigris to irrigate as large an area as it hopes, it will probably be for this reason and not because of the effect of Turkish abstractions.

The impact of the GAP on Syrian hydro-power production is harder to predict. Syria has already complained that low flows in the Euphrates have reduced the generating capacity of the Tabqa Dam from 880 megawatts to 150. It seems more likely, however, that the main reason for this fall in generating capacity is lack of maintenance; difficulties of this nature have been apparent since 1980.[68]

The Tishreen Dam, with a generating capacity of 630 megawatts, is under construction upstream from Lake Assad. However, other projected power-stations in Syria are thermal.[69] The discovery of large reserves of gas in the north-eastern part of the country is likely to strengthen the trend away from hydro-power, and should enable Syria to rely much less on the flow of the Euphrates for the generation of electricity.

Iraq's needs

For many years, the Iraqi leadership has followed a policy of promoting national self-sufficiency in all sectors. Agriculture has been part of this. Self-sufficiency in food was one of the goals of the 1976-80 Five-Year Plan.[70] This was not achieved, but in 1980 Saddam Hussein declared that agriculture was Iraq's 'permanent oil', and that he wanted the country to become self-sufficient and a net exporter of food before the end of the century.[71] Moreover, it is clear that the UN embargo has reinforced this emphasis.[72] This is partly in response to the immediate situation, in which Iraq feels a need to increase agricultural production to minimise the effects of the embargo. But Iraq's recent experiences have also highlighted the dangers involved in a dependence on the outside world, giving self-sufficiency a longer-term aspect as well.

The more Iraq seeks self-sufficiency, the greater the area it will seek to irrigate, and the larger the volume of water it will require.

---

[68] Butter (1993).

[69] See *Mideast Mirror,* 14 January 1994: 'Syria plans $1.3 plants to end electricity shortages'.

[70] Al-Nasrawi (1992).

[71] Mofid (1990).

[72] Republic of Iraq Radio, 28 August 1991, translated by BBC Monitoring*SWB* ME/1164, 30 August 1991: 'Iraq: agricultural campaign launched to counter UN embargo.'

However, soil salinity has proved to be an obstacle to the expansion of the overall area irrigated. Thus can be overcome with effective drainage: if schemes such as the Third River are successful, the area of land under irrigation in Iraq could increase substantially.

At first sight, this seems to imply a higher demand for water. But the avoidance of soil salinity also requires greater care in the application of irrigation water: if more water than necessary is applied to fields, this creates conditions in which salt rises more rapidly through the soil and into the layer from which the roots of crops draw their moisture. Like Syria, Iraq needs to introduce less wasteful methods of irrigation and to concentrate the minds of its farmers on the value of water by charging them for it. Such measures should produce a substantial reduction in the amount of water used per hectare. Indeed, an assessment produced in the late 1970s concluded that improvements in irrigation systems could cut Iraq's demand for water by over 40%, with the same irrigated area.[73] The net effect of the measures needed to reduce soil salinity would probably be a reduction in the volume of water required by Iraq. It should also allow Iraqi farmers to achieve higher yields, perhaps resulting in reduced pressure to extend the area of irrigated land.

Without improvements in efficiency, Iraq is unlikely to regard the volume of water which it will receive across its border with Syria as adequate. If that volume turns out to be the 9.3 bcm. a year, on average, that Iraq should receive under its 1990 agreement with Syria, this would barely be enough to irrigate 620,000 hectares – between a half and two-thirds of the area irrigated with Euphrates water at present. If Syria's ability to use Euphrates water for irrigation falls well below the official target, as it probably will, Iraq would have more water available, perhaps as much as 10.5 bcm. a year, which would be sufficient to irrigate about 780,000 hectares, around three-quarters of the present area irrigated from the Euphrates.[74]

Of course, Iraq is much less dependent on the Euphrates than is Syria. If Turkey takes 5 bcm. a year from the Tigris, that would leave 14.7 bcm. of flow from Turkey to be shared between Syria and Iraq. The latter also has the flow of the tributaries that join the main river in Iraq, amounting to 29.5 bcm. Even if Syria were to abstract 5 bcm. a year from the Tigris (which it could only do with the agreement of Turkey and probably of Iraq too), Iraq would still have access to 39.2

---

[73] Al-Hadithi (1979).

[74] This calculation assumes that 13,300 cubic metres will be applied each year to each irrigated hectare. This is a high 'water duty' but one that has been observed to apply in Iraq (Ubell, 1971). Nasser (1987) estimated that about 1 million hectares were irrigated with water from the Euphrates in the mid-1980s.

bcm. of Tigris water each year, enough to irrigate over 2 million hectares, even on the basis of existing conveyance and irrigation techniques. This is roughly the present area irrigated from the Tigris.[75]

Clearly, Iraq is likely to have much more water available in the Tigris than in the Euphrates in the years to come. At the same time, it may be that a shortfall in the Euphrates basin will mean that cultivable land will be deprived of irrigation water. In this situation, it seems reasonable for Iraq to transfer large quantities of water from the Tigris to the Euphrates, via Lake Tharthar, if the level of salinity of the water transferred in this way turns out to be acceptable. Considering the country as a whole, it appears that Iraq will have enough water to irrigate more land in the Tigris and Euphrates basins than Turkey, and much more than Syria. Moreover, Iraq has hardly started to tap the substantial aquifers which lie beneath its soil.[76]

It seems likely, therefore, that Iraq will have enough water to maintain a very large agricultural sector. It will probably not be adequate to enable Iraq to achieve its goal of self-sufficiency in food, but then it was always doubtful if this was a realistic or even a particularly desirable goal anyway, in normal circumstances. It could perhaps be argued that Iraq under Saddam Hussein will never enjoy the peaceful relations with the outside world which would enable it to depend on international trade for a large part of its food supply. Whether that argument can be sustained or not, the results achieved so far suggest that self-sufficiency will remain out of reach: for example, before the imposition of the UN embargo, Iraq was importing around three-quarters of its food needs – and this after two decades of effort explicitly aimed at the attainment of self-sufficiency.[77]

Iraq has seen water as a means of producing energy after oil and gas run out.[78] By the time of the Gulf war of 1991, Iraq had a number of major hydro-power stations, only one of which was on the Euphrates.[79]

Iraq's ability to generate hydro-power on the Euphrates may be affected by greater consumption of water in Turkey and Syria. But the potential is limited anyway by the lack of suitable sites: the terrain is

---

[75] Iraq would receive 9.7 bcm. of water in the Tigris from Turkey and Syria. Together with the 29.5 bcm. from tributaries, this makes 39.2 bcm. Assuming a water duty of 13,300 cubic metres per hectare per year (and no other use of Tigris water, and ignoring losses to evaporation from reservoirs), 2,215,000 hectares could be irrigated.

[76] Nasser (1987).

[77] Al-Nasrawi (1992).

[78] Independent estimates suggest that this may be an unnecessary 'insurance policy', as Iraq's reserves of hydro-carbons may last for over a century.

[79] At the Saddam, Darbendikhan, Dukan, Qadisiya and Samarra Dams, the generating capacity of which was 808, 160, 400, 660 and 60 MW. respectively. These stations were damaged by coalition bombing in the Gulf war, but have since been repaired.

very flat, and as a result, a reservoir capable of generating a given amount of power has to have a much larger surface area than in more mountainous country. The consequence, in turn, is very heavy losses to evaporation, exacerbated by very high temperatures and low humidity. This important consideration has not prevented Iraq from building a sizeable dam to generate hydro-power: evaporation from the reservoir may result in a loss of over 1.1 bcm. a year, which could have been put to other uses downstream in Iraq.[80]

There are better sites for dams on the Tigris and especially its tributaries, and evaporation losses would be much smaller than on the Euphrates; some of these sites have already been developed. The Tigris basin is also a better place for hydro-power stations in that Iraq's ability to generate power on the Tigris is much less likely to be impaired by abstractions in Turkey and Syria than is that of the dams on the Euphrates, while the output of power-stations on the tributaries cannot be affected significantly by consumption in upstream states.

In any case, Iraq has enormous reserves of both oil and gas.[81] Since almost all Iraq's gas is associated with oil – in other words, it has to be produced if oil is – it offers great possibilities for low-cost electrical generation that could make up for any loss of hydro-power capacity.

The effect of pollution

Until large areas of the GAP region have been under irrigation for some time, it will be difficult to make any estimate of the impact of the project on the quality of the water which Syria and Iraq receive down the Tigris and Euphrates. Only just over a third of the land earmarked for irrigation in the Euphrates basin in Turkey will produce return flows to the main stream of the river, as the most extensive areas earmarked for irrigation are in the upper basins of the Belikh and Khabur. Return flows to the Euphrates in Turkey may reach around 1 bcm. a year. If the flow from Turkey into Syria does not fall below 16 bcm. a year, even heavy use of agri-chemicals will probably not make a noticeable difference to the quality of water in the main channel of the Euphrates.

Return flows from the areas lying in the upper basins of the Belikh and Khabur will be very large, probably of the order of 2 bcm. Unless intercepted, these flows will reach the aquifers which extend under the

---

[80] The Qadisiya Dam, with installed capacity of 660 MW. The figure for evaporation loss is from Manley (1994).

[81] Iraq's proven gas reserves were estimated at 3,000 billion cubic metres in 1995: see *Middle East Economic Survey*, 20 March 1995: 'Iraq opens window on upstream oil development potential'.

Turkish-Syrian border, to emerge in the flow of the Belikh and Khabur rivers. Given that the combined flow of these two is only 2.1 bcm. a year, there could be a significant deterioration of the quality of the water reaching Syrian farmland in the basins of these two rivers.

However, the situation may not be quite as alarming for Syria as it seems at first sight, for two reasons. The first is that the passage of water through an aquifer has some purifying effect, although this will not be great in the case of the aquifers in question because they are composed of limestone which is a poor filter compared with other rocks, sandstone especially. The second and more important is that, as already mentioned above, Turkey is aware of the danger and is developing drainage systems that are intended to intercept this flow. But it is impossible to predict how successful this will be.

Return flows from areas to be irrigated from the Tigris under the GAP would amount to around 1.7 bcm. a year. These flows would be diluted by the unused and therefore unpolluted flow, which would be at least six times larger.

Although industrial development is part of the GAP, few of the industries which the GAP planners hope to attract to the region are major polluters.[82] Similarly, there are no major cities in the GAP region: domestic effluent should not have any serious effect on the quality of the water.

In sum, the GAP schemes will certainly cause some deterioration in the quality of Syria's supply of water from the Tigris and the main channel of the Euphrates, but this will probably not be severe enough to damage agricultural production, or to render Lake Assad unsuitable as a source of water for Aleppo. More problematical is the effect of irrigation in Turkey on the quality of the water emerging in the Belikh and Khabur. If the Turkish measures to intercept return flows are not successful, Syrian farmers in the basins of those two rivers might find that the deterioration in the quality of their water supplies damages yields.

In comparison with Syria, Iraq is in a more favourable position on the Tigris, since any polluted flows that Iraq receives will be diluted by the Iraqi tributaries. There are no such tributaries to freshen the waters of the Euphrates which has, moreover, received return flows from both Turkey and Syria by the time it reaches Iraq. This is especially worrying for Iraq, since the country already has a serious problem of salinity in its soil. A substantial increase in the salinity of irrigation water applied to Iraqi farmland within the Euphrates basin could render uncultivable large areas that are still producing crops.

[82] See the list published in Table 6 of the Executive Summary of the GAP Master Plan (1990).

One assessment even goes so far as to suggest that the flow of the Euphrates received by Iraq could become essentially unusable, because of high salinity.[83] But the authors of this assessment recognise that the conditions under which this would occur are extreme, requiring that all the projects which Turkey and Syria have for the Euphrates eventually become operational. The assessment also assumes that substantial return flows will reach the 'Syrian' tributaries of the Euphrates from the Urfa-Harran and Mardin-Ceylanpinar irrigation schemes, whereas such flows will be at least partly eliminated if Turkish plans are successful. Moreover, if the 1990 agreement between Syria and Iraq holds good, the overall flow of the Euphrates would be between 50 and 100% higher than the assessment assumes, and the level of salinity therefore much lower.

Iraq will almost certainly be able to continue to use the waters of the Euphrates. To do so, however, it will probably need to improve their quality by supplementing them with better-quality water from the Tigris or from ground-water. At the same time, considerable investment will have to be put into controlling the amount of irrigation water applied to fields and draining the surplus away.

Increased use of the Karun by Iran will reduce the volume of fresh-water reaching the Shatt; in turn, this would cause the level of salinity in the Shatt to rise, because there would be less fresh-water to dilute the salinity of the water from the Tigris and Euphrates, because return flows from irrigation in Iran would give the rivers a higher salt content, and also because tidal water from the Gulf would penetrate further upstream. However, the dams which Iran is building on the Karun at the moment are mainly for the generation of hydro-power rather than for irrigation, so the depletion of the flow of the river will be limited to evaporation losses from the reservoirs. Some reduction of both the quantity and quality of flow into the Shatt, or at least to the waters of the marshes of southern Iraq adjacent to the lowest reaches of the Tigris, is likely to be caused by the dam under construction on the Karkheh which will impound water for the irrigation of 220,000 hectares of Iranian farmland. But any such effect is likely to be obscured by Iraq's own engineering projects in the marshes.

Strategic questions

Syria and Iraq seem to fear that Turkey might use its reservoirs on the Euphrates as a weapon. In other words, in times of tension or hostilities, Turkey could use the storage capacity behind the GAP dams to deprive the downstream states of much the flow of the Euphrates and Tigris,

[83] Kolars and Mitchell (1991).

as a means of doing them deliberate damage – or at least the possibility of such an action could be brandished by Turkey as a threat in the same way as missiles or tank divisions could be.

Whether such an action would be possible or not would depend on the circumstances at the time. It would clearly be possible for Turkey to deprive Syria and Iraq of large quantities of water if its own reservoirs were low, following a run of dry years. It would not be possible following years of average or above average flow. And it is not something that Turkey could prepare for by emptying its reservoirs in advance, as that would simply allow Syria and Iraq to store the water themselves.

Whether such an action would be desirable strategically for Turkey is another question altogether. It could not bring the sort of swift results which could quickly win a war, since the amount of water needed for the physical survival of a population is only a tiny fraction of the amount normally consumed by a national economy. The amount needed to maintain industrial production is also rather small. Assuming that Syria and Iraq were able to import food or to rely on stockpiles, the effect of such a cut-off would be unlikely to bring them to their knees – at least it would probably not do so before Turkey had run out of storage capacity in its reservoirs and had to release water again.

Much would also depend on the identity of Turkey's enemy. If that enemy were both Syria and Iraq, it would be possible for Turkey to deprive both Arab states of water from the Euphrates (assuming that Turkey had the capacity in its reservoirs to do so). If the enemy were Iraq, Turkey could use the 'water weapon' if Syria was in alliance with Turkey: enough water could be released into Syria for Syrian needs, but no surplus for Iraq. The effectiveness of such an action would be undermined by Iraq's supply of water from the Tigris, which could not be cut to anything like the same extent (since over half of the flow effectively originates in Iraq itself). If the enemy were Syria, but Turkey had no wish to harm Iraq, the 'weapon' could not work, as Turkey could not cut Syria's water supply without cutting Iraq's too.

All this suggests that Turkey's control of the Tigris and Euphrates is less of a strategic asset that it might appear to be at first sight. There are at least two other hefty reasons why Turkey (and Syria in collusion with Turkey) might wish to avoid using it. Any attempt to withhold water in response to strategic aims would do economic damage to the state withholding it, because its capacity to generate electricity would be reduced. The other question is one of the reaction of the international community. A state using water as a means of damaging its neighbours would forfeit international support, since the action would be seen as directed against a basic human need on the part of the civilian population. This would almost certainly be a major element in the calculations of any foreseeable government in Ankara.

These considerations did not prevent Turgut Özal from suggesting (in October 1989) that the waters of the Euphrates might be withheld if cross-border raids by the PKK continued.[84] Of course, he may have had no intention of doing so, but must at least have believed that such a suggestion would cause the Syrian regime to think about reining in the PKK.

The withholding of water from Iraq was certainly suggested (e.g. in the press) in the crisis following Iraq's invasion of Kuwait, as a means of compelling Iraq to withdraw. However, Turkey gave no indication that it was interested in acting in accordance with these suggestions.

Syria and Iraq also fear that the GAP will make Turkey more powerful economically, and therefore a neighbour to be feared. It is certainly true that Turkish planners envisage that the GAP will make a major contribution to the development of their country. According to a brochure published by the Turkish Prime Ministry, 'GAP is the Turkish Republic's most meaningful milestone towards its target of a Great Turkey'; it is a 'contemporary monument of development that is being built to make Turkey great and mighty'.[85] If fully completed, the GAP will increase Turkey's irrigated farmland by a third, and double its capacity to generate electricity.

Turkey's Arab neighbours have not managed to match Turkey's economic growth over the last decade. Syria's state-dominated economy has failed to keep pace with the expansion of its population; Iraq's money and energies have been dissipated in two futile wars. Nor does either state have the capacity to match Turkey's development potential over the next decade. Syria will be constrained by the anxiety on the part of the leadership that its grip on the country would be undermined by far-reaching economic liberalisation, without which the Syrian economy cannot grow at any worthwhile rate. Even without such a constraint, the process of re-structuring an economy that has been under state direction for many decades would prove long and difficult, as the experience of Eastern Europe testifies. And it will take Iraq many years to recover from the effects of the coalition bombing and the post-Gulf-war UN embargo, which recovery cannot start in earnest until without the lifting of the UN embargo.

It seems unavoidable, therefore, that the GAP and economic development more generally will make Turkey a relatively more powerful neighbour in economic terms. While Syria and Iraq may find this uncomfortable, they will have to come to terms with it: economic success

---

[84] *MEED*, 13 October 1989.

[85] GAP brochure, issued by the Prime Ministry, South-eastern Anatolia Project and Regional Development Administration, n.d.

on the part of a neighbour cannot ever be *casus belli*. With time, they may find that this success benefits them by offering enhanced opportunities for trade with Turkey.

Conclusions

The first conclusion which emerges from this discussion is that Syria and Iraq probably have less reason to fear the GAP than they appear to believe. From the economic point of view, despite a considerable increase in the consumption of water by Turkey, there should be enough water left to permit both Arab states to realise the expansion of irrigated agriculture up to limits imposed by other constraints. In other words, Syria and Iraq may well not be able to attain their targets, but it will be factors other than water that prevent them from doing so. For Iraq, water may have to be taken from the Tigris to the Euphrates to make up for shortfalls in the flow of the latter, but this does not seem to pose insuperable difficulties. Both states could achieve their current production in agriculture with less water than they consume now, by introducing less wasteful irrigation practices.

On the basis of present knowledge, Syria and Iraq should not suffer great damage as a result of reduced water quality in either river. However, both countries already have problems of soil salinity, and will need to manage their irrigation and drainage with greater care than they have done so far if large areas of land are not to become unproductive. The potential to produce hydro-power from the Euphrates downstream of Turkey may be reduced by the GAP. But both states have alternative sources of energy that could be used for the generation of electricity.

From the strategic point of view, greater control of the Euphrates and Tigris does not seem to offer Turkey a weapon of critical importance. It would only be available in certain sets of circumstances and, even then, would probably not be used because of the international repercussions.

A rather more unsettling conclusion must also be drawn, however. It is that, for the moment, a number of crucial questions cannot be answered with confidence. Newly-irrigated land in Turkey may turn out to need more water than predicted, or a different mix of crops from that foreseen may be chosen, resulting in higher water requirements. The demand for electricity in Turkey might not grow as rapidly as it has in recent years, so that less water might have to be released through the turbines of GAP dams. Turkey might find that it was unable to intercept return flows in irrigated lands on the border with Syria to the extent which it had planned, with serious consequences for Syrian farmers in the Belikh and Khabur basins.

Moreover, the foregoing discussion has assumed that the variations in the volume of water available in the Tigris and Euphrates basins will remain within the range experienced over recent decades. The period over which measurement of these rivers has taken place is, however, rather short: about seventy years in the case of the Euphrates, forty-five in the case of the Tigris. Quite apart from the effect of any climatic change, it is impossible to be sure that future series of dry years will not be longer and drier than those experienced within this period.

If such dry periods occur, the conclusions might not hold. Turkey might feel that the needs of its farmers and consumers of electricity outweighed its obligations under whatever agreement it might have with its Arab neighbours to maintain a certain flow in the Euphrates, especially if its relations with those neighbours were being undermined by disputes over other issues. In such circumstances, real economic damage could result downstream while Turkey retained the water which it felt it required. Very low flows would also increase the potential for the deliberate use of water as a weapon (although the constraints imposed by the existence of two states downstream rather than one would remain).

While there are strong grounds for not making pessimistic predictions about the future, there are equally good reasons for tempering any optimism with caution.

The Outlook: Policy Responses Downstream

We saw in the previous section that, on the basis of the available evidence, Turkey's GAP is unlikely to do critical economic damage to either Syria or Iraq, and that the Syrian and Iraqi fear of a Turkish 'water weapon' was almost certainly exaggerated. But these re-assuring conclusions were based on uncertain information: the outcome could well be more difficult to bear for the downstream states, which have themselves taken a pessimistic view of the future.

There are other considerations, too. States like to retain sovereign control over as many areas of decision-making as possible. Even in the relatively harmonious circumstances of the European Union, a number of states have found it difficult to yield such control. Among Middle Eastern states that have traditionally regarded one another's motives with great suspicion, it is not surprising that the ability to dispose freely of a known quantity of water is seen as being of fundamental importance, all the more so when it is a commodity that has strategic and emotional as well as economic qualities.

Moreover, governments do not wish their citizens to see them as weak and unable to respond in the face of external challenges. This is particularly true of regimes that have obtained and retained power through

The Outlook: Policy Responses Downstream 139

strength rather than popular choice, and for which any show of weakness at home or abroad is potentially very damaging. This is certainly so in the case of the Syrian regime. It also applied to Saddam Hussein's regime in Iraq before the Gulf War of 1991. Even in its present enfeebled condition, the Iraqi regime continues to put up whatever shows of resistances to external pressure it can.

With such thoughts in mind, Syria and Iraq are continuing to seek a permanent agreement with Turkey that would allocate the waters of the Euphrates between the three states. As long as such an agreement is not forthcoming (or in order to persuade Turkey to take seriously their demand for it), they will attempt to prevent the further development of the GAP. Both states will undoubtedly consider what assets they could deploy if a confrontation over water developed with Turkey. With Iraq currently weak, these observations apply mostly to Syria – but a revived Iraq could be expected to take a similar line.

One of the most valuable defences which downstream states can use to prevent an upstream riparian from constructing works that they regard as damaging is financial. Major water projects are hugely expensive, and beyond the means of many states. Moreover, much of the cost of such projects must be paid to foreign consultants and contractors, who normally insist on hard currency. Those states which are unable to raise the necessary funds must seek them from international financial institutions or the governments of richer states.[86]

The largest institutional lender of money for water projects is the World Bank. The Bank has a very clear policy of refusing to lend for a project that another riparian has objected to, provided that the objection has been found to have some substance.[87] Other lending institutions follow similar if less formally defined policies. Individual governments are free to lend or give money as they wish, but must take into account the effect on their relations with the state which regarded itself as harmed by the project which they were supporting. More general considerations of 'image' would also be important: governments would not wish to be seen to be promoting the economic development of one state at the expense of another.

As we have seen in the previous section, the 'financial defence' has not been as effective in the case of the GAP as it has elsewhere. But in forcing Turkey to raise much of the funding from its own sources, it has undoubtedly caused difficulties: for example, about half of the 70% annual inflation which the country endures has been attributed to the GAP. Moreover, the delays which the GAP has suffered are mainly

---

[86] For a fuller discussion of this question, and other 'defence mechanisms' available to downstream states, see Shapland (1995).

[87] See Krishna (1995).

due to financial constraints. As a result, the original target of full completion by 2005 has been reduced to the completion of priority hydropower and irrigation schemes by the same date. This inconvenience will not, however, prevent Turkey from continuing to implement the GAP, a project of major national importance.[88] This is especially so now that the most costly element of the project, the Atatürk Dam, is complete.

Nevertheless, Syria and Iraq will almost certainly maintain such financial pressure as they can on Turkey. An Arab League 'committee of experts' has recommended that international financial institutions should be discouraged from funding projects on the Euphrates and Tigris 'until a tripartite agreement concerning the apportionment of waters is reached.'[89]

This does not seem likely to induce Turkey to sign the sort of agreement on the Euphrates which Syria and Iraq are demanding. Rather, Turkey will probably continue to exploit its position of strength by offering an agreement of the sort which it would itself prefer, linking the Tigris and Euphrates, knowing that rejection by the two Arab states allows it to continue building what amount to *faits accomplis*.

As the rest of the GAP projects are implemented, Syria and Iraq may find that the water which they had hoped to use for the expansion of their own irrigated areas is not available, and that a flow of 500 cusecs in the Euphrates looks likely to become a permanent fact rather than a temporary inconvenience. They may also find that higher levels of salinity and pollution begin to affect the yields of their crops. In these circumstances, they might well wish to take action against Turkey, both to dissuade the Turks from going further, and to demonstrate to their own citizens that they were protecting their interests and to potential enemies that Syria and Iraq should not be expected to absorb damage without retaliation.[90]

The options open to the two Arab states are limited. As the damage that the GAP might do to them would manifest itself in economic terms, the Syrian and Iraqi regimes might consider that some form of economic retaliation would be appropriate. But Syrian trade with Turkey is very small, and so a trade boycott would not have much impact on Turkey. In any case, it would do as much damage to Syria as it would

---

[88] The realisation of all components of the Southeastern Anatolia Project is one of the main national objectives of Turkey': Kamran Inan, State Minister (Inan (1990)).

[89] Recommendations of the Special Committee formed by Resolution 5233 of the Arab League Council, dated 13 September 1992, quoted by Armanazi (1993).

[90] Statements by Saddam Hussein in July 1990 indicate, however, that the Iraqi regime was prepared to come to terms with a reduced flow in the Euphrates, including reconsideration of its 'reclamation' programmes. See WAKH (Gulf News Agency) report from Baghdad, 4 July 1990, translated by BBC Monitoring *SWB* 6 July 1990.

to Turkey. Before the invasion of Kuwait, the economic relationship between Iraq and Turkey was more significant than that between Syria and Turkey. In the mid-1980s, Iraq was one of Turkey's main export markets, while Turkey gained royalties and a large proportion of its oil supplies from two pipelines running from Kirkuk to Turkey's Mediterranean coast.[91] Nonetheless, by shutting down the pipeline in August 1990 and complying with the other international sanctions against Iraq, Turkey has shown that it can make do without Iraqi trade.

Legal measures offer little hope for the downstream states. There is no international court to which they can have recourse: the International Court of Justice will only consider a case if all parties to the dispute agree to its doing so. Given the lack of a universally-accepted body of international law on the subject of shared rivers, the results would be highly uncertain in any case.[92] In early 1993, Iraq threatened to take legal action against commercial firms involved in the construction of the Birecik Dam but does not seem to have followed this up.[93]

At first sight, reducing the flow of the Orontes mights seem to be a suitable form of retaliation for Syria. But Syria has already done this to a very large extent, for its own economic purposes: there is little potential left for further action. In any case, the flow of the Orontes is very small compared to that of the Euphrates and Tigris: the damage which could be done to Turkey would have only a local impact.[94]

The weakness in the Turkish body politic caused by separatist feelings on the part of much of Turkey's Kurdish population is a more readily exploitable asset. Indeed, for some years the Syrian regime appears to have used its relationship with the PKK to demonstrate to Turkey that it is not without assets. But Syria must be aware of the strength of Turkish feelings about the PKK. The Syrians almost certainly realise that increased support for the PKK's violent campaign in Turkey (and against Turkish interests abroad) might well provoke Turkish retaliation, which could take the form of a reduction in the volume of Euphrates water crossing the border into Syria. It would be dangerous, and quite possibly (if Turkey *did* retaliate by reducing the flow of the Euphrates)

---

[91] Medzini (1994). A disagreement over oil prices led to the halving of Turkish oil imports from Iraq in 1989 relative to their highest level (in 1987), when they represented nearly half of those imports; over the same period, Turkish exports to Iraq fell by three quarters.

[92] On the short-comings of international law as a mechanism for resolving disputes over fresh-water as a resource for consumption, see Chapter 7: 'Some common themes'.

[93] See *Financial Times*, 10 February 1993: 'Iraq muddies water of Turkey-Syria dam deal.' In February 1996, Iraq and Syria both said that they were considering taking action against European companies involved in the Birecik Dam project: see the *Financial Times*, 15 February 1996: 'Euphrates power plant generates new tension.'

[94] See Chapter 5: 'The Orontes'.

counter-productive. Syria probably also has in mind the unsettling effects on its own Kurdish minority which might result from promoting Kurdish separatism just across the border in Turkey.

Before the 1991 Gulf War, Iraq had cooperated with Turkish efforts to suppress the PKK, to the extent of allowing the Turkish armed forces to cross the border with Iraq in 'hot pursuit' of PKK groups. At the moment, the Iraqi authorities are not able to take any action against the PKK, which has used Iraqi territory as a base for raids into Turkey. Whatever regime is in power in Baghdad is unlikely to provide significant support for Kurdish separatism in Turkey, as Iraq (where Kurds make up a fifth of the population) is equally vulnerable.

Nor is the use of military force a promising option for either of the two downstream states. Syria's armed forces are inferior in size and equipment to Turkey's, and are deployed on the front with Israel. Given its continuing suspicions of Israeli intentions, the Syrian regime would be reluctant to move them from that front, especially as their presence may have value as a bargaining counter in the peace process. It might be obliged to do so as part of the security arrangements consequent upon a peace settlement, but would probably wish to keep them facing south-eastwards to cater for a possible breakdown of those arrangements rather than move them to its northern borders.[95] Still less would it want to launch them against a neighbour as strong as Turkey.

It will be many years before Iraq's armed forces again possess anything like the capabilities which they had before the 1991 Gulf war. Even when they do, it seems improbable that an Iraqi government would wish to mount an attack on Turkey, which was at least as strong militarily as Iraq even before the destruction of the Iraqi armed forces in the 1991 Gulf war and would probably continue to be a match for Iraq.[96] The lesson of Iraq's war with Iran – in which Iraq had hoped for a quick victory and found itself bogged down in a war that lasted eight years – is also unlikely to be forgotten by Iraqi military planners.

There remains the theoretical possibility of a joint attack on Turkey by armed forces of Syria and Iraq, acting in concert. This would require the reconstruction of Iraq's military strength, and a peace settlement between Israel and Syria that left the Syrian regime feeling confident that an Israeli attack was no longer possible and that Syrian forces could therefore be deployed against Turkey. The former is predictable over the long term; the latter is less certain, and would involve a change in basic Syrian attitudes that could not be brought about by security arrangements alone, however carefully devised. Moreover, the history

---

[95] Paradoxically, Turkey has tried to persuade Syria to move more troops to their common border, to counter Kurdish infiltration, but Syria has not felt able to do so.

[96] IISS (1990-1).

The Outlook: Policy Responses Downstream 143

of Iraqi-Syrian relations suggests that the sort of close co-ordination needed for sustained joint military action would be hard to achieve. Other factors also argue against military action. Turkey is a member of NATO, and could be expected to call on the organisation to come to its defence. Moreover, the only target whose destruction would make a worthwhile impact on the supply of water to Syria and Iraq is the Atatürk Dam. The Dam is very well defended against aerial attack, which would have to be on a massive scale to do any significant damage: it is designed to withstand an earthquake measuring 8 on the Richter scale.[97] The task could not be accomplished by Scud missiles, which would not be accurate enough or carry a sufficiently large warhead. Capture by land against what one assumes would be determined resistance in hilly terrain by Turkish forces would be even less likely. There are no other attractive targets in the areas of Turkey bordering Syria and Iraq. An attack on Turkey would not make sense for Syria or Iraq on quantifiable economic calculations, which would argue for internal adjustments to a reduced or poorer-quality supply of water rather than the expense and – more important – the risks of military action.

All these are good reasons to believe that Syrian and Iraqi reactions to the GAP will remain verbal. Since they lack the means to prevent its implementation or to retaliate against Turkey if it manages the rivers in a way they consider damaging to their interests, it would certainly make sense for the two Arab states to accept the fact of the GAP and find ways of taking advantage of its installations. For example, co-operative management of the project's reservoirs could enable Syria and Iraq to lower the normal operating levels in their own reservoirs, thus avoiding the loss of large quantities of water through evaporation.

Nevertheless, in regions where water is short, the desire for sovereign control of water is so fundamental as to be described as atavistic. In the case of the three riparians of the Tigris and Euphrates rivers, this feeling is aggravated by a long-standing mutual suspicions.[98] For the foreseeable future, therefore, it seems to be asking too much of Syria and Iraq willingly to place their trust in Turkey. This future appears to hold more of the same: that is, accusations and counter-accusations between the downstream states on one side and Turkey on the other, and poor or tense relations, with the water issue being exacerbated by other disputes. But armed conflict is unlikely to break out.

---

[97] Asked during the Gulf war of 1991 if he was concerned that Iraq might attack the Dam, a Turkish official remarked that 'it would take a nuclear bomb to dent it'. *Financial Times Survey:* Turkey's South East Anatolian Project', 24 July 1992.

[98] See for example *Mideast Mirror*, 30 November 1993: Turkey accused of blocking deal with Syria over Euphrates water.'

5

THE ORONTES (ASI)

The Orontes, also known as the Asi, is a small river in comparison with the Tigris or Euphrates. However, it is of some importance for two reasons. First, it supplies irrigation water to productive agricultural regions in Syria and, on a much smaller scale, in Lebanon. Secondly, it serves as a possible parallel to the situation of Turkey and Syria on the Euphrates.

The Orontes rises in the northern part of the Bekaa valley in Lebanon. It flows northwards through Syria and into the province of Hatay in Turkey. Its principal tributary is the Afrin, which rises in Turkey and flows first into Syria and then back into Turkey, to join the Orontes in Hatay. Of the main stream of the Orontes, 33 km. are in Lebanon, 471 in Syria and 67 in Turkey.

The average natural flow of the river at Antakya (ancient Antioch) near its mouth is around 1,100 mcm. a year. Of this, some 420 mcm. come from Lebanon and 370 mcm. from Syria; the remaining 310 mcm. come mainly from the Afrin, mostly from Turkey. Like the Tigris and Euphrates, the Orontes exhibits considerable variation from season to season: the river is at its highest in February or March, and at its lowest in late summer.[1]

Use of the Orontes by Lebanon is slight: in recent years, some 50 mcm. may have been taken annually.[2] However, the Lebanese have plans to irrigate a further 6,000 hectares with water from the Orontes basin.[3]

In September 1994, following twenty years of discussions, Lebanon and Syria signed an agreement to divide the waters of the Orontes between them. The terms of the agreement reflect the strength of Syria's position in Lebanon. They entitle Lebanon to take 80 mcm. annually from the Orontes and its Lebanese tributaries; this allocation includes

---

[1] Kolars (1992). The figure for the flow within Lebanon is supported by the terms of the Lebanese-Syrian agreement of 20 September 1994 (see below), which defines average flow as between 403 and 420 mcm. a year.

[2] Ibid. All the figures in this chapter are net of return flows: i.e. they assume that about a third of water supplied to farm-land will find its way back to the river.

[3] 'The waters of the Orontes: source of conflict?' (in French) in *Proche-Orient*, 30 September 1994.

present use within Lebanon. The Lebanese are permitted to continue drawing water from existing wells within the basin, but not to drill new ones. The allocation of 80 mcm. a year would be enough to allow Lebanon to supply water to the areas which it plans to irrigate, as well as to maintain present uses

The agreement also provides for a joint technical committee that would settle a number of questions not regulated by the agreement. One of the most important of these is to determine which of the Lebanese tributaries of the Orontes (in addition to those already specified in the agreement) are to be considered as part of the permanent flow of its basin for 'accounting' purposes: in other words, those which cannot be exploited by Lebanon without the water which is withdrawn being considered as part of Lebanon's 80 mcm. If the technical committee adopts a liberal definition of the terms of the agreement, Lebanon will be able to take little or no water from within the basin over and above the limit of 80 mcm.

That Lebanon would only get around 20% of the waters of the Orontes which arise on its territory has led to criticism of the agreement.[4] There has also been disappointment within the Bekaa valley that the agreement makes no provision for a large dam on the Orontes, which had been seen locally as crucial to the development of the area.

In contrast to Lebanon, Syria has made extensive use of the river for irrigation since the early 1950s. Two main agricultural areas are supplied with water from the Orontes: the region between Homs and Hama, and the Ghab, a large, previously swampy valley. The latter is the more important of the two, with 70,000 hectares under irrigation, consuming some 330 mcm. of water per year from the river (and another 105 mcm. from ground-water). The Homs-Hama region uses about 310 mcm. a year. Because towns and industries along the river empty their effluent into the Orontes untreated, little water is taken from the river in Syria for municipal and industrial users, who are mainly supplied with ground-water.

During the 1950s, Syria built two dams on the Orontes, at Rastan and Mhardeh. They are very small compared with later Syrian dam-building: their combined capacity is less than 3% of Lake Assad's.[5] More recently, Syria has built a dam at Homs, and plans two further dams, one at Kremish on the main stream of the Orontes, and the other

---

[4] Ibid. According to a statement by the Lebanese Minister of the Interior, Lebanon would get 22% of the water, and Syria 78%. See *al-Hayat*, 22 September 1994: 'Al-Marouta and Rufail laud the agreement on the waters of al-Asi' (in Arabic). It is not clear on what calculation the Minister's figures are based. The same percentage is also given in a report in *L'Orient-Le Jour*, 21 September 1994: 'Lebanon will exploit 22% of the waters of the Orontes' (in French).

[5] The capacity of the reservoirs is 250 and 65 mcm. respectively.

on the Afrin: with capacities of 275 and 230 mcm. respectively, these would be on a similar scale than existing dams. These dams are under construction but have been delayed, mainly as a result of inadequate equipment.[6]

Turkey has shown some sensitivity to Syrian use of the Orontes. In the 1950s, Syria sought World Bank funding for its projects in the Ghab. Turkish protests led the Bank to subject Syria's request to further examination (causing Syria to withdraw it), and also stimulated it to develop a systematic policy to deal with similar cases of disputed projects on shared rivers.[7] Syria then proceeded with its plans for the Ghab, using its own capital.

Syria is upstream of Turkey on the Orontes. The situation is therefore the mirror-image of that on the Euphrates and Tigris. With this consideration in mind, it would seem good policy for Syria to consult and negotiate with the Turks on every Syrian project for the Orontes, with a view to undermining any claim by Turkey to be able to do what it wanted on the Euphrates and Tigris because Syria had done so on the Orontes.

However, there is a complicating factor for the Syrians. In response to Turkish claims to the region, the Hatay province into which the Orontes flows was detached from Syria in the late 1930s when Syria was under the French Mandate – essentially as a sop to Turkey to prevent it from siding with Nazi Germany. Although the Syrians must be well aware that there is no prospect of getting the region back in the foreseeable future, they maintain officially that it is part of their country. They therefore refuse to discuss the Orontes with Turkey, since this could be construed as tacit recognition of Turkish sovereignty over the Hatay. Syria's reluctance to contemplate such a move is probably strengthened by the fact that the Golan Heights remain under Israeli occupation: it would be harmful in domestic political terms and to Syria's negotiating position as regards Israel if the regime were to give up its claim to one 'occupied' area while it was still working to regain another.

Since their objections to the Ghab project in the 1950s, the Turks do not seem to have made further protests about Syrian use of the Orontes until late 1995. At this time, the Turkish Foreign Ministry complained that the Hatay was only receiving a tenth of its previous supply; according to one media report, the flow had been reduced from 50 cusecs (or 1.55 bcm. a year) to 4.5 cusecs (or 0.14 bcm. a year). The charge was rejected by the Syrian Irrigation Minister, who declared that the quantity flowing into Turkey was greater than that being used

---

[6] *Al-Baath* (Syrian daily newspaper), 20 July 1995, FBIS translation.
[7] Krishna (1994).

by Syria, and blamed the lack of rain for any shortages being experienced by Turkey.[8]

Whatever the case may be, the timing of the resurrection of Turkey's case against Syria over the Orontes appears to have been motivated more by a desire to counter Syrian objections to the Birecik Dam project on the Euphrates than by water shortages in the Hatay. In themselves, these shortages are not likely to bring about a significant deterioration of relations between Turkey and Syria. Indeed, it may well be the case that the Turks see the value of being able to point out (at a relatively small cost in terms of lost water) that Syria, the upstream state on the Orontes, has not behaved as well in terms of consultation and proffered cooperation as Turkey, the upstream state on the Euphrates and Tigris.

---

[8] Interview broadcast on Istanbul Show Television on 30 January 1996 (in Turkish: BBC Monitoring *SWB* translation).

6

GROUND-WATER DISPUTES

It will be clear from the discussion in earlier chapters that surface water resources in the Middle East are less and less able to meet the demands made upon them. In response, the countries of the region are turning increasingly to ground-water. Like rivers, aquifers are often divided by boundaries.

The two main aquifers in contention in the Middle East (those underlying the West Bank and the Gaza Strip) form an indivisible element in the whole complex of water issues in the Arab-Israel dispute, and have already been dealt with in Chapter 2. We have seen (in Chapter 4) that Syrian expectations of a deterioration in the quality of ground-water reaching Syria from Turkey are beginning to aggravate the existing friction over the Euphrates. Elsewhere in the region, disputes over ground-water, where they have occurred, have been much more low-key.

The Qa Disi aquifer: Jordan and Saudi Arabia

This aquifer extends under southern Jordan and north-western Saudi Arabia.[1] Unlike the West Bank and Gazan aquifers, which are renewed by rainfall, the Qa Disi aquifer contains 'fossil' water that accumulated perhaps 40,000 years ago. There is a perceptible flow from the Saudi side into Jordan, with water from the aquifer eventually emerging at the surface near the Dead Sea. The reserves are large but, because much of it is more than 250 metres below ground (the conventional economic pumping limit), it may not be cost-effective to abstract more than a small proportion.

At present, water from Qa Disi is used by both countries. On the Saudi side, 650 mcm. a year are being abstracted for irrigated agriculture. Jordan has not taken water from the aquifer on anything like the same scale. It is abstracting a total of around 75 mcm. a year, mainly for local irrigation but also to supply the town of Aqaba.[2]

For the future, Jordan envisages that the annual supply to Aqaba

---

[1] Qa Disi is the name by which this aquifer is most widely known, and is thus used here. In hydro-geological terms, it is more accurately known as the 'Rum-Saq aquifer': see ODA (1995).
[2] ODA (1995).

The Qa Disi aquifer: Jordan and Saudi Arabia

will rise to 25 mcm. by 2005, while abstractions for irrigation will rise to 55 mcm. and remain at that level. Jordanian planners also see water from Qa Disi as part of the answer to the growing problem of providing water to Amman. They aim to abstract 80 mcm. each year for this purpose; a scientific evaluation indicates that this is likely to be sustainable for over 200 years.[3] Water from Qa Disi would be well suited as a supply for urban consumption, being of high quality.

The location of the aquifer is less advantageous: a pipeline some 300 km. long would be needed to convey the water to Amman. The associated capital and operating expenses would add greatly to the cost of the water per cubic metre. A leading Jordanian water expert has estimated that the cost of delivering water to the point where it would enter the Amman network would be 60 US cents, making the cost to the final consumer between 80 and 90 cents.[4] Nevertheless, this is not prohibitive for urban supply, and appears to be cheaper than other possibilities such as desalination or importing water from neighbouring countries. A former head of the Water Authority of Jordan has described the pipeline from Qa Disi as 'the most viable option'.[5] The Jordanians are likely to go ahead with the project as soon as finance can be found; the work may take anything between three and five years.

Assessments of the longevity of the resource on the Jordanian side depend on an assumptions about abstractions on the Saudi side as well. Because of the nature of the Qa Disi aquifer, heavy pumping on that side could cause the water level to fall on the Jordanian side too, especially if Saudi abstractions were to take place closer to the border than they do at the moment, or were to reach an annual rate of over 1,000 mcm.

In November 1992, the Jordanian Minister of Agriculture publicly charged Saudi Arabia with over-using the aquifer.[6] There was no Saudi response. This may have been partly for political reasons, as the Saudis were still keeping Jordan at arm's length as a result of its position during the Gulf crisis of 1990-1. They may also have been reluctant to be drawn into a discussion of their policy of paying farmers for wheat and barley prices above those at which these cereals could be obtained on the world market and subsidising the diesel fuel used to pump ground-water to the surface to irrigate them. This policy was

---

[3] Statement by the Jordanian Minister of Water, reported in the *Jordan Times*, 8 December 1992, and ODA (1995).

[4] Comment by Haddadin at SOAS Conference 'The hydro-politics of the Levant', March 1993.

[5] Interview given to *Jordan Times* by Mumtaz Bilbeisi, quoted in *Mideast Mirror*, 11 September 1991.

[6] Statement by Dr Awn Khasawneh, Head of Legal Department, Jordanian Ministry of Foreign Affairs, at SOAS Conference 'Water in the Middle East: legal, political and commercial implications', 19 and 20 November 1992.

widely criticised as economically unsound and environmentally unsustainable, and has now been changed.[7]

Whatever the reason, the lack of contact between the two governments on this issue can only stand in the way of the most effective exploitation of the resource for the benefit of both countries. At worst, it could lead to a pumping race, in which each party would attempt to extract as much water as it can in order not to see it taken by the other. Such a race would exacerbate the existing mis-use of expensive and high-quality water for irrigation. Saudi Arabia would inevitably emerge the winner, as it not only has the capital to install as much equipment as it wants, but also has cheap energy to power the pumps.

Jordan has no such advantages. Nor does it have any means of preventing its neighbour from continuing to exploit the aquifer as they wish: Saudi Arabia is more powerful militarily and economically, and (despite Jordan's positive role in the Middle East peace process) more influential internationally. Jordan can only hope to secure a more co-operative Saudi attitude on Qa Disi as part of the improved overall relationship which is now developing. The Saudi decision to cease subsidising wheat production should also help, by reducing abstractions on the Saudi side (albeit for economic reasons rather than in the interests of bilateral co-operation).

Other shared aquifers

Other shared aquifers in the region have not become the subject of disputes, at least not in public. They may have the potential to do so if the pressure on other sources of water increases, or political relationships deteriorate.

The Azraq aquifer. Water is abstracted in Jordan from the Azraq aquifer for local irrigation and to supply the cities of Irbid and Amman. Since the early 1980s water levels in the aquifer have fallen by between three and five metres; salinity has increased from 500 mg/l to 700.[8]

These unwelcome developments may have been caused mainly by abstractions within Jordan, but may also have been accelerated by abstractions in southern Syria, into which the aquifer extends. So far, however, no dispute has developed between Jordan and Syria over the aquifer.[9]

---

[7] For an example of the sort of criticisms levelled at this policy, see the *Daily Telegraph*, 28 September 1994: 'Draughts that spell danger'. The change in policy was reported by Reuter on 5 September 1995 ('Saudi farmers seen planting less wheat, barley').

[8] Fataftah and Abu-Taleb (1992).

[9] Author's interview with Ziad Elias Shawwash, Head of Water Demand and Supply Section, Ministry of Water and Irrigation, Jordan, June 1993.

Other shared aquifers 151

Eastern Arabia.   As with the Qa Disi aquifer, Saudi Arabia has exploited ground-water reserves in its Eastern Province for irrigation. These aquifers extend into the sub-soil of Qatar and Bahrain, where the level of water underground has fallen.

Libya, Egypt and Sudan.   An extensive aquifer, known as the Nubian Sandstone aquifer, lies beneath the area where Libya, Egypt and Sudan meet. Concern has been expressed that Libya's Great Man-made River might abstract so much water from this aquifer that its level in Egypt and Sudan would fall, making it more expensive (perhaps prohibitively so) for them to exploit the ground-water themselves.[10] The volume of water which Libya plans to take from the aquifer is certainly large: some 1,900 bcm. a year when all five stages are complete. On the basis of present knowledge, it is difficult to know whether Libyan abstraction will have any effect on its neighbours. One view is that, because the 'transmissivity' of the aquifer is low (in other words, water cannot move through it very quickly), the water level in the Libyan well-fields will fall so low that no further extraction is possible, *before* any effect is apparent on the other side of the border.[11]

As is the case with shared rivers, there is nothing inherent in shared aquifers that dictates that the states sharing them will fall out over the way in which the resources is exploited. The development of a dispute, or the lack of one, will be essentially a function of the nature of the political relations between the states concerned. There is no doubt, however, that pressure on these reserves of water will increase.

---

[10] For Egyptian and Sudanese plans regarding this resource, see Chapter 3.
[11] Author's interview with Dr Jean Khoury, ACSAD (Arab Centre for the Study of Arid Zones and Dry Lands), June 1993.

7

SOME COMMON THEMES

As the central issue under discussion on this book is international competition for a shared resource, it falls within the purview of political geography. A useful term, 'successive rivers', has evolved to describe water courses shared sequentially by states. However, the treatment in the standard texts of political geography, such as those by Muir (1981) and Prescott (1987), is very skimpy. This is especially remarkable given the importance of the issue as a potential cause of international disputes, and the large number of rivers that are shared internationally – over 200, globally, even before the break-up of the Soviet Union. And this figure does not include major shared aquifers that are not connected with surface water-courses.

A number of writers have attempted to derive general principles or establish analytical frameworks to aid the examination of shared river basins. These constructs may seek to predict whether the riparian states are more or less likely to co-operate in the management of the resource they share, or whether disputes over shared rivers might degenerate into armed conflict.[1]

Each river basin is unique. There is a large number of geographical, economic and political factors involved in each case. Some of these can be quantified. Others cannot, either because the data are not available or because they are impossible to express in numbers. Moreover, all these factors – whether quantifiable or not – occur in permutations that vary enormously from one dispute to another. It is therefore difficult to produce general principles that assist in analysis.

Nonetheless, some common themes emerge from this study of Middle Eastern water disputes. It may be useful for those working on international water disputes in other parts of the world for these to be identified. They may help in examining other water disputes by providing pointers to the demands on a shared resource which riparian states are likely to make, and the policy options available to them – and consequently the likely evolution of the particular dispute under consideration.

These common themes can be seen most clearly with shared rivers,

---

[1] As examples of the former, see LeMarquand (1977), Waterbury (1990) and Mandel (1991); for the latter, see Naff and Matson (1984).

but also apply in most cases to shared aquifers, especially where there is a strong flow from the sub-soil of one state to that of another.

Because of the uniqueness of each source of water, these points cannot be ranked in an order of importance that will hold true in all cases. The listing below begins with geographical-cum-hydrological factors, followed in turn by those which are economic and financial; legal and political; and military.

Geographical-cum-hydrological factors

Position. The first and most obvious of these themes is the importance of position. An international river is a resource that moves sequentially from one state to another (and this is also true of many international aquifers). At the same time, part or even all of it can be prevented from doing so, or its quality can be impaired. It is clear that, other things being equal, the state furthest upstream is best placed: no other state can reduce or pollute its supply from the shared river. States further downstream are vulnerable to abstractions by upstream riparians, the state furthest downstream being the most vulnerable of all.

Position may make downstream states more vulnerable in a less direct way. Such states often develop earlier and faster than those upstream, which are usually more sparsely populated, have more difficult terrain and are further from the sea, but have higher rainfall.[2] A downstream state may thus have become heavily dependent on the shared water resource while an upstream riparian may so far have made little use of it. This point is clearly illustrated by Egypt with respect to most of the rest of the Nile basin. It also held true until recently for Iraq and Syria *vis-à-vis* those regions of Turkey which are within the Tigris-Euphrates basins.

These factors are likely to condition the attitude of the riparian states to agreement on water-sharing or the cooperative development of the shared resource. Downstream states could be expected to be keen to come to arrangements with upstream riparians that would guarantee them a known volume of water, or even increase the volume through the development of the river basin or aquifer as a unit. Upstream states could be expected to resist being drawn into such arrangements, which can only constrain their freedom of action.

However, this pattern is not observed everywhere. A downstream state may already be using all or almost all the water which reaches it down the shared water-course. Moreover, political mistrust may make cooperation and its benefits seem utopian. In such a situation, a downstream state may attempt to preserve the *status quo* by preventing

---

[2] See for example Waterbury (1990) and Dellapenna (1995).

any significant use upstream, rather than countenance the concessions necessary to reach agreements with upstream riparians. In the past, this has sometimes seemed to be the attitude of Egypt towards Ethiopian use of the Blue Nile, and of Israel towards Palestinian use of the West Bank aquifer.

Where three (or more) states share a river in a sequential fashion, one (or more) will have both a downstream and an upstream position. Sudan and Syria are Middle Eastern examples. A state may also be downstream in respect of one water-course within the basin, and upstream in respect of another. For example, Israel is downstream of Lebanon on the Hasbani, of Syria on the Banias and of both Syria and Jordan on the Yarmuk – but upstream of Jordan and the West Bank on the River Jordan. Moreover, a state may be upstream of another in respect of one shared river but downstream of the same state on a second shared river. Syria is an example: it is upstream of Turkey on the Orontes, but downstream of Turkey on the Euphrates. Rivers may be shared contiguously, as well as sequentially: in other words, a boundary line may follow the course of a river rather than cross it. It is not uncommon for the same river to be shared in both ways in different parts of its course: for example, the Tigris forms the boundary between Turkey and Syria before it crosses into Iraq (see Map 5). In such a situation, no advantage is conferred by position on either state. There may be competition for water between the states on opposite banks of the river – but such exploitation will be limited by the difficulty which either state would have in undertaking any major hydraulic works without the consent of the other.

Similar considerations apply to ground-water. Where there is a strong underground flow from the sub-soil of one state of that of another, the 'downstream' state is vulnerable to abstractions by the state 'upstream'. This is the situation with respect to the aquifers which Israel shares with the West Bank, where the Palestinians are in the upstream position.

Where underground flow is absent or insignificant, the case is somewhat analogous with the river which is shared contiguously. Neither state will have an inherent advantage over the other. The only way one state's activities can have a harmful effect on the volume of water available to the other is by pumping at much faster rate: this lowers the water-table on the side of the state which is pumping faster, and creates an underground water flow towards its sub-soil.[3] This situation appears to have arisen in the case of the Qa Disi aquifer.

Degree of dependence on the shared resource. The degree of dependence on the shared resource or, put another way, the availability

---

[3] Robin Herbert (Institute of Hydrology), personal communication.

of other supplies of water can also affect the intensity of a dispute. A downstream state may be well supplied with alternative sources of water in the shape of other rivers or aquifers. In such a situation, it will be less likely to regard any reduction in flow caused by upstream states as a threat. As far as the Middle East is concerned, it is clear that the opposite situation is more common. Egypt is the most extreme case, drawing around 95% of its total water supply from the Nile.

Variability of flow. The degree to which the flow of a shared watercourse varies may have an influence on the development of a dispute. If a river's minimum flow is small relative to the average, dry years could cause crises that might have been avoided, had the fluctuations from year to year been less. As in most arid areas, the rivers of the Middle East show a high degree of variability from year to year. The volume of water which they carry also varies greatly through the year: it is usually at its lowest in summer, when the demand is greatest.

In the dry season of a drought year following a run of similar years, an upstream state would want to maintain the levels in its reservoirs so that it could continue to generate electricity and provide irrigation water for its farmers. At the same time, consumers and farmers in a state downstream might be suffering cut-backs as the volume held in its own reservoirs fell to an abnormally low point. It would be surprising if such a situation did not have an impact on bilateral relations.

Proportion of flow derived from within each state. The proportion of the flow derived from within each state may also affect the seriousness of any dispute. If two states share a river, the larger the proportion of the flow which arises in the upstream state, the greater the potential impact on the upstream state's abstractions – and the more sharply a downstream state is likely to react to any plans the upstream state may have for the shared river. A couple of notional examples may help.

A river rises in one state and flows into another, where it enters the sea. Its natural flow at that point is 1,000 mcm. a year; 900 mcm. of this flow come from precipitation in the upstream state, only 100 mcm from precipitation in the downstream state. The latter can be absolutely sure only of a continued, unpolluted flow of 100 mcm. a year. In an extreme case, the upstream state might divert the entire flow of the river to another river basin in a different part of its territory. Alternatively, it might make greatly increased use of the river for irrigation and industry within the same basin. In this latter situation, the downstream state would receive return flows from use upstream – but these might be heavily polluted as well as being far less than the original flow.

However, in a second example, the contributions of the two states to the flow of the river might be more evenly balanced: say 500 mcm.

of the total annual flow of 1,000 mcm. were derived from precipitation in the downstream state, rather than 100. In such circumstances, the upstream state's activities can only have an impact on half the flow into the downstream state, rather than on 90% of it, as in the first example.

The Nile and the Euphrates provide striking examples of the first situation. None of the flow of either river comes from precipitation in the state furthest downstream. The Tigris illustrates the second situation, around half the flow in Iraq coming from within Iraq itself.

Economic and financial factors

Extent to which the source of water is already utilised. The extent to which the waters of a river are already utilised may well have a bearing on whether new projects lead to a dispute, and how intense it becomes. If there is a large enough flow to cater for all foreseeable uses by all riparians, there may be no dispute of any kind. In many parts of the world, however, and certainly in the Middle East, the flow of shared rivers is often almost fully utilised, in the sense that any additional abstraction by an upstream riparian is likely to harm economic interests downstream. Present worries about difficulties to come are heightened by the realisation that demand is increasing everywhere – a result of both population growth and rising expectations. Naturally, such conditions make for strong reactions (at least verbally) on the part of downstream governments.

Opportunities for obtaining 'new' water. The existence of opportunities for obtaining 'new' water should make it easier for a state to adjust to increased use of a shared source of water.

The state affected may look to the importation of water by pipeline or other means as an alternative source of supply. But governments considering such schemes must take into account the possible risks of depending on supplies controlled by other states, especially in situations where they may already be depending on those states for the continued flow of water in a shared river.

Desalination, either of brackish ground-water or of sea-water, has been introduced to make up for deficiencies in existing sources of water. Its use has been particularly developed in the Arabian Peninsula, where cheap energy is available. But even in such favourable circumstances, the cost of desalinated water makes it uneconomic for uses that do not bring high returns. For countries without cheap energy, it is currently uneconomic for virtually all uses.

Using the same water twice seems more promising. Since domestic use requires higher quality water than other uses, the costs of treating for re-use can be kept down by supplying domestic consumers first, and then treating the water to make it safe for use in irrigation. Reclamation of waste-water therefore offers the greatest possibilities where the proportion of the total water supply used by domestic consumers is relatively high. This is the case in Israel (where domestic consumers now take over a quarter of the total water supply), but not so in Egypt (where domestic consumers only take about a twentieth of the total).

Ability to reduce wastage. The ability to reduce wastage is another factor that can work in a positive way, by enabling states to adjust to decreased availability of water from a shared source, as a result of increased use by other riparians.

There is a variety of ways of reducing wastage of water in downstream states in the Middle East (and indeed in all arid lands).

In the Middle Eastern countries considered in this study, the lion's share of available water is used in irrigation. The proportion varies from 65 to over 90%. Small improvements in efficiency in this sector can therefore have a big impact. Conveying water by pipes rather than open channels reduces evaporation losses; so does applying irrigation water at night. The same yields can be obtained with less water by installing drip or sprinkler systems in place of traditional flood methods. More realistic pricing, combined with metering, makes farmers more careful in using water. It can also encourage them to abandon the cultivation of crops that require a lot of water in favour of less thirsty ones.

As a result of population growth, domestic use will take an increasingly large share of national water budgets. In this sector, consumers can be encouraged to make savings by a combination of meters and the introduction of pricing structures that penalise heavy use. Substantial quantities of water are lost from leakages in urban distribution networks. Water can be saved if the capital can be found to repair the public plumbing.

Finding alternatives to water. Savings on a qualitatively bigger scale can be made by finding alternatives to water. Since such a large proportion of water is allocated to agriculture in arid lands, a small shift away from irrigation can make a considerable difference to a national water budget. Moreover, the economic returns to water used in irrigated agriculture are far less than in domestic and industrial uses. Indeed, in some countries the returns for certain irrigated crops may be less than the value of the water supplied if all the costs are taken into account. Cutting back the supply of water to agriculture therefore seems a doubly attractive policy.

However, it will be apparent from the discussion of specific examples in earlier chapters that this course of action is rarely adopted with enthusiasm by political leaders. It may be helpful to summarise the causes again.

Food security and self-sufficiency in food production are often cited as reasons for wishing to maintain or expand activity in the agricultural sector relate to the sector's contribution on export earnings, to the national economy, and to employment. There is considerable variation in this contribution among Middle Eastern states. In Egypt, Sudan and Syria, the sector is a substantial part of the economy, especially in employment terms. In Iraq, agriculture is an important part of the economy for the employment it provides. Moreover, the United Nations measures against Iraq since its invasion of Kuwait in August 1990 have increased the value of the sector in the eyes of the regime. In Jordan, agriculture makes only a small contribution to the economy (but continues to be regarded as important by the country's leaders).

A shortage of foreign exchange and an unwillingness to depend on aid are other reasons for wishing to grow your own food. Social policy – discouraging migration to already over-crowded cities – may also play a part. Internal political considerations are at least as important: farming lobbies can exert a powerful influence. (This issue is examined a little more fully later in this section.)

For varying combinations of strategic, economic and domestic political considerations, Middle Eastern leaders have avoided the public elaboration of a policy of re-allocating water away from agriculture. They have preferred to cling to the rhetoric of self-sufficiency, despite the widening gap between this rhetoric and reality. In fact, self-sufficiency in food has proved unattainable in the Middle East, with all countries in the region importing large quantities of food, especially cereals.

States may also need to come to terms with a reduced supply of water for hydro-power generation, as well as for irrigation. Increased abstractions by an upstream state may leave those downstream without enough water to generate the amount of electricity they have come to rely on, or at least face them with a difficult choice between holding back water for power generation and releasing it for irrigation.[4]

For states with access to alternative sources of energy, such a situation can be avoided. Following the crisis of the late 1980s, Egypt accelerated its programme of building new thermal power stations, mainly gas-powered, to reduce its dependence on the High Aswan Dam. Egypt's

---

[4] Or vice versa, depending on the season of the year and hence the needs of the agricultural sector: in seasons when water was needed for irrigation, the pressure on the operators of the dam would be to release water, whereas in other seasons it would be to store water against future demand.

difficulties in 1988 were caused by drought in Ethiopia, not by Ethiopian or other upstream abstractions. But the Egyptian response shows that downstream states need not be at the mercy of river flow, if alternative sources of energy can be used for the generation of electricity.

Financial resources. The financial resources available to riparian states, especially those upstream, can be an important determinant of the course of a dispute. Major water projects are expensive. Most Third-World countries cannot pay for them themselves, and have to seek funds from international lending institutions, or richer countries. However, the World Bank, the main international lending institution, will not lend for a project involving a shared river if another state can show that the project would cause it appreciable harm.[5] Other international financial institutions, as well as individual lending or donor countries, often take a similar (if less formal) position. In many cases, therefore, riparians have what amounts to a veto on their fellow riparians' projects. This is a valuable form of protection for downstream states.

Nevertheless, this does not necessarily work in all situations: in the case of one major river in the Middle East, the upstream state concerned (Turkey) proved capable of doing without foreign currency.[6]

Political and legal factors

Water-sharing agreements. The existence of water-sharing agreements evidently reduces the risk of disputes. So do other, less advanced forms of cooperation, such as agreements to exchange meteorological data, or informal joint activities of a practical nature.

Even water-sharing agreements embodied in international treaties cannot, however, provide a guarantee against disputes arising. There may still be differences over the interpretation of an agreement, or one party may surreptitiously breach its provisions (water-sharing agreements rarely include provision for monitoring).

More disturbing, in terms of the possibility of shared rivers becoming the focus of serious disputes, is the absence of the sort of agreements that are really needed – those that embrace *all* states of a river-basin, or at least all those that matter in terms of potential abstractions. All the currently recognised water-sharing agreements in the Middle East are bilateral, and this is unsatisfactory. Bilateral agreements between downstream states can be undermined by the actions of states upstream;

---

[5] Krishna (1992).
[6] See Chapter 4.

bilateral agreements between upstream states provide no protection for riparians downstream.

General rules of international law on shared water resources. The importance of effective water-sharing agreements is enhanced by the absence (so far) of universally accepted legal rules on the sharing of international watercourses.

This is not to say that legal rules have not been devised. In 1991, after twenty years' work, the International Law Commission (ILC), an organ of the United Nations, submitted to the General Assembly a set of Draft Articles on The Law of the Non-Navigational Uses of International Watercourses. These have as their central theme the principle that 'Watercourse States shall in their respective territories utilize an international watercourse in an equitable and reasonable manner.'[7] To safeguard the interests of all concerned, this principle is balanced by the provision that states shall seek, in their use of an international watercourse, to avoid causing 'significant harm' to other riparians.

The Articles have two great strengths: they represent the consensus of many distinguished international lawyers, and have the authority of a UN body. But these strengths may not be enough to secure their acceptance as a convention by the UN as a whole. Governments that believe national interests to be at stake in water disputes may feel that acceptance of the Articles could compromise their negotiating positions.

In these circumstances, it remains possible for a state to cite the ILC Articles when to do so supports its case but, when they do not, to refer instead to other principles. In other words, the Articles provide the strongest available legal basis for a state's claims (and a source of superior propaganda), but not the only one possible.

Prominent among the other principles which may be cited when expedient are the notions of 'absolute territorial sovereignty', 'historic rights', and the 'absolute integrity of the river'.[8] The first of these, in asserting the right of a state to do whatever it wishes with the water within its territory, is much favoured by upstream states, but it is nowadays rarely employed without supporting argument relating to other factors (e.g. economic need).

The other principles are more popular downstream. The principle of 'historic rights' asserts that a state is entitled to the same volume of water as it has always received and used in the past. (Sometimes the terms 'established', 'acquired' or 'vested' are used by downstream states: their import is very similar.) The 'absolute integrity' principle enables downstream states to claim that nothing may be done by upstream

---

[7] ILC (1994): Chapter III.

[8] The Principle of 'absolute territorial sovereignty' is also known as the 'Harmon doctrine'

riparians that would affect the quantity or quality of the water flowing down the shared river.

If the ILC is successful in having its Draft Articles accepted by the UN as a whole, their legal and moral authority will be greatly enhanced: they will become *the* international law on the subject. Nonetheless, they will not provide an automatic solution to all disputes over international watercourses. They will not provide a formula that dictates how the water available in a particular river basin should be divided between the states concerned (and here it should be clearly understood that using water in an 'equitable' manner means sharing it fairly but not necessarily equally). Rather, the Articles offer a framework of principles within which those states must negotiate for themselves the terms of water-sharing agreements. There is much room for disagreement over the interpretation of individual rules, which are necessarily expressed in very general terms. There is also ample scope for the use of negotiating muscle based on non-legal considerations.

Ground-water is touched on by the ILC rules, but only that ground-water which is associated with a surface watercourse.[9] Rules for the sharing of other transboundary ground-waters were drawn up at Seoul in 1986 by the International Law Association, and in the form of a 'draft treaty' at Bellagio, Italy, in 1989. These are based on similar principles to those of the ILC's Draft Articles. There is no more reason why states should consider themselves bound by these rules than by those of the ILC – if anything, rather less, as they do not have the authority of a UN organisation.

International law in general suffers from the lack of a judicial body with automatic jurisdiction. There is no equivalent of the US Supreme Court, which has involved itself in water disputes between states of the Union, however reluctant one of the states may have been to see such involvement. The nearest equivalent for sovereign states is the International Court of Justice (ICJ). The ICJ, however, cannot consider a case unless the contending parties have agreed to accept its jurisdiction.[10]

Of course, there is nothing to stop states from agreeing to submit their water disputes to the ICJ. But until very recently, this had never occurred; even now, only one water dispute has been taken to the Court.[11] This almost certainly reflects a general reluctance to surrender sovereignty. It is probably also because those states which have a strong

---

[9] Khasawneh (1995). The law on ground-water not associated with a surface watercourse is on the ILC agenda for codification at a future date.

[10] UN (1968).

[11] The dispute in question is that between Hungary and Slovakia over the Danube. The two states agreed to submit the case to the ICJ in May 1994.

position in non-legal terms prefer to rely on those sources of strength, rather than accept the uncertainties of the law, where it might turn out that the opposing state had a more convincing case.

Political relationships. The condition of political relationships within the basin is of crucial importance to the evolution of any dispute over water. However, given that there are often more than two states involved, and any number of issues, this is difficult to express as a general principle.

Basically, if the states of the basin are on good terms with one another, and co-operating in non-water areas to their mutual benefit, then they are more likely to be able to cooperate over water too. Certainly the possibility of a dispute over water getting out of hand is greatly reduced. This sort of situation is found 'where relations are routinized and there is tradition of easy communication such as between Canada and the United States'.[12] In such cases, it is much easier to isolate particular bilateral issues such as water and avoid retaliation in other areas.

Conversely, if states harbour deep-seated suspicions or antagonisms, or are already quarrelling over other specific issues. a water dispute will be more difficult to solve. Indeed, there is a danger that it will seriously exacerbate existing tensions. A state with a grievance over water may hit back over another issue (or vice versa), leading to a vicious circle of tit-for-tat actions that in extreme cases may lead to the collapse of the whole bilateral relationship.

Where relations are poor, downstream states may even fear that river control works constructed by upstream riparians could be used for strategic as well as economic purposes: in other words, water could be withheld as a form of leverage, or as a weapon.

Nevertheless, a downstream state may believe that the linking of water with other issues on which the upstream state is more vulnerable would have positive effects. This may be so if the linkage leads to a realisation on the part of the upstream state that it stands to benefit from not pushing to the limit the advantage conferred by its position. Of course, the state which initiated the linkage cannot be certain that the effect will be the one intended. The linkage could turn out to be counter-productive, leading to reprisals over water.

Related to the question of linkage is that of incentives. A downstream state may be able to offer something positive to an upstream neighbour to encourage the latter to be more understanding of its water needs, or at least to create an atmosphere conductive to such understanding. Incentives could take a number of forms. The most obvious is economic aid. However, this is not the only possibility. A downstream state that

[12] LeMarquand (1977).

is unable to spare money for this purpose could offer technical or military assistance instead if (as is often the case) it is more advanced than the states upstream.

It could work in the opposite direction. An upstream state might give its downstream neighbour an incentive to drop its complaints about a declining water supply by offering to provide water from another source, or other benefits such as cheap electricity or food. Turkey has offered such inducements to its Arab neighbours.

Domestic political pressures. These pressures are felt in two main ways. First, those whose livelihoods are gained from farming will be likely to resist the suggestion that the way to avoid water disputes with neighbouring states is to cut back on irrigation. How seriously the government has to regard such resistance will vary: in Israel, for instance, the agricultural lobby has an influence out of proportion to the number of voters it represents, especially as regards the allocation of water. The equivalent interest groups in, say, Syria or Iraq do not have the same strength.

The second form of domestic political pressure is the need on the part of political leaders to be seen to be defending national interests against the perceived depradations of neighbouring states. This need is particularly pressing where neighbours are regarded by domestic opinion with suspicion or hostility.

Dictators as well as democratically accountable politicians are susceptible to this sort of pressure. Indeed, dictators may feel is necessary to respond vigorously, as an image of strength serves to secure their position. They may also sometimes find it useful to exploit external disputes as a means distracting the public from hardships at home, or of demonstrating that the nation needs a strong, unchallenged leader.

Both forms of domestic pressure make it harder for governments to make the kind of compromises necessary to reach agreement over internationally-shared water. But political leaders can at least to some extent use rhetoric to cater for the need to be seen to be defending vital national interests. While this may not be well received by neighbouring states, it is less damaging than more practical measures such as economic reprisals, subversion, or military action.

Policies of outside states. The policies of outside states may play a role in a number of ways. Where a powerful state enjoys a good relationship with states that are engaged in a water dispute, or for other reasons sees a strong interest in preventing a degeneration of the dispute, it should be possible for it to exercise a calming influence. In the present global political situation, the USA is by far the most likely candidate for this role. However, a regional power could also perform such a function.

A downstream state with good relations with the USA would be very likely to enlist American help if it felt threatened by developments upstream. A state may also make efforts to convince the USA and the international community more generally that its projects do not conflict with international law, or agreements it has made with other riparians. (Both Israel and Jordan did so before proceeding with their respective projects for the waters of the Jordan basin, following the failure of the Johnston negotiations.)

Where the USA or another outside power favours one party to a dispute more than the other, this may well affect the outcome of an application for international funding for a particular project.

Internal cohesion of upstream states. The internal cohesion of upstream state may be a factor in determining the course of a dispute. A downstream state that feels threatened by an upstream riparian's plans for a shared river may be able to respond by exploiting the upstream state's vulnerability to subversion. It may, for example, be possible to offer training facilities or at least a safe haven to groups representing disaffected ethnic minorities. This support can then be introduced into concessions by the upstream state over the shared river. In other words, a linkage of the sort discussed earlier in this chapter has been established. Syria seems to have exploited its support for the PKK in such a way.

Military strength

The relative military strength of the states in the basin is a factor that usually remains in the background. Military action is very rarely even threatened to dissuade other states from proceeding with water projects. Even in the Middle East, where states have resorted to force with depressing frequency in the recent past, military action has only been used over water in the particular circumstances of the Arab-Israel dispute, where the states concerned were already in a state of belligerency.

Nonetheless, the military aspect must be an element in the calculations of states that share the region's sources of water. A militarily weak upstream state would clearly be unwise to start on a project that a stronger downstream state might regard as a threat to its vital interests. Military strength can thus reverse or at least reduce the disadvantage which a downstream state would otherwise suffer because of its position.

The changing picture

Just as the factors involved occur in a bewildering variety of combinations from one shared water resource to another, so they also change over time. The increasing demand for water, already mentioned, is an important element in this changing picture. As pressure on existing sources of water grows, pollution is likely to play a larger part in international water disputes. Technological advances may make processes for desalinating water more economic. Changes of regime in states sharing a source of water may make for a greater or a lesser degree of willingness to cooperate with one another.

A further difficulty is added to attempts to predict the evolution of disputes by the fact that different developments have different time-scales. Major water projects take many years from the commencement of construction to operation. This time-scale is even longer if one includes feasibility and design studies, and the raising of finance. Political changes, however, may take place over a much shorter period. Between the initial announcement of a water project and its first effects on the flow of a river, regimes may have changed and relations between the states sharing the river may have already radically. Similar changes may occur in the relationship between the states in a basin and outside powers.

For all these reasons, predictions about the evolution of international disputes over water are risky. This does not make it any less necessary to try to make them.

8

OUTLOOK

In the Middle East, increasing pressure on water resources is manifesting itself in falling volumes of available water for some states, in less water per head of population in all parts of the region, and in lower water quality. At the same time, nearly all the opportunities for large-scale increases in the supply of cheap water have been exhausted.

In the Tigris-Euphrates basin, reductions in the volume of water available to Syria and Iraq caused by the GAP, and the possibility of greater reductions to come, have already had a harmful effect on those states' relations with Turkey. By contrast, in the Nile basin, political rapprochement has put an end to the war of words between Ethiopia and Egypt, and opened up the possibility of cooperation between the largest 'supplier' of Nile water and the largest 'consumer'. Moreover, the slow pace of economic development in Ethiopia and the upstream states of the White Nile means that, for the moment, demand for Nile water is not increasing upstream in a manner that is threatening to Egypt (or Sudan). For the Egyptian government, the pressure on water supplies is coming at present from the country's own development and population growth.

Israel, Jordan, and the West Bank and Gaza Strip already have some of the world's lowest levels of water supply per capita, and these levels are declining as their populations increase. In these circumstances, water has inevitably been one of the most sensitive problems in the Middle East peace process, although the Jordan-Israel treaty demonstrates that agreement can be reached. An agreement on water-sharing between Israelis and Palestinians will be a necessary part of a permanent settlement on the Palestinian track. The cooperative arrangements in the Interim Agreement suggest the form which an agreement might take, built on the foundation of joint management of shared aquifers. Water has been added to the list of contentious issues to which a solution must be found if Israel is to make peace with Syria; it must also have a place in any peace agreement between Syria and Lebanon. However, by providing a framework for negotiations under superpower supervision, the peace process has taken a great deal of the heat out of the area's water disputes.

While sharp words continue to be uttered by Middle Eastern governments regarding the use of water by fellow riparian states, the experience of the last few decades has been that armed conflict over water (or even the threat thereof) is extremely rare. Instead, governments have resorted much more to diplomatic and economic muscle, with the concepts of international law being employed less to resolve disputes than to dignify positions based on individual state interest. At the same time, those states which have found their water supplies reduced by the actions of other riparians have managed to adjust – just as they have done when they have found themselves with less water for other reasons, whether (per capita) as a result of population growth, or because of drought. In terms of their consequences, these situations are the same, and similar practical measures can be adopted to deal with them.

That such adjustments have been possible, and continue to take place, suggests that there is more 'slack' in Middle Eastern water budgets than may appear at first sight. There are two reasons for this situation. The first is the availability of substitutes for water. Imported food can substitute for crops produced locally by irrigated agriculture, while gas or oil can be used instead of water-power to generate electricity (thus saving water lost to evaporation from reservoirs). The second is the existence of considerable room for improvement in the efficiency with which water is used on farms and in homes and factories, and the great potential for the re-use of waste-water from the region's ever-growing urban agglomerations.

Out of necessity, Middle Eastern states will continue to make these adjustments. Those which relate to improved technical efficiency are likely to be favoured more than those which involve the re-allocation of water away from agriculture, a step with domestic political implications. However, such re-allocation is already under way (albeit without fanfare) in many parts of the region; its continuation is well nigh inevitable. The completion of the Middle East peace process should, by reducing the likelihood of further conflict, encourage governments to accept a greater reliance on imported food. In turn, this would allow water to be released from irrigation: given the large proportion of water used in agriculture, relatively small incremental shifts in this direction should make sufficient water available to meet the needs of increasing populations for direct consumption, and of industry.

This does not mean that water will not remain an important factor in the international politics of the Middle East. Indeed, it is likely to be a source of discord, and possibly tension, as unwelcome and sometimes costly measures are forced on states by higher consumption or pollution on the part of fellow riparians. Equally, governments may feel that increased use by other riparians requires a visible foreign-policy response, either to avoid accusations of failure to defend national interests, or to impede the attempt of a neighbouring state to increase its economic power. Nevertheless, in none of the disputes considered in this book does it seem at all likely that armed conflict will break out over water alone. The alternatives to war (financial or political means of obstructing the plans of other riparians, or making internal adjustments) are much cheaper and far less risky.

The existence of disputes in the region unrelated to water remains, however, a complicating factor. It makes the resolution of water disputes much harder to achieve, as they can rarely be dealt with in isolation from these other quarrels. It also creates the disturbing (if remote) possibility that water disputes will become caught up with others in a downward spiral of deteriorating relations that leads to the sort of breakdown of relations between states which opens the way for the use of force.

In the particular case of the Palestinian and Syrian tracks of the Middle East peace process, water issued will make agreement on the Palestinian, Syrian and Lebanese tracks more difficult to attain. But the realisation that all major areas in dispute (including water) must be tackled before a lasting peace is secured will give impetus to the solution of water problems.

BIBLIOGRAPHY

Political geography

Muir, R., *Modern political geography* (London, 1981).
Prescott, J.R.V., *Political frontiers and boundaries* (London, 1987).

Water in general

Le Marquand, D.G., *International rivers: the politics of co-operation,* 1977.
Mandel, R., 'Sources of international river basin disputes', unpublished conference paper, 1991.
Newson, M., *Land, water and development* (London, 1992).
Pearce, F., *The dammed* (London, 1992).

International law

Hayton, R.D. and Utton, A.E., 'Transboundary ground-waters: the Bellagio draft treaty', *Natural Resources Jnl,* vol. 29, summer 1989.
ILC, *International Law Commission Report,* 46th session, 1994.
Khasawneh, A., 'The International Law Commission and Middle East Waters' in Allan and Mallat, *Water in the Middle East.*
Krishna, R., 'International watercourses: World Bank experience and policy' in Allan and Mallat, *Water in the Middle East.*
UN Office of Public Information, *Everyman's United Nations,* 8th edn, 1968.

Middle East water in general

Allan, J.A., and C. Mallat (eds), *Water in the Middle East: legal, political and commercial implications* (London, 1995).
Beschorner, N., *Water and Instability in the Middle East,* Adelphi Paper no. 273, International Institute of Strategic Studies (London, 1993).
Kolars, J., 'Water Resources of the Middle East', *Canadian Jnl of Development Studies,* Special Issue on Sustainable Water Resources Management in Arid Countries (Ottawa, 1992).
Naff, T., and R.C. Matson (eds), *Water in the Middle East: conflict or co-operation?,* (Boulder, CO, 1984).
Shapland, A.C., 'Policy options for downstream states in the Middle East' in Allan and Mallat, *Water in the Middle East.*

US Army Corps of Engineers, 'Water in the Sand: a survey of Middle East water issues', draft (Washington DC, 1991).

Arab-Israel dispute

Aboudi, S., 'Agriculture: the bread-basket of the Palestinian economy' in V. Yorke (co-ordinator), *Peace-media 1994, Economic Dimensions of the Middle East Peace Process* (London, 1994).

Abu-Maila, Y., 'Water resource issues in the Gaza Strip', *Area*, vol.23, no. 3, (1991).

Abu Taleb, M.F., *et al.*, 'The Jordan River Basin' (draft World Bank paper, 1991).

Ahiram, E, and H. Siniora, 'The Gaza Strip water problem – an emergency solution for the Palestinian population' in Isaac and Shuval, *Water and Peace*.

Allan, J.A., 'Jordan catchment and the peace talks' (review article), *MEWREW*, 3 (London, April 1995).

Alpher, Y., *Settlements and borders – Final Status Issues – Israelis-Palestinians*, Study no. 3, Tel Aviv University, Jaffee Center for Strategic Studies (Tel Aviv, 1994).

Anderson, E.W., 'The vulnerability of Arab water resources', *Arab Affairs*, summer/autumn, 1988.

Armanzani, G., 'Water issues in the Arab World', unpubl. paper given at EURAMES conference, Univ. of Warwick (July 1993).

Baasiri, M., 'Water Resources in Lebanon' (in Arabic) in Salameh, E. and M.A. Bakheit, proceedings of a conference on the water resources of the Arab states and their strategic importance, University of Jordan (Amman, 1990).

Baskin, G., 'The West Bank and Israel's water crisis' in Baskin (ed.), *Water: conflict or co-operation* (Jerusalem, 1992).

Ben Meir, M., 'Water management policy in Israel: a comprehensive approach' in Issac and Shuval *Water and Peace*.

Brecher, M. *Decisions in Israel's Foreign Policy*, 1974.

Bruins, H.J., A. Tuinhof and R. Keller, *Water in the Gaza Strip* (Netherlands Ministry of Foreign Affairs 1991).

Comair, F., text of lecture given on 2 December 1993 by Dr Fady Comair, President of the National Authority for the Litani River.

Cooley, J., 'The hydraulic imperative', *Middle East International* (London, 22 July 1983).

Dellapenna. J.W., 'The Jordan basin: the potential and limits of law', *Palestine Yearbook of International Law*, 1989.

Dillman, J.D., 'Water rights in the Occupied Territories', Jnl of Palestine Studies, vol. XIX, no, 1 (Berkeley, CA, autumn 1989).

Eban, A., *My Country, the Story of Modern Israel* (London, 1972).

Elmusa, S.S., *The water issue and the Palestinian-Israeli conflict*, in-

formation paper no. 2, Center for Policy Analysis on Palestine (Washington DC, 1993).
— 'The Jordan-Israel water agreement: a model or an exception?', *Jnl of Palestine Studies*, vol. XXIV, no. 3 (Berkeley, CA, spring 1995).
European Community, *Prospects for Brackish Water Desalination in Gaza, Commission of the European Communities, Directorate General for External Relations* (Brussels, 1993).
Fataftah, A.A. al-, and M.F. Abu-Taleb, 'Jordan's water action plan', *Canadian Jnl of Development Studies*, Special issue: Sustainable Water Resources Management in Arid Countries (Ottawa, 1992).
Fischer, S., 'Building Palestinian prosperity', *Foreign Policy*, no. 93, winter 1993/4.
Foreign Office, File FO 371, Eastern 1946, Syria File No. 11699.
Garfinkle, A., *Israel and Jordan in the Shadow of War*, 1992.
—, *War, Water and negotiation in the Middle East: the case of the Palestine-Syria border, 1916-1923* (Tel Aviv, 1994).
Gruen, G.E., 'The contribution of water imports to Israeli-Palestinian-Jordanian peace' in Isaac and Shuval, *Water and Peace*.
Gvirtman, H., 'Groundwater allocation in Judea and Samaria' in Isaac and Shuval, *Water and Peace*.
Haddadin, M., 'A view from Jordan' in *Water and the peace process: two perspectives*, Policy Focus: Washington Institute for Near East Policy, Research Memorandum, no. 20, (Washington DC, September 1992).
Hadid, B., 'Rapport national syrien', *Séminaire des stratégies de gestion des eaux dans les pays méditerranéens, horizon 2010*, CCE/Gouvern. algérienne/CEFIGRE (Algiers, 1990).
Harrosh, J.H., *Rivers of Eden: The struggle for water and the quest for peace in the Middle East* (Oxford, 1994)
Hudson, J., 'The Litani River of Lebanon: an example of Middle Eastern water development', *Middle East Jnl*, vol. 25, 1971.
Hurewitz, J., *Diplomacy in the Near and Middle East* (Princeton, 1956).
Hussein bin Talal (HM King Hussein of Jordan), *Uneasy lies the head*, (London, 1962).
Inbar, M., and J.O., Maos, 'Water resources planning and development in the northern Jordan valley', *Water International*, vol. 9, no. 1, 1984.
Isaac, J., and H. Shuval (eds), *Water and Peace in the Middle East* (Amsterdam, 1994)
Israel, *Statistical Abstract of Israel*, 1992.
Jordan, Government of, 'Water Management Practices', paper prepared for the Multilateral Water Resources Working Group, Middle East Peace Process (Amman, 1992a).
—, 'Enhancing Water Supply', paper prepared for the Multilateral Water

Resources Working Group, Middle East Peace Process (Amman, 1992b)

Kahan, D., *Agriculture and Water Resources in the West Bank and Gaza (1967-1987)* (Jerusalem, 1987).

Kolars, J., 'The Litani River in the context of Middle Eastern water resources', unpublished conference paper, 1991.

Khouri, R.G., *The Jordan Valley* (1981).

Longergan, S.C. and D.B. Brooks, *Watershed: the role of fresh water in the Israel-Palestinian conflict* (Victoria, BC, Canada, 1995).

Lowi, M., *Water and power: the politics of a scarce resource in the Jordan river basin* (Cambridge, 1993).

Mekorot, *Israel National Water Carrier: 50 years of Mekorot* (Tel Aviv, 1987).

Merhav, M., *Economic Co-operation and Middle East Peace* (London, 1989).

Musallam, R., *Water: The Middle East problem of the 1990s* 1991.

Naff, T., 'Israel and the waters of South Lebanon', unpublished conference paper, 1991.

Neff, D., 'Israel-Syria: conflict at the Jordan River, 1949-1967', *Jnl of Palestine Studies,* vol. XXIII, no. 4 (Berkeley, CA, summer 1994).

Omran, A.R., and F. Roudi, 'The Middle East Population Puzzle', *Population Bulletin*, vol. 48, no. 1 (July 1993).

Palestine, Government of, *A Survey of Palestine, prepared for the information of the Anglo-American Committee of Inquiry* (Jerusalem, 1946/7), [3 vols].

Pearce, F., 'Wells of conflict on the West Bank', *New Scientist* (London, 1 June 1991).

Peters, J., *Building Bridges: The Arab-Israeli multilateral talks* (London, 1994).

Richard Morris & Associates (Energy and Environmental Consultants), *Dead Sea Hydro Projects Review* (Glasgow, 1994).

Rodan, S., 'Divided Waters', *Jerusalem Post Magazine* (Jerusalem, 1 Sept. 1995).

Saliba, S.N., *The Jordan River Dispute* (The Hague, 1968).

Schiff, Z., *Security for peace: Israel's minimum security requirements in negotiations with the Palestinians,* policy paper no. 15, Washington Institute for Near East Peace (Washington DC, 1989).

Schwartz, J., 'Water resources in Judea, Samaria and the Gaza Strip' in D.I. Elazar (ed.), *Judea, Samaria and Gaza* (1982).

Shuval, H.I., 'Approaches to finding an equitable solution to the water resources problems shared by Israel and the Palestinians over the use of the mountain aquifer' in G. Baskin (ed.), *Israel/Palestine: Issues in Conflict, Issues for Co-operation*, vol II, no. 2: *Water, conflict or co-operation* (Jerusalem, March 1993).

Smith, C. G., *The disputed water of the Jordan*, Institute of British Geographers, Transactions and Papers, publication no. 40, 1966.
Soffer, A., 'The relevance of the Johnston Plan to the reality of 1993 and beyond' in Isaac and Shuval *Water and Peace*.
Tahal, *Israel Water Sector Review* (Tel Aviv, 1990).
United Nations, *Report of the Economic and Social Council: Assistance to the Palestinian People* (annex), A/44/637 (New York, 1989).
—, *Report of the Economic and Social Council: Israel: Land and water practices and policies in the occupied Palestinian and other Arab territories*, A/46/263 (New York, 1991).
—, *Water resources of the Occupied Palestinian Territory*, A/AC.183 (New York, 1992).
Wachtel, B., 'The Peace Canal project: a multiple conflict resolution perspective for the Middle East' in Isaac and Shuval, *Water and Peace*.
Wishart. D.M., 'The breakdown of the Johnston negotiations over the Jordan waters', *Middle Eastern Studies*, no. 4 (London, Oct. 1990).
WRAP (Water Resources Action Programme – Palestine), *A rapid interdisciplinary sector review and issues paper*, (Gaza, 1994).

The Nile

Abate, Z., *Water resources development in Ethiopia* (Reading, 1994).
Abdalla, I.H., 'The Nile Waters Agreement in Sudanese-Egyptian Relations', *Middle Eastern Studies*, vol. 7 (London, Oct 1971).
Abu-Zeid, M., 'Environmental impacts of the High Dam at Aswan' in N.C. Thanh and A.K. Biswas (eds), *Environmentally sound water management* (Oxford, 1991).
— and A.K. Biswas, 'Some major implications of climatic fluctuations on water management', *Water Resources Development*, vol. 7, no. 2, June 1991.
Adam, A.M., *et al.*, 'Co-operative environmentally sound and integrated development of the Nile Basin' in *Proc. Nile 2002 Conference* (Aswan, February 1993).
Ahmed, S., 'Context and precedent with respect to the development, division and management of Nile Water' in Howell and Allan, *The Nile* (1990).
Allan, J.A., 'Nile water basin planning', unpublished paper presented at FAO Symposium on the Nile in Bologna, March 1991.
—, 'Water in the Arab world', unpublished paper presented at Harvard conference, 1993a.
—, 'The impact on Egypt of the High Dam at Aswan', unpublished paper presented at SOAS, Nov. 1993b.
Assen, J.H., 'Land reclamation in Egypt', *Land and Water International*, vol. 58, 1986.

Bigirimana, M., and M. Ndorimana, 'Surveillance, prévisions et simulation des bassins fluviaux. Cas de la Ruvubu au Burundi', *FAO Workshop on monitoring and forecasting of river basins for agricultural production*, Bologna, March 1991.

Chesworth, P.M., 'The history of water use in Sudan and Egypt' in Howell and Allan, *The Nile*.

Collins, R.O., *The waters of the Nile* (Oxford, 1990).

Ethiopia, 'Nile Basin integrated water resources management: a strategy for co-operation', unpublished paper by 'Ethiopian Technical Experts' for Nile 2002 Conference, Aswan, Egypt, 1-6 February 1993.

Conway, D., 'The development of a grid-based hydrologic model of the Blue Nile and the sensitivity of Nile river discharge to climate change', unpublished Ph.D. thesis, Univ. of East Anglia (1993).

Evans, T.E., 'History of Nile flows' in Howell and Allan, *The Nile*.

Gasser, M.M., and M.I. Abdou, 'Nile water management and the Aswan High Dam', *Water Resources Development*, vol. 5, no. 1, March 1989.

Guariso, G., and D. Whittington, 'Implications of Ethiopian water development for Egypt and Sudan', *Water Resources Development*, vol. 3, no. 2, 1987.

Howell, P.P., and J.A. Allen, *The Nile: resource evaluation, resource management, hydropolitics and legal issues* (London, 1990).

Hunt, R.C., 'Agricultural ecology: the impact of the High Dam reconsidered', *Culture and Ecology*, no. 31, 1987.

Kahangire, P.O., 'Water resources mointoring and hydrological data availability in Uganda', unpublished paper for Nile 2002 Conference, Aswan, Egypt, 1-6 Feb. 1993.

Kenya, Republic of, 'A report of the co-operative environmentally sound and integrated development of the Nile Basin', unpublished paper for Nile 2002 Conference, Aswan, Egypt, 1-6 Feb. 1993.

Knott, D.G., and R.M.G. Hewitt, 'Water resources planning in the Sudan' in Howell and Allan, *The Nile*.

Matondo, J.J., 'Management of international river basin conflicts: case studies in Tanzania' in E. Vlachos, A. Webb and I. Murphy (eds), *The management of international river basins conflicts* (Laxenburg, Austria, 1986).

Nkurunziza and Rushemeza, 'Atelier sur la gestion des bassins fluviaux' in *FAO Workshop on monitoring and forecasting of river basins for agricultural production*, Bologna, March 1991.

Okidi, O., ' A review of treaties on consumptive utilisation of waters of Lake *Victoria* and Nile drainage basins' in Howell and Allan, *The Nile*.

Pacific Consultants (for USAID, Cairo), *Egypt: New Lands productivity study*, 1980.

Stoner, R., 'Future irrigation planning in Egypt' in Howell and Allan, *The Nile*.
Waterbury, J., *Hydropolitics of the Nile Valley* (Syracuse, NJ, 1979).
—, *Riverains and Lacustrines: toward international co-operation in the Nile Basin*, discussion paper no 7, Research Program in Development Studies, Princeton University, 1982.
—, 'Legal and institutional arrangements for managing water resources in the Nile Basin', *Water Resources Development*, vol. 3, no. 2, 1987.
Whittington, D., and E. McClelland, 'Opportunities for regional and international co-operation in the Nile Basin', *Water International*, vol. 17, 1992.
Wolde-Mariam, M., *An introductory geography of Ethiopia* (Addis Ababa, 1972).
Zaki, E.A.A., 'Water resource management: Sudan', unpublished paper presented to World Bank International Workshop on Comprehensive Water Management Policies, Washington DC, June 1991.

The Tigris-Euphrates basin

Abu Daoud, Z.F., 'The case of the Euphrates River: the Syrian side', *The Arab Researcher*, no. 23 (London, April-June 1990).
AMER (Association for Middle Eastern Research Institute, AMER staff), *Water Technology in the Tigris and Euphrates River Basins* (Philadephia, 1992).
Bagis, A.I., *GAP, South-eastern Anatolia Project: The Cradle of Civilisation Regenerated* (Istanbul, 1989).
Beaumont, P., 'The Euphrates River – and International Problems of Water Resources Development', *Environmental Conservation*, vol. 5, 1978, no. 1.
Bilen, O. and S. Uskay,'Comprehensive Water Resources Management Policies: an Analysis of Turkish Experience', unpublished paper given to World Bank International Workshop on Comprehensive Water Management Policies, Washington, June 1991,
Butter, D., 'Public Investment, Infrastructure and Industrial Strategy', unpublished paper given to conference on Current Economic and Political Change in Syria, SOAS, May 1993.
EIU (Economist Intelligence Unit), *Iraq: Country Profile* (London, 1992-3).
Gischler, C., *Water resources in the Arab Middle East and North Africa* (Wisbech, UK, 1979).
al-Hadithi, 'Optimal utilization of the water resources of the Euphrates river in Iraq', unpublished Ph.D. thesis, 1979.
Haigh, F.F., *Report on the control of the rivers of Iraq and the utilisation of their waters* (1951).

IISS (International Institute of Strategic Studies, London), *The Military Balance, 1990-91* (London, 1991).

Inan, K., 'Southeastern Anatolia Project and Turkey's Relations with The Middle-Eastern Countries', *Middle East Business and Banking* (Istanbul, March 1990).

Kienle, E., *Bàth v. Bàth: the conflict between Syria and Iraq, 1968-89* (London, 1990).

Kolars, J., 'The future of the Euphrates River', unpublished paper prepared for the World Bank International Workshop on Comprehensive Water Management Policy, Washington DC, June 1991.

—, 'Water Resources of the Middle East', *Canadian Jnl of Development Studies*, special issue: 'Sustainable Water Resources Management in Arid Countries' (Ottawa, 1992).

— and W.A. Mitchell, *The Euphrates River and the Southeast Anatolia development project* (Carbondale, IL, 1991)

Manley, R.E., 'Hydrological report for environmental and ecological study of the marshlands of Mesopotamia' (unpublished, 1994).

Medzini, A., 'The Euphrates River: an analysis of a shared river system in the Middle East', unpublished M.Phil. thesis, SOAS (1994).

Mofid, K., *The economic consequences of the Gulf War*, (London, 1990).

al-Nasrawi, A., 'Iraq: economic consequences of the 1991 Gulf War and future outlook', *Third World Quarterly*, vol. 13, no. 2, 1992, pp. 335-52.

Nasser, M.H., 'Land and water resources in Iraq: an updated assessment', *Jnl of Arid Environment*, vol. 12 (London, 1987), pp. 191-8.

Schofield, R.N., *Evolution of the Shatt al-'Arab boundary dispute*, 1986.

Ubell, K., 'Iraq's water resources', *Nature and Resources*, vol. VII, no. 2 (Carnforth, England, June 1971).

Waterbury, J., 'Dynamics of basin-wide co-operation in the utilization of the Euphrates', unpublished conference paper, 1990.

Ground-water

Fataftah, A.A. al-, and M.F. Abu-Taleb, 'Jordan's water action plan' *Canadian Jnl of Development Studies*, Special Issue: 'Sustainable Water Resources Management in Arid Countries' (Ottawa, 1992).

ODA (Overseas Development Administration), *Qa Disi Aquifer Study, Jordan* (London, 1995).

Some common themes

Dellapenna, J., 'Building international water management institutions: the role of treaties and other legal arrangements' in Allen and Mallat, *Water in the Middle East*.

INDEX

Abdullah, King, 16
Abbasid caliphate, 107
'acquired rights', 80-1, 117, 160
Adawa, battle of, 71
Addis Ababa, 78, 89, 100
Addis Ababa Agreement, 70, 71
African Development Bank, 78
Afrin, river, 144, 145
Agreement for the Full Utilisation of the Nile Waters, *see* Nile Waters Agreement
agriculture, 14, 51, 53, 54, 77, 83, 90, 96, 111, 129, 137, 157, 159
agricultural lobby, 51
Aleppo, 110, 126, 133
Allenby, General, 7
Amazon, river, 58
Amman, 44, 46, 149, 150
Antakya, 144
Aqaba, 148-9
Arab League: 2, 16, 122, 140; Technical Committee, 15, 16; Council, 16
Arafat, 38
armed conflict: 1, 118, 167, 168; *see also* military action
Armistice Agreement (1949), 11, 37
Asi, river: *see* Orontes
Aswan, 57
Aswan Dam: first, 61, 64; High, 61, 62, 63, 65, 72, 73, 74, 87, 89, 92, 95, 158
Atatürk Dam, 46, 113, 120, 121, 124, 140, 143
Atatürk reservoir, 114, 124, 127, 128
Atbara, river, 59, 60, 69, 70, 85, 89
Auja basin, 8
Awali, river, 19
Azraq aquifer, 150

Baath Dam, 110-11
Baathist regimes, 117, 119
Baghdad, 106, 117, 119, 121, 142
Bahr el Ghazal, 92
Bahrain, 151
Banias, river, 7, 9, 12, 15, 16, 17, 21, 27, 39, 40, 154
Banias spring, 13
Baro, river, 79
Barak, Ehud, 39
Basra, 106, 115
Batman Dam, 125
Beersheba, 48
Bekaa, 19
Bekaa valley, 145, 146
Belgian Congo, 70
Belikh, river, 104, 127, 132-3, 137
Bellagio, 161
Ben Gurion, 19
Ben Meir, 43
Birecik Dam, 122, 141, 147
Blue Nile: 58, 59, 60, 61, 66, 67, 68, 69, 70, 78, 79, 81, 85, 88, 89, 154; variations in flow, 85; hydro-power dams, 87; flood, 92
Blue Nile basin: 77, 79, 82; climatic changes, 90-1
Boutros-Ghali, 79
brackish water, 48, 50, 55, 156
Bridge of Jacob's Daughters, 14
Britain, 69, 70, 86, 116
Burundi, 59, 77, 83, 85

Cairo, 62, 89, 92, 95
Canada, 45, 162
Central African Republic, 76
'century storage', 61-2, 68
Ceyhan, river, 40, 46
Cizre, 105, 106, 125

cloud-seeding, 49-50, 55
coastal aquifer, 22, 26, 32
Convention of 23 December 1920, 116

Damascus, 117, 119, 121, 122
Dan spring, 7
Dan Waste-water Reclamation Project, 48
Dead Sea, 7, 13, 48, 55, 148
Declaration of Principles (Oslo Agreement), 28, 31-4, 38
Delta (Nile), 61, 63, 65, 69, 89
desalinated water, 30
desalination, 47-8, 94, 149, 156
Deymirel, Suleyman, 111-13
Dezful, 114
Dicle Dam, 125
Dinder, river, 85
Directorate of State Water Works (DSI) (Turkey), 113
Diyala, river, 105
domestic consumption/use/water, 22, 27, 34, 42, 44, 52, 67, 68, 123, 124, 156, 157
Draft Articles on The Law of Non Navigational Uses of International Watercourses, 160-1
drought, 90, 105, 158

East Ghor canal, 16
East Ghor project, 16
Eastern Aquifer, 11, 21, 22, 23, 24, 33, 37, 45
Eastern Arabia, 151
Egypt: 1, 11, 52, 55, 58, 59, 60, 98, 102, 103, 151, 153, 154, 157, 158, 166; regulating the Nile, 61-6; quality of Nile waters, 68-9; colonial agreements, 69-72; 1959 Agreement, 72-4; and White Nile states, 75-7, 85-6; and Ethiopia, 77-82, 87-9, 99-100; new demands, 83-5; making more water available, 91-7; and Sudan, 100-1
Egyptian Fund for Technical Cooperation in Africa, 76
Eisenhower, President, 14

el-Himmeh, springs, 28
Equatorial lakes, 58, 61, 68, 89, 92
equitable entitlement, 82
'equitable use', 80
'established rights', 36, 160, 166
Eritrea, 83
Ethiopia: 2, 46, 59, 60, 68, 75, 83, 91, 98, 101, 154, 159, 166; colonial agreements, 69-72; treaties and disputes, 77, 82; meeting new demands, 87-9; and Egypt, 99-100
Ethiopian Highlands, 58, 61, 68, 89, 92
Euphrates, river: 1, 9, 18, 40, 47, 104-5, 106, 115, 126, 128, 129, 130, 131, 132, 134, 138, 140, 143, 139, 144, 146, 147, 154, 156; conveying water from, 45, 46; history of use, 107-8; use by Iraq, 108-9; use by Syria, 109-11; agreements over, 115-23; and GAP scheme, 123-6; water quality, 132-3; strategic questions, 134-7; see also Tigris-Euphrates basin
evaporation: 10, 85, 90, 134; Lake Nasser 65, 87, 88, 93; Turkey, 114; Tigris-Euphrates basin, 115; Iraq, 132

Finchaa Dam, 78
Finchaa hydro-power project, 78
Finchaa tributary, 68
First World War, 115
France, French, 70, 116, 146
flood(s), flood-waters, flooding, 9, 59, 60, 61, 63, 73, 74, 107, 108
fossil aquifers, 94
'fossil' water, 93, 148

GAP (South-east Anatolia Project), 113-14, 118, 119-20, 123-5, 127, 129, 132, 133, 134, 136-7, 138-40, 143, 166
Gaza (Strip): 8, 11, 12, 17, 22, 25-7, 32, 34, 42, 44, 48, 50, 51, 53, 166; environmental degradation, 27; population, 41; conveying water to, 45, 47

Index

Gaza/Jericho Agreement (Cairo agreement), 26, 29, 32
Gazan aquifer, 12, 34, 44, 148
Gaziantrep, 127
Geneva Convention, 25
Germany, 146
Gezira cotton scheme, 66-7
Ghab, 145, 146
Golan, 13, 16, 27-8, 39, 146
Great Man-made River, 151
Greater Cairo Sewerage Project, 66
Green Line, 11, 33
ground-water(s), 1, 3, 7, 11-12, 27, 37, 54, 93-4, 109, 124, 127, 134, 148-51, 154, 161
Gulf, the: 134; *see also* Persian Gulf
Gulf crisis, 42, 149
Gulf war, 131, 139, 142
gypsum deposits, 110

Habib, Philip, 18
Haditha Dam: *see* Qadisiya Dam
Haifa, 48
Haigh Report, 109
Hama, 145
Harran plain, 127
Hasbani, river, 7, 9, 12, 15, 16, 40, 154
Hatay province, 122, 144, 146-7
Hebron, 6
High Aswan Dam: *see* Aswan Dam
Hindiya, 107
Hit, 104, 105
Homs Dam, 145
Hurst, H.E., 61, 62, 63
hydro-power: 3, 19, 48, 62, 64, 67, 68, 78, 87, 90, 107, 110, 134, 137, 158; Turkey, 111-13, 120, 121, 140, Iran, 114; Syria, 129; Iraq, 131-2
Hydromet, 75, 80

importing water, 45-7
industrial use, 68, 82, 123, 124
Interim Agreement on the West Bank and Gaza (Oslo II/Taba Agreement), 29, 33, 34, 35, 36, 38, 44, 52-3, 166

International Court of Justice (ICJ), 141, 161
international law, 42, 72, 80, 141, 160-1, 164, 167
International Law Association, 161
International Law Commission (ILC), 160-1
Iran, 18, 106, 114, 120, 134
Iraq: 2, 18, 19, 42, 46, 104, 105, 106, 107, 110, 115, 126, 128, 129, 134, 138-43, 153, 154, 156, 158, 163, 166; use of Tigris and Euphrates, 108-9; agreements on Tigris and Euphrates, 115-23; impact of GAP, 123-5; water needs, 129-32; strategic questions, 134-6
Irbid, 150
irrigation: 3, 6, 18, 41, 49, 51, 52, 53, 54, 55, 60, 61, 63, 66, 67, 69, 77, 79, 86, 88, 89, 95, 150, 156, 158, 163; Tigris- Euphrates basin, 107, 128; Iraq, 108, 109, 123, 129-30; Syria, 110, 111, 123, 126, 127, 128; Turkey, 111, 114, 119, 120, 122, 124, 125, 137; Iran, 114, 134; Jordan, 149, 150
irrigation water, 96, 97, 107, 111, 155
Isango, river, 70
Israel: 2, 11, 94, 118, 142, 154, 157, 163, 164, 166; establishment of, 8; boundaries not agreed, 12; national water plan, 13; disputing waters to 1967, 13-17; disputing waters to 1991, 17-28; water in peace process, 28-41; population, 41-2; increasing water supply, 43-50; conserving water, 50; managing demand, 51-5
Italy, 70

Jebel Auliya Dam, 61, 70, 92, 93
Jerablus, 104, 121
Jericho, 32
Jerusalem, 6, 11, 32
Jewish Agency, 51
Johnston, Eric, 14, 15, 16, 18, 30-1
Johnston Plan, 38

180 Index

Johnston 'share', 40
Joint Water Committee (JWC), 33, 35, 37, 38, 55
Jonglei Canal, 67-8, 76, 85, 91-2, 98
Jordan, basin: 8-9, 12, 17, 18, 39, 41; Main Plan for, 14; Revised Unified Plan, 15, 16; surface waters of, 35, 38
Jordan-Israel peace treaty, 29-31, 44, 166
Jordan, Kingdom of: 9, 12, 13, 14, 15, 16, 18, 19, 38, 56, 154, 158, 164, 166; treaty with Israel, 29; population, 41-2; increasing supply, 43-50; managing demand, 53-5; conserving water, 50; Qa Disi aquifer, 118, 148-50
Jordan, river: 1, 7, 9, 10, 15, 28, 36, 38, 154; diversion of, 14; in Jordan-Israeli peace treaty, 30; Lower, 7, 10, 29; Upper, 7, 12, 13, 15, 17, 39, 40
Jordan valley: 24, 44; Lower, 15, 48
Jordan Valley Authority, 44
Jordan Valley Commission, 17

Kagera Basin Organisation (KBO), 77, 85
Kagera, river, 68
Karameh Dam, 44
Karakaya Dam, 113, 120
Karasu, river, 104
Karkheh, river, 114, 134
Karun, river, 106, 114, 134
Keban Dam, 113, 117, 120
Kenya, 59, 72, 76, 77, 83, 85, 86
Khabur, river, 104, 109, 111, 127-8, 132-3, 137
Khan al-Baghdadi Dam, 107
Khartoum, 60, 61, 69, 73, 81, 92, 95, 96
Khasm al-Girba Dam, 67
Khasm al-Girba reservoir, 69
Khuzestan, 114
King Abdullah Canal, 16, 29, 44, 56
Kiralkizi Dam, 125
Kremish Dam, 145
Kurds: 118, 120, 141, 142; *see also* PKK

Kuwait, 2, 19, 42, 46, 107, 120, 122, 141, 158

Lake Albert, 70
Lake Assad, 109-10, 111, 114, 117, 133
Lake Haffaniya, 107
Lake Hammar, 104
Lake Huleh, 9, 13
Lake Nasser: 62, 63, 67, 91; evaporation, 65, 87, 88, 93
Lake Tana, 61, 68
Lake Tharthar, 108, 131
Lake Tiberias, 7, 9, 10, 13, 14, 15, 16, 28, 29, 39
Lake Victoria, 62, 68, 77, 86
League of Nations, 7
leakages, 157
Lebanon: 1, 7, 10, 12, 15, 28, 31, 40, 41, 144-5, 154, 166; selling water to Israel, 45
Lebanese track: *see* peace process
Libya, 79, 151
Likud, 23
Litani, river: 7, 10, 11, 19, 20, 56; conveying water from, 45

Madrid Conference, 28
Madrid peace process, *see* peace process
Main, Chas. T., Inc., and Main Plan for the Jordan Basin, 14
Malakal, 89
Manavgat, river, 47
Maqarin, 14, 17, 18
Mara, river, 77
Mardin-Ceylanpinar, 128, 134
marshes of southern Iraq, 108
Master Plan of the Nile Waters, 89
'Med-Dead' canal, 48
Mediterranean, 46, 48, 55, 65, 69, 95
Mekorot, 27, 51
Menelik, Emperor, 71
Mengistu, 81
Merowe Dam, 90, 98
Mesopotamia, 104, 107
Mhardeh Dam, 145
military action, 55, 56, 100-1

Index

military force, 142
Mills Bunger, 14
Mississippi, river, 58
Mountain Aquifer: 11, 20, 23, 24, 33, 35, 36, 45, 55; in Interim agreement, 34
Mubarak, President, 79, 100-1
Muhammad Ali Pasha, 61, 63
Murat, river, 104
Muslim Brotherhood, 18

Nasiriya, 104
Nasser, President, 62, 89
National Water Carrier (Israel), 10, 14, 16, 26, 33, 55
NATO, 143
Negev, 16, 45, 48
New Valley project, 94
Nile basin, 8, 45, 59, 93, 98, 153, 166
Nile Basin Commission, 75
Nile Basin Organisation, 81
Nile, river: 1, 8, 45-6, 52, 58-98; *passim*, 154, 156; *see also* Blue Nile, Delta, Egypt, Ethiopia, Nile basin, Nile Waters Agreement, Sudan, White Nile
Nile Waters Agreement (1959 Agreement): 58, 66, 72-4, 80-1, 82, 83, 88, 90, 92, 100, 101; Permanent Joint Technical Committee, 73-4, 86
North-Eastern aquifer, 11, 20, 22, 45
'Nyere doctrine', 72

OAU, 79
Ocalan, 122
Occupied Territories: 2
Ogaden region, 79
Orontes, river (Asi), 1, 18, 109, 122, 141, 145-8, 154
Ottoman Empire, 107, 115
Owen Falls Dam, 62, 68, 71, 72
Özal, Turgut, 46, 111, 113, 136

Palestine, 6, 7
Palestine Electric Corporation, 8
Palestinian National Authority (PNA), 26, 32, 33, 52, 53
Palestinian track: *see* peace process

Palestinian Water Authority, 32
Palestinian(s), 20, 22, 23, 24, 25, 26, 31, 34, 35, 36, 37, 38, 41, 45, 52, 53, 55, 154, 166
Paris Peace Conference (1919), 7
peace process: 4, 24, 28-9, 56, 150, 167; Water Resources Working Group, 28; multilateral track, 28; Palestinian track, 31, 32, 40, 166, 168; Syrian track, 40, 168; Lebanese track, 168
'Peace Pipeline', 46
Peres, Shimon, 39
Persian Gulf: 48, 104, 115; *see also* Gulf, the
PKK (Kurdish Workers' Party), 120, 122, 136, 141-2, 164
PLO, 26, 31, 33
pollution, 2, 37, 68, 122, 124, 130, 132-4, 140, 153
population, 50, 82-3, 125-6
population growth, 2, 3, 26, 41-2, 156, 157
Protocol of Economic Cooperation, 120-1
Protocol of 10 October 1932, 116
pumps, pump schemes, pumping, 64, 66, 89, 93, 109, 127, 149, 150, 154

Qa Disi aquifer, 44, 46, 148-51, 154
Qadisiya Dam, 107
Qatar, 151
Qiraoun, 20
Qurna, 104, 106

Rabin, Yitzhak, 39
Rahad, 85, 88
rain(s), rainfall, 10, 37, 44, 58, 60, 61, 68, 85, 88, 89, 106, 108, 147, 153
Ramadi, 115
Rastan Dam, 145
reclamation, 63-4
recycled water, 95-6
Red Sea, 48, 55
refugees, 14, 15, 26, 27
Revised Unified Plan, 15, 16
return flows, 39, 46, 123, 132-3, 134, 137

Index

Roseires Dam, 66, 69, 72, 73, 88, 90
Rusumo, 85
Rutenberg Concession, 8
Rwanda, 59, 77, 83, 85

Sadam Hussein, 107, 109, 129, 131, 139
Sadat, President, 46, 78, 79, 80
Sajur, river, 104, 127
saline water, 10, 108
salinity: 27, 68, 69, 86, 124, 134, 150; Iraq, 109, 115, 130, 131, 133, 134, 137, 140
salt-water, 26
Samarra, 105
Saudi Arabia, 44, 46, 148, 149-50, 151
sea water, 3, 26, 48, 69, 156
'security zone' 12, 19
Semliki, river, 70
Sennar Dam, 66
Sennar reservoir, 69
settlement, Israeli, 32, 37
settlers: West Bank, 23-5, 26; Gaza Strip, 25; Golan, 28
Seyhan, river, 40, 46
Shatt al-Arab, 104, 106, 115, 119, 134
Shi'ite dissidents, 108
silt, 64, 65, 69
Sinai, 46, 64, 79
Sir Alexander Gibb and Partners, 93
Sobat, river, 60, 70, 79, 85
Somalia, 79
South-east Anatolia Project: *see* GAP
Soviet Union, 42, 73, 77, 78, 81, 152
SPLA (Sudanese People's Liberation army), 81
storage, 44, 61, 62, 68, 69, 70, 76, 87, 91, 92, 114, 128, 134; *see also* 'century storage'
Sudan, 46, 58, 59, 60, 72, 75, 78, 98, 151, 154, 158; regulating the Nile, 66-8; quality of Nile waters, 68-70; 1959 Agreement, 72-4; and Ethiopia, 80-2, 87-9; new demands, 85-6, 89-90; making more water available, 91-7; future prospects, 99-102
Sudd: 76, 85, 86, 91; evaporation, 59, 60, 61

Sumerian civilisation, 107
Syria: 1, 2, 7, 9, 14, 15, 17, 18, 19, 28, 31, 43, 53, 55, 104, 105, 107, 115, 130, 133, 134, 138-42, 148, 153, 154, 158, 163, 166; boundary with Israel, 12-13; in peace process, 39-41; conveying water to, 47; use of Euphrates, 109-11; agreements on Tigris and Euphrates, 116-23; impact of GAP, 123-5; water needs, 125-9; strategic questions, 134-6; and Orontes, 144-7; and Qa Disi aquifer, 150
Syrian track: *see* peace process

Tabqa Dam, 109-10, 117, 129
Tahal, 49
Tanzania, 59, 72, 77, 85
Tantawi, General, 80
Tel-Aviv, 48
Tennessee Valley Authority (TVA), 14, 54
Third River, 107, 130
Tiberias, 6
Tigris-Euphrates basin(s): 115, 131, 138, 166; one or separate basins, 119
Tigris, river: 104, 105-6, 111, 114, 115, 128, 130-1, 132, 138, 143, 144, 146, 147, 154, 156; history of use, 107-8; use by Iraq; agreements over, 115-23; and GAP scheme, 123-5; water quality, 132-4; strategic questions, 134-7
Tikrit, 105
Tirat Zvi, 30
Tishreen Dam, 129
Transjordan, 7, 8
Treaty of Friendship and Good Neighbourliness, 116
Treaty of Lausanne, 116
Treaty of Ucciali, 71
Turabi, 100-1
Turkey: 1, 2, 39-40, 46, 47, 55, 104, 105, 106, 107, 111, 115, 123-5, 126, 127, 128, 130, 131, 132, 133, 134, 138-44, 148, 153, 159, 166; use of Euphrates, 111-16; agreements on

Index

Tigris and Euphrates, 116-23; strategic questions, 134-7; and Orontes, 144, 146-7; *see also* GAP
Turkish rivers, 45, 46, 47

Uganda, 59, 62, 68, 70-1, 72, 77, 85, 86
Undugu Group, 76, 80
UN embargo, 129, 131, 136
United Nations: 25, 107, 160-1; Security Council, 25
United Nations measures, 158
United States: 16, 18, *see also* USA
Unity Dam, 18-19, 20, 44, 56
UNRWA, 14
Urfa-Harran irrigation scheme, 134
USAID, 64
US Bureau of Reclamation, 77-8, 87, 88, 91
US Supreme Court, 161
USA: 77, 162-3; *see also* United States
Uzayam, river, 105

Vale of Esdraelon, 48

Wadi Araba, 30, 48
Wadi Gaza, 27
Wadi Yabis, 30
war of June 1967, 12, 17, 55
waste, wastage: 50, 128; reduction of 94, 157
waste-water, 26-7, 33, 35, 36, 48-50, 66, 96, 157
Water Authority of Jordan, 149
'water duty', 125, 127
'water gap', 101

water-power, 167
'water rights': 28; Palestinian, 29, 33, 34
water-saving, 50
water-sharing agreements, 159-61
'water weapon', 123, 135, 138
West Bank: 8, 11, 12, 18, 19, 26, 31, 48, 52, 53, 154, 166; aquifers, 21-3; 148, 154; Israeli settlers, 23-5; in peace process, 31-8; population growth, 41-2; conveying water to, 45, 47
West Ghor Canal, 17
Western aquifer(s), 11, 12, 22, 35, 36, 37, 45
Western desert, 64, 94
White Nile, 58, 59, 60, 68, 70, 72, 85, 86, 87, 92, 93, 166
White Nile basin, upper, 75-7, 83, 85-6
White Nile states, 75-7
World Bank, 19, 73, 78, 117, 120, 139, 146, 159

Yarmuk basin, 53
Yarmuk, river: 7, 9, 10, 13, 14, 15, 16, 17, 18, 20, 27, 38, 43, 44, 56, 154; in Jordan-Israel treaty, 29-31
Yarmuk triangle, 18

Zab, river, (Greater/Lesser), 105
Zagros mountains, 106
Zaire, 59, 85
Zerqa, river, 9
Zionist(s), Zionism, 6, 7, 8, 10, 45, 51